Gospel of John
JESUS THE GOD/MAN

MIKE MAZZALONGO

LINE BY LINE BIBLE SERIES

Line by line, verse by verse. These studies are designed to bring out the simple meaning of the biblical text for the modern reader.

ISBN: 978-0-9904155-4-1

BibleTalk Books
14998 E. Reno
Choctaw, Oklahoma 73020

TABLE OF CONTENTS

1.
PROLOGUE

JOHN 1:1-18

The book of John is named after and attributed to John, the Apostle. There is much internal and external evidence to support this and it has never been seriously contested so we will not dwell on arguments concerning its authorship.

We do have a good profile of John from the Scripture itself:

- Son of a wealthy fisherman (Zebedee) – Mark 1:20
- Had a brother, James (not writer of the epistle)
  – Matthew 4:21-22
- Close to Jesus, inner circle (Transfiguration) and it is said Jesus loved him – Matthew 17; John 21
- Zealous, impatient, intolerant – Luke 9:54
- Jesus entrusted Mary to his care – John 19:26-27
- Worked with Peter in Jerusalem – Acts 3

We also have writers of the period referring to John in their letters that give us more information about him. Polycarp, bishop of Smyrna reveals that:

- He made his home and work in Ephesus after the destruction of Jerusalem in 70 AD, which was a key influence on him and his writings.
- From here he wrote this gospel and three of his epistles around 80 AD.

- He was eventually exiled to the Isle of Patmos by the Roman emperor Domitian around 94-96 AD and from here he wrote the book of Revelation.

Purpose of the gospel of John

Each gospel writer had a purpose in writing their books:

- Matthew writes with the Jew in mind in order to show that Jesus is the Messiah/King.

- Mark and Luke have the Gentiles in mind in order to show that Jesus is the Redeemer that the nations longed for.

- John wrote when the difference between Jew and Gentile had disappeared (after the destruction of Jerusalem and the temple in 70 AD). He is writing from Asia Minor where false doctrines such as Gnosticism are challenging the claims of Christianity and so his purpose is to show Jesus as the Son of God and that salvation is found by faith in Him alone.

This purpose is summarized in John 20:30-31...

> Therefore many other signs Jesus also performed in the presence of the disciples, which are not written in this book; but these have been written so that you may believe that Jesus is the Christ, the Son of God; and that believing you may have life in His name.

… and developed throughout the book by using 3 main themes (think of braiding someone's hair):

1. Jesus is presented as a true man as well as the divine Son of God.
2. The rise and development of belief.
3. The rise and development of disbelief.

These themes are not presented in sequential order but rather, like three strands, they are braided together to form one single narrative.

1 strand: He demonstrates Jesus' humanity and divinity by alternately showing him as a man, doing human things (eating, weeping) and showing Him as divine (doing miracles).

The other 2 strands: He interweaves the two other strands, belief and disbelief by describing how people reacted to Jesus with faith or rejection as they witnessed His dual human/divine nature.

John's gospel describes the object of faith (Jesus Christ) and why He should be considered as such (miracles, resurrection). He also describes the development of belief or disbelief as people react to Him.

Outline

When we understand this idea of braiding these three themes the outline of the book makes sense.

Prologue – 1:1-18

In this opening section John introduces Jesus as the Son of God, the God/Man. He traces Jesus' existence from the pre-creation era to His incarnation as a human being.

Proof of His divinity through ministry – 1:19-12:50

The next large section of the book simply braids together the two strands of episodes of belief and disbelief around the description of His ministry. John presents accounts of His teachings and miracles with alternating responses of belief and disbelief.

Proof of His divinity through His death, burial and resurrection – 13:1 – 21:25

In the final chapters John uses the same technique of describing alternating responses of belief and disbelief, but this time they are set against the backdrop of His final days as He is arrested, tried, tortured, crucified, buried and resurrected.

John's focus was quite narrow in this gospel. Jesus Himself and who He was are presented along with a whole series of believing and unbelieving responses from people around Him. The idea is that the reader will see not only Jesus, but will also see himself in the reaction of the various people.

Prologue – 1:1-18

So we begin our study with what is called the "prologue" because it is not a narrative about Jesus' life or actions, but describes Him before coming to earth in human form.

This is where John is different. He begins with a statement clearly declaring Jesus' divine nature whereas the other three gospel writers allow the reader to conclude this from the evidence they present in their gospels.

There was a certain concept of the idea of "word/logos" that existed at that time:

For Jews: The Word/Logos (Greek) was a revelation from God. It was something to be understood and put into practice as well as respected.

For Gentiles/Greeks: Word represented the great "Reason" or "Power" or "Force" as we would say today. To be in accord with this Word/Power was to have a happy and balanced life.

John, in his prologue, explains that the full meaning of this concept is revealed through Christ: He is the Word, He is the Logos, He is the Force.

Vs. 1 – In the beginning…

This refers to the time before creation, that dimension that existed before the space/time continuum that we live in was created.

John takes the reader to that point where one is standing at the beginning of time and looking backwards into eternity.

…was the Word…

The "Word" is a title for Jesus. The Jews would see 'revelation from God'. The Gentiles would read – 'force/power.' John uses "Word" for Jesus because what you say is a reflection of what is in your heart and mind. This opening title for Jesus describes Him as being the perfect expression of the mind of God in human form.

…and the Word was with God,…

Not a power coming from God as in a created thing or an attribute of God. No, Jesus as person co-existing with God on an equal basis. In other words when God speaks, when the power is realized, Jesus is what is said, what is expressed.

…and the Word was God.

The Word was God/God was the Word.

John, a devout Jew, would never say, "…and the Word was a god.." as the Jehovah's Witnesses claim in their New World translations. This would violate his monotheistic belief, to him this would be idolatry. And so in the 1st verse, John asks and answers some basic questions:

- Who is the Word? God is the Word.
- Why is the Word God? It is eternal (before time); it coexists with God; its nature is divine.

John, therefore, gives substance to this idea of Word/Logos, far beyond what the Jews or Gentiles had thought:

- The Word is Almighty God.
- God expresses Himself in the Word.
- God and the Word are one.

> Vs. 2 – He was in the beginning with God.

Once having made the connection between God and the Word, John now begins to connect Jesus with the Word.

He does not mention Him by name but uses the personal pronoun – He – to connect Jesus (who he will mention by name later) with the Word and ultimately to God.

His reasoning is quite mathematical:

- If A (God)   = B (Word)
- And B (Word)   = C (Jesus)
- Then A (God)   = C (Jesus)

So in the next verse he will complete this equation.

> Vs. 3 – All things came into being through Him, and apart from Him nothing came into being that has come into being.

The Jews attributed the creation to the power of God's Word ("let there be light..." in Genesis 1:3). God literally spoke the creation into existence. The Gentiles also saw the power of the "force" as the agent for creation.

In this verse John is connecting the Word to the person of Jesus, making Him and the Word as One. The idea is that Jesus, in the form of the Word, was the agent of creation. This teaching is also presented by Paul in Colossians 1:16: "For by Him all things were created, both in the heavens and on earth..."

> Vs. 4-5 – In Him was life, and the life was the Light of men. The Light shines in the darkness, and the darkness did not comprehend it.

Here John makes the bridge from divinity to humanity in three steps:

1. God is the Word in eternity.
2. The Word is Jesus creating the universe.
3. Jesus is the life bringing light into the world.

John also summarizes Jesus' earthly ministry:

- He is life (the essence of God).
- His life brings light (the truth of God).
- His Word does not disagree with anything true but reveals the final answer to all questions about God and salvation, etc.

John briefly explains at the beginning of his gospel what happens at the end of his gospel: Jesus brings the truth and is rejected.

> Vs. 6-8 – There came a man sent from God, whose name was John. He came as a witness, to testify about

the Light, so that all might believe through him. He was
not the Light, but he came to testify about the Light.

In these verses John describes the role of one of the major
figures in Christ's ministry: John the Baptist. He will later
describe John's work and connection to Jesus, but at this point
he summarizes John's purpose. John was a witness, according
to Scripture, to prepare the people for the coming of the
light/truth. The majority of John's ministry was to alert the people
that the Messiah was coming. In the end, after he baptized
Jesus, he began to directly point to the Lord as the One who
was to come. With his death, most of his disciples began to
follow Jesus.

Vs. 9-11 – There was the true Light which, coming into
the world, enlightens every man. He was in the world,
and the world was made through Him, and the world
did not know Him. He came to His own, and those who
were His own did not receive Him.

In this passage, John reviews and expands on what he
mentioned briefly in verse five. He makes three major points:

1. He brought with Him and within Him the capability to
    bring every person into the knowledge of the truth (light).
2. Even with this ability the world, which He created,
    rejected Him.
3. The people (the Jews) that He had especially blessed
    were especially hard and refused to accept Him.

Vs. 12-13 – But as many as received Him, to them He
gave the right to become children of God, even to those
who believe in His name, who were born, not of blood
nor of the will of the flesh nor of the will of man, but of
God.

This is the gospel in capsule form

It does not explain everything in detail but rather gives a bird's eye view of what Jesus did accomplish with some. For those who received (believed) Him, He transformed them into spiritual beings. Not created by normal reproductive means but by the will of God.

The details are spelled out later, for now he merely summarizes the fact that some rejected Him and others accepted Him. And for these, the blessing was to become a new creation he calls "child of God".

> Vs. 14 – And the Word became flesh, and dwelt among us, and we saw His glory, glory as of the only begotten from the Father, full of grace and truth.

The Word becoming flesh is the Incarnation. From God/Word to Word/Jesus to Jesus/Man. Jesus = the God/Man. In a few words John proclaims that Almighty God took on a human body.

Now he speaks of his own experience of this. We (the Apostles/John) saw (experienced) this glory (God/Man) – a kind of glory that only the Son (God/Man) could radiate. And the substance of His glory (what it was about Him that made Him glorious) was His Godly nature, grace and truth (the mind of God clearly expressed).

The only begotten from the Father.

- Some never become sons of God.
- Others become sons by adoption as God forgives and cleanses them from sin and adopts them as His children.
- Jesus, however, is a Son by nature. He is the only one (only begotten) related to God by having an identical nature.

John is also reminding his readers of the incredible "presence" that Jesus had, which makes the rejection of Him a terrible sin.

> Vs. 15 – John testified about Him and cried out, saying, "This was He of whom I said, 'He who comes after me has a higher rank than I, for He existed before me.'"

Reinforcing this idea of the impact of Jesus' presence, the gospel writer reaches back and talks about John the Baptist's work again. He says that even John the Baptist, in his witness, testified to the eternal quality and preeminent position of the One who was to come. For example, "…the One to come was before…" and John was conceived before Jesus. John the Baptist knew and preached about Jesus' God/Man status.

Again the implication is that their rejection was a grave sin because they had plenty of preparation of His coming from a credible source.

> Vs. 16 – For of His fullness we have all received, and grace upon grace.

Jesus is the Word and the Word is divine and for this reason the Word is completely full.

You cannot exhaust the supply of truth and grace coming from the Word/Jesus/God just like you cannot use up the supply of oxygen by breathing in the open air. You cannot exhaust the amount of grace and truth that Jesus/Word/God has towards sinners who breathe in God's grace and truth through faith in Jesus Christ.

> Vs. 17 – For the Law was given through Moses; grace and truth were realized through Jesus Christ.

Moses received the Law (which contained the promise of the grace and truth to come - Hebrews 10:1) and he administered this Law.

Jesus is the substance of the promises that were only contained in the Law. It is like the difference between having a picture of an item you have ordered from a catalogue or on the internet and finally having the product in your hands.

John speaks to Jews here by giving them a graphic illustration to show them the difference between the Old Testament and the New Testament. One is of promise (Old Testament) and one is of presence (New Testament).

> Vs. 18 – No one has seen God at any time; the only begotten God who is in the bosom of the Father, He has explained Him.

No man has ever seen God. Moses spoke directly and saw the back of His glory. But Jesus, the God/Man, gives us an experience of God not available until now. He is able to do this because of His intimate knowledge of God, having the same nature and being part of the Godhead with Him. Jesus is able to relate to man what He knows about God from firsthand experience as a divine being within the Godhead Himself.

Summary

John begins his gospel by establishing the fact that with his own eyes he has experienced God taking on a human nature in order to give man an intimate experience and knowledge of Himself. Since we could not transfer to His realm, He transferred to ours.

This knowledge he calls "truth"/"light". This experience he calls "life". He says that for the most part, men rejected this knowledge and experience. He also lists 3 witnesses that proclaimed this knowledge/experience but were not believed:

- John the Baptist and his witness of preaching.

- Jesus Himself and His witness of miracles and teaching.
- John the Apostle and his eye witness.

With the prologue John sets up the three braids of his gospel.

1. The presence of Jesus the God/Man.
2. Reactions of belief.
3. Reactions of disbelief.

Beginning in verse 19, he will start to intertwine these three strands to make up his gospel record.

2.
JOHN'S WITNESS

JOHN 1:19:34

We are studying the book of John and in this gospel John presents three themes or strands which he intertwines to create a single narrative.

1. The first strand is the presentation of Jesus as the divine Son of God who has come in the flesh as Jesus Christ. John establishes this theme immediately in the first 18 verses of his gospel, called the prologue. He calls Jesus the "Word" and explains that Jesus, the divine Word, created the world and then entered His own creation as a man.

2. The next strand is belief. John briefly mentions in his prologue that some believed that Jesus was God and their belief led them to life and truth.

3. The third strand is disbelief. In the prologue John also mentions that even though Jesus provides proof/witnesses of His identity, His people and the majority of others do not believe.

As I mentioned previously, John takes these three ideas and weaves them together to show Jesus in various situations: teaching, performing miracles (as proof of His divinity) and the reactions of belief and disbelief from those who witness these things.

Once John has set forth the pattern for his gospel in chapter 1:1-18, he begins with the introduction of a major New Testament character, John the Baptist. John called him this because this is what Jesus called him in Matthew 11:11.

In the pattern of how the book is written, John serves as the first response of belief: John believes that Jesus is the Messiah and even begins to make a witness for it.

John the Baptist was the second cousin of Jesus (Mary was the cousin of Elizabeth, who was John's mother). Elizabeth and Zacharias (his father) were very old and childless when an angel appeared to Zacharias while he ministered at the temple (he was a priest). This angel announced that Elizabeth would conceive a child and he would be named John.

From an early age John the Baptist was set apart for a special ministry which, as he grew, was defined as one who prepared the way for the Lord. This was in accordance with what the angel said about him and what the Old Testament said would happen before the Messiah would come. According to the prophets (Malachi 3:1-3) God would send a messenger, a prophet in the spirit of or in the style of Elijah, to announce the imminent coming of God's Messiah. John and his ministry were the fulfillment of that prophecy and promise from God.

And so John (the gospel writer) puts John (the Baptist) as the first example of one who believed. Jesus had not taught or performed miracles before His baptism and so John's faith and belief in Jesus were based on a special sign that God would give him so he could know who the true Messiah was. In John 1:33, John the Baptist says that God revealed to him that the one over whose head a dove would appear after their baptism, this would be the one he was preparing a way for. This is one of the reasons Jesus had to be baptized, to witness to John so he could fulfill his mission. We know that this is exactly what happened when Jesus was baptized as a signal to John among others.

John believed this sign and began to point to Jesus as the Messiah, the one for whom he was preparing a way.

John the evangelist introduces John and his story as the first example of those who believed.

Reaction of a believer

So we pick up the witness of the first believer, John the Baptist in chapter 1, verse 19.

> Vs. 19 – This is the testimony of John, when the Jews sent to him priests and Levites from Jerusalem to ask him, "Who are you?"

The gospel writer introduces John the Baptist by telescoping directly to an encounter between him and the priests/Levites of the time concerning his true identity. The Baptist's parents and connection to Jesus' family is detailed by Luke in his gospel, so John skips all of that and goes directly to an event in his public ministry.

The "Jews" were the religious leaders (Pharisees). They were scribes who were zealous in keeping and enforcing the Law.

Priests and Levites were those who ministered at the temple.

John was drawing crowds, proclaiming the imminent coming of God's kingdom, God's Messiah and in doing so he was stirring up the people. The religious leaders, fearing the loss of their position or a backlash from the Roman authorities, sent a delegation to check out this preacher/prophet.

In response to their question John makes his witness and confession of belief in the One to come.

> Vs. 20-21 – And he confessed and did not deny, but confessed, "I am not the Christ." They asked him, "What then? Are you Elijah?" And he said, "I am not." "Are you the Prophet?" And he answered, "No."

They ask him 3 questions:

1. They ask if He thinks He is the Messiah (because there were many religious radicals that claimed this), and he answers no.
2. Are you Elijah? This was a reference to Malachi 4:5 where the Old Testament prophet said that Elijah would return as a forerunner of the Messiah. Many Jews believed that Malachi meant that God would actually resurrect Elijah and send him to the people. In Matthew 11:14, Jesus explained that John the Baptist was the person Malachi spoke of, that John the Baptist was a prophet in the "spirit" of Elijah: powerful preacher; man of the desert; man of vision. And so John, knowing their confusion, answers no, he is not the resurrected Elijah (even though he is the fulfillment of Malachi's prophecy).
3. Are you the prophet? In Deuteronomy 18:15 Moses said that one day God would raise up a prophet to lead the people just as he (Moses) had led the people. They wanted to know, did he think of himself as that prophet? John answers no, he is not that prophet. Actually Jesus is that prophet. He is the fulfillment of that prophecy and promise (Acts 3:22-23 – Peter).

Vs. 22 – Then they said to him, "Who are you, so that we may give an answer to those who sent us? What do you say about yourself?"

They have run out of questions and possibilities concerning his identity according to Scriptures. This was the key: who he was according to prophecy. If not Christ, Elijah or the prophet, then who? The Pharisees wanted to know (probably so they could plan an attack to discredit him).

Vs. 23 – He said, "I am a voice of one crying in the wilderness, 'Make straight the way of the Lord,' as Isaiah the prophet said."

John answers that he is two things:

1. A voice. The significance is that he is a proclaimer and messenger. In the wilderness refers that his is not a popular messenger and he is not part of the establishment.
2. One who makes straight. He challenges them. He goes against convention. He is here to prepare a new way (crooked was the old way).

His ministry is spoken of by Isaiah, as this is whom he is quoting.

Vs. 24 – Now they had been sent from the Pharisees."

John adds an editorial comment in order to put their questions and motives in context.

Vs. 25 – They asked him, and said to him, "Why then are you baptizing, if you are not the Christ, nor Elijah, nor the Prophet?"

Their question shows their reaction to John the Baptist and his witness: they disbelieve. See the third strand being woven in here?

They are stung by his message because if he had said he was Christ, they would accuse him of blasphemy or of being a lunatic or an imposter. If he had said he was Elijah they would have demanded proof through miracles, since Elijah did miracles. If he had said he was the prophet they would have denounced him as a troublemaker and reported him to the Romans.

Instead he claims that his source for ministry was the prophet Isaiah who wrote extensively about the coming of the Messiah and the circumstances surrounding this event.

At this point they become defensive. They do not respond with belief, instead they question his authority to baptize. If you are not Elijah or the prophet, they say, what gives you the right to baptize?

When we are challenged with the truth, there are only 3 ways to respond:

1. Become defensive. Get mad, run away, reject, deny.
2. Rationalize. Give yourself good reasons to disbelieve or disobey.
3. Submit. Listen carefully, obey the truth, do the right thing.

The reaction of the priests and Levites and by extension, the Pharisees, was to become defensive and challenge John's right to baptize, which in essence was a challenge and rejection of his message: "Get ready (by baptism) because the Messiah is coming."

> Vs. 26-28 – John answered them saying, "I baptize in water, but among you stands One whom you do not know. It is He who comes after me, the thong of whose sandal I am not worthy to untie." These things took place in Bethany beyond the Jordan, where John was baptizing.

John responds to their attitude rather than to their question which was: "If you are not the Christ, Elijah or the prophet, what gives you the right to baptize? In essence he says:

Yes I am baptizing, even though you think I have no right to do so because you do not believe my message. This is just like you. But, there is one here among you today that people like you do not know. You are threatened by what I say and do, but the one of whom I speak is so great, I (who threaten you so much) am not even worthy to untie His sandal. What will you say and do when He comes?

His reference to the Jordan situates the place where this confrontation took place and where John did much of his work.

In verses 29 to 34 the gospel writer now describes John the Baptist's own witness about Jesus. This action takes place after Jesus' baptism that is described in detail in the other gospels.

His witness contains four elements:

1. The purpose of Christ's coming

> Vs. 29 – The next day he saw Jesus coming to him and said, "Behold, the Lamb of God who takes away the sin of the world!"

Jesus did not come to start a movement, do miracles, begin a revolution or a new philosophy. He came to die for men's sins. Everything else serves this purpose or stems from it. John came to announce it; the Apostles reported it; we remember it. This is what faith is about: His death for us and what that means.

2. The character of the One to come

> Vs. 30 – This is He on behalf of whom I said, 'After me comes a Man who has a higher rank than I, for He existed before me.'

John was conceived before Jesus was, he was 6 months older. By saying that Jesus was before him, he declares that Jesus has a divine nature, not simply a human one. We come into being when our bodies are conceived; Jesus existed before his body was conceived.

3. The nature of his ministry

> Vs. 31 – I did not recognize Him, but so that He might
> be manifested to Israel, I came baptizing in water.

His ministry was to baptize those who believed his preaching
and wanted to prepare for the coming One. His ministry would
be validated because the One to come would also come first
through his ministry of baptism.

4. The source of his ministry

> Vs. 32-34 – John testified saying, "I have seen the
> Spirit descending as a dove out of heaven, and He
> remained upon Him. I did not recognize Him, but He
> who sent me to baptize in water said to me, 'He upon
> whom you see the Spirit descending and remaining
> upon Him, this is the One who baptizes in the Holy
> Spirit.' I myself have seen, and have testified that this is
> the Son of God."

John was recognized as special from his birth, people wondered
how God would use him. In this passage he claims the authority
of a prophet based on what he has received from the Lord. It
has been 400 years since the last legitimate prophet spoke in
Israel (Malachi) so this is quite a challenge and excitement for
the people. However, it is not something new: the Jews were
familiar with the presence of inspired men speaking from God.

John says that God gave him his ministry and the sign to identify
the One for whom he was preparing the way. He says that the
sign was the Spirit descending and remaining on one individual,
this would be the One.

In Matthew 3:16, Matthew describes the Spirit as a dove descending on Jesus and a voice from heaven declaring His Sonship. This was the fulfillment of the sign John looked for.

John was told that the one to whom this happened, this would be the one who baptized with the Holy Spirit. In some cases this meant to empower someone to do miraculous things. In all cases this meant the authority to send the Holy Spirit to dwell within a believer. John says that the fulfillment of this sign was the proof to him that Jesus was indeed the God/Man, the Messiah. And so John acknowledges that he had a sign from God to direct him to the true Messiah and that sign was given at the time of Jesus' baptism.

Summary

We have our first episode where John entwines all three of his themes.

1. Jesus the God/Man. John explains the supernatural way John the Baptist was alerted to Jesus' coming.

2. Disbelief. The first examples are the Pharisees, priests and Levites who challenge John's authority to baptize which indirectly disregarded his message (which required him to baptize).

3. Belief. John the Baptist himself was the first true believer and we see him explaining the things (signs) that led him to belief.

And so in his description of John the Baptist's ministry, John sets forth yet another claim of Jesus' divine nature and provides two reactions to this claim (the challenge by the Jews) as well as the belief and witness of John the Baptist.

3.
THE PATTERN OF WITNESS

JOHN 1:35-51

We are studying John's gospel and John's presentation of Jesus as both fully man and fully God. He makes this presentation by using three different strands of narratives:

1. The first strand is made up of accounts of Jesus' ministry and miracles that show both His divine nature and human nature.

2. The second strand contains stories of how some people react to Jesus with faith and trust.

3. The third strand contains other stories that show people reacting to Him with disbelief and rejection.

John does not recount these events in the order I have just explained them. Instead he weaves the three strands into a single narrative with each strand coming into view from time to time.

So far we have seen John begin with a statement that presents Jesus as the divine Messiah and how some would believe and others would disbelieve this claim. This section is in chapter 1:1-18 and is called the prologue. In these 18 verses John summarizes his entire gospel and also demonstrates the three strand approach he will use in writing his information.

After the prologue we looked at John the Baptist, the first character introduced by the gospel writer. As far as the gospel and its approach are concerned, John the Baptist is the first example of someone who believed.

In our last chapter we examined John's witness of faith and his role in preparing the way for Jesus the God/Man's coming.

Witness – Background

Let's leave off our main framework of study (the three strands made up of Jesus' witness and the dual responses of belief and disbelief) for a moment and open a "sub file" entitled: "Power of witness."

In verses 35 to 51 we will notice an early pattern for evangelism beginning with John and spreading out to bring in the first six close disciples of Jesus. They had no Bible school, worship service, correspondence courses or home Bible studies. Their main method of evangelism was through personal witness.

Before we begin to describe the approach or pattern, let's examine what the word "witness" means, because it was a word used to describe John the Baptist and the Apostles. A witness is a person who declares as true what he has seen, heard or knows.

The Greek word for witness is *MARTUS/MARTUR* from which comes the word MARTYR. And martyr describes a person who witnesses the truth of something with their death.

The Apostles were chosen to be witnesses of the death, burial, resurrection of Christ (Acts 1:8).

I explain all this because it is through a witness that the first six disciples come to Jesus, and John explains the pattern and power of witnessing in John 1:35-51.

GOSPEL OF JOHN | 29

The pattern and power of witness

When we read John 1:1-18, we were reading, in summary form, John's witness concerning Jesus.

In verses 19 to 34 we looked at John the Baptist and what we saw was his witness concerning Jesus.

In verses 35 to 51 we will see how the pattern of witnessing works to produce disciples and new witnesses who in turn bring other disciples, etc.

> Vs. 35-37 – Again the next day John was standing with two of his disciples, and he looked at Jesus as He walked, and said, "Behold, the Lamb of God!" The two disciples heard him speak, and they followed Jesus.

This brief description is about John and two converts he makes. The question is, "How do witnesses become witnesses?" The answer is that they hear a witness about someone or something from another person. For example, John became a witness because of what God witnessed to him concerning the coming Messiah (He confirmed with the scriptures). John believed the witness and in turn began to witness what had been revealed to him.

Jesus' first two disciples heard John's witness, believed it and consequently began to follow Jesus.

> Vs. 38-39 – And Jesus turned and saw them following, and said to them, "What do you seek?" They said to Him, "Rabbi (which translated means Teacher), where are You staying?" He said to them, "Come, and you will see." So they came and saw where He was staying; and they stayed with Him that day, for it was about the tenth hour.

What do you think happened that day? Did they sleep, play video games? No, there were questions and discussions about who Jesus was (what did John mean by the term 'lamb of God'?). We see by their following actions that they had to make a decision about Him and they did.

> Vs. 40-42 – One of the two who heard John speak and followed Him, was Andrew, Simon Peter's brother. He found first his own brother Simon and said to him, "We have found the Messiah" (which translated means Christ). He brought him to Jesus. Jesus looked at him and said, "You are Simon the son of John; you shall be called Cephas" (which is translated Peter).

What does Andrew do the next day? He himself becomes a witness for Jesus. So in these brief verses we see a pattern or cycle begin to develop:

1. God witnesses to John about the Messiah and his role in preparing the way. He does this through signs and His Word.
2. John makes his witness about Jesus to the people.
3. Two believe John's witness and follow Christ.
4. They themselves become witnesses for Christ and bring others to Him.

We see then that the witness for Jehovah is Christ, the witness for Christ was John and from John's witness came others who were ready to witness for Christ as well.

> Vs. 43-46 – The next day He purposed to go into Galilee, and He found Philip. And Jesus said to him, "Follow Me." Now Philip was from Bethsaida, of the city of Andrew and Peter. Philip found Nathanael and said to him, "We have found Him of whom Moses in the Law and also the Prophets wrote—Jesus of Nazareth, the

son of Joseph." Nathanael said to him, "Can any good thing come out of Nazareth?" Philip said to him, "Come and see."

Here we see the very same cycle repeated. The crowds that followed Jesus, who waited for Him to teach, how did they know where He would be or who He said He was? The disciples were the ones who provided the crowds. How? Through their witness.

Vs. 47-49 – Jesus saw Nathanael coming to Him, and said of him, "Behold, an Israelite indeed, in whom there is no deceit!" Nathanael said to Him, "How do You know me?" Jesus answered and said to him, "Before Philip called you, when you were under the fig tree, I saw you." Nathanael answered Him, "Rabbi, You are the Son of God; You are the King of Israel."

In these verses John gives more details concerning Jesus' witness and the disciples' reaction.

1. Jesus convinced them or witnessed to them concerning His true identity with His teaching, His knowledge and His power. His claims were backed up by His power. His was a power-based witness.
2. The decision, regardless of who it was, was always the same: He was or He was not the Son of God. The decision remains the same today: to believe in Jesus as the Son of God or to deny His claims. Nathaniel is very clear in his confession of faith.

Vs. 50-51 – Jesus answered and said to him, "Because I said to you that I saw you under the fig tree, do you believe? You will see greater things than these." And He said to him, "Truly, truly, I say to you, you will see the heavens opened and the angels of God ascending and descending on the Son of Man."

Truly, truly; verily, verily means amen, amen… what I am about to say is very important.

Nathaniel has just experienced the supernatural knowledge of Jesus, but in the future he will actually see with his eyes Jesus' supernatural works.

The reference to the heavens opening up and angels ascending and descending means that while Jesus was on earth, all of heavens' power was at His disposal.

The reference to "the Son of Man" comes from Daniel 7:13-14. This is a unique term applied to Jesus:

- It is always "the" and not "a" when used.
- It is a generic term casting Jesus as the Son of Mankind.
- It suggests that Jesus is a man who possesses a human nature in a way that no man has ever possessed it.
- Of course, we know that Jesus' unique status is that He is the only man possessing both a human nature and a divine nature simultaneously.

Jesus' words finish off this section by stating that His witness will only grow stronger for those who believe in Him.

Summary on Christian Witness

As we close out this chapter I would like to make a few comments about witnessing and its importance in our Christian lives.

Each of us owes our salvation to someone's witness.

Whether it was through VBS, a book, an invitation to worship, a newspaper article (as was the case with me), everyone who is a Christian today is one because somebody, somehow provided a witness of Christ to him. The idea is that not every witness is done the same way, not all have the same talent, but all need to witness in some manner. Either you witness directly for Christ through a direct one on one contact; or you do it indirectly by participating in the many works of the church.

The bottom line is that we are each responsible to continue the cycle of witness which first brought the disciples to Christ and eventually brought us to Him as well. There are many methods but we all must make a witness for Christ.

The subject of our witness is Jesus Christ.

Our basic witness is not that the church of Christ is the true church; we are the purest doctrinally of all the religious groups; the Bible is inspired. These are worthy ideas and goals, but not the subject of our essential witness.

No, our witness is that Jesus is the divine Son of God and the Savior of our souls. Our witness is that Jesus is the Lord of our lives. The purpose of our witness is to bring people face to face with this reality.

Now they may not like this witness because this reality will interfere with lifestyle, family, peace, friends, prestige, etc.

This negative response may be an obstacle to us, but we need to remember that Jesus said that if we do not witness (confess) Him here on earth, He will not witness (confess) our names in heaven (Matthew 10:32). We need to witness here if He is to witness there.

Our witness should be confirmed with our lifestyle.

Jesus said, "Let your light (witness) shine before men in such a way that they may see your good works and glorify your Father who is in heaven." (Matthew 5:16)

If our lifestyles have no moral power then our witness will have no saving power.

In the Bible, the witnesses were prepared and often forfeited their very lives as a confirmation that what they said was true. All were willing to lay down their lives so that others would be assured that their witness was sincere, true and powerful. People do not give up their lives for what they know is a lie or a mistake, and people are never impressed by a lukewarm witness.

Exhortation

I know a lot of us have received a witness of Christ's person and power in some way, and I am persuaded that most have decided to believe the witness and become disciples of Jesus. True maturity comes, however, when we complete the cycle and begin to make our witness for Christ.

Many Christians often feel a lack of joy, purpose or peace in their souls. Often times the reason for this condition is because they are not completing the cycle of witness in their lives. They have received the witness from someone, they have believed and responded to it, but they themselves have not begun to witness to others and in so doing they are denying their calling in Christ.

They fail to witness in several ways:

1. They are not witnessing directly or indirectly to anyone.
2. They are eliminating the power of the gospel and their own witness for Christ with low moral standards or a lack of commitment to the church.

We will never see the heavens open up and God's power working in our lives if we do not begin making a powerful moral witness to the world with our lives, and a powerful witness of loving service to others.

People expect this from Christ's disciples and our witness falls short when we do not deliver on people's expectations of us in spiritual matters.

Preview

We have digressed a bit in order to examine the evangelistic pattern outlined for us in these few verses:

- Step 1 – Hear the witness (Romans 10:17)
- Step 2 – Believe the witness (Mark 16:15-16)
- Step 3 – Make a witness to others (Matthew 28:18-20)

In the following chapter we will go back to our main outline and review the first burst of ministry Jesus accomplishes as He begins to preach in the northern part of the country.

4.
MIRACLE
AT CANA

JOHN 2:1-12

We are beginning chapter 2 of John's gospel where Jesus will go public with His ministry in a first demonstration of His power and authority.

Wedding at Cana

Until this time Jesus' ministry is largely practiced among the disciples of John the Baptist and within the confines of His home area and family. There is little, if any resistance to Jesus at this point, just as there is little resistance at our efforts to confess Christ so long as it is confined to the church building and our own Christian family. It is when we reveal ourselves publicly that the trouble starts, and so it was with Jesus when He began His public ministry at Cana.

Wedding feasts were great and joyous occasions during those times. Life revolved around the religious calendar and family events. A betrothal (engagement) meant that the couple were legally joined as man and wife, but usually remained with their families until co-habitation was arranged. The wedding feast signaled that the couple would begin actually living together as husband and wife. Many times the groom and his party would parade through the streets in order to fetch his bride and bring her to the wedding feast from which they would eventually leave to spend their first night together in their home. The feast itself could be an elaborate event which lasted seven days or more as guests arrived to wish the couple well. This type of celebration required an ample supply of food and drink. It was to such a feast Jesus was invited along with His disciples in Cana.

> Vs. 1-3 – On the third day there was a wedding in Cana of Galilee, and the mother of Jesus was there; and both Jesus and His disciples were invited to the wedding. When the wine ran out, the mother of Jesus said to Him, "They have no wine."

Cana in Galilee was near Jesus' adult home located in Capernaum. Mary was at the wedding as friend and helper, it could well have been some family member being married. The wine ran out early and losing the main beverage so soon would spoil the feast and embarrass the family. Mary comes to Jesus (rather than the host) and states the problem, and in so doing intimates that He should solve this problem.

> Vs. 4-5 – And Jesus said to her, "Woman, what does that have to do with us? My hour has not yet come." His mother said to the servants, "Whatever He says to you, do it."

"Woman what does that have to do with us?" literally means never mind; do not worry about it; this is my affair, not yours; what common thing do we share in this?

Her question contains a suggestion that she expects her action to move Him to a solution. His answer reveals that He is aware of what is going on and in control of the situation. He does not act because of her insistence. His time is not yet come; God initiates His actions, not man. Note also that the term "woman" is not a harsh or derogatory term for that time. See John 19:26 for comparison "Woman, behold your son."

His mother understands His response and since she was there as a helper, she gives instructions to the other helpers to follow His directions. Note that she leaves the problem in His hands after stating it. Many times we add solutions along with our prayers, but God's solutions to our prayers are not always the same as ours.

> Vs. 6-8 – Now there were six stone water pots set there for the Jewish custom of purification, containing twenty or thirty gallons each. Jesus said to them, "Fill the water pots with water." So they filled them up to the brim. And He said to them, "Draw some out now and take it to the headwaiter." So they took it to him.

Water pots were needed for purification as well as the washing of utensils, etc. as was the custom of Jesus before eating. Jesus has them filled with water and then had a sample taken to the host for a taste. Note how effortlessly the miracle is produced: Jesus only intentioned it and it was done.

> Vs. 9-10 – When the headwaiter tasted the water which had become wine, and did not know where it came from (but the servants who had drawn the water knew), the headwaiter called the bridegroom, and said to him, "Every man serves the good wine first, and when the people have drunk freely, then he serves the poorer wine; but you have kept the good wine until now."

When the host or head-waiter tastes, he compliments the groom on the excellence of the wine. A side benefit of the miracle is that it not only saved the family from embarrassment and maintained the joy of the feast, but also blessed the groom in the eyes of his guests.

The head-waiter's compliment rested on the common practice of serving the sweet, fresh wine first and after much eating and drinking the taste buds are dulled so then they would serve the older, less tasty wine which would, by that time, not be noticed. The groom was complimented on serving good wine at the beginning and then the best at the end.

There are several comments I would like to make about this first miracle of Jesus at Cana.

The secretiveness of it

Only a few (His mother and a few of the servants along with His disciples) knew that a great miracle had taken place. Jesus managed to demonstrate His power to a few people without upsetting or overshadowing the happy moment that this couple and guests were sharing.

The miracle would be spoken of for all time, but for that precious moment, Jesus limited its impact to accommodate his hosts, while providing a witness to His disciples.

The nature of the miracle

The basic nature of the miracle is that Jesus transformed water into wine with only His will.

Many debate whether the water turned into pure grape juice or wine with an alcohol content. The argument is based on the Greek word OINOS and if it only refers to fermented wine or to grape juice or both. Here are some links to arguments for both sides of this issue so you can read and decide for yourselves:

- letgodbetrue.com/bible/heresies/did-jesus-make-wine.php
- letgodbetrue.com/proverbs/commentaries/20_01.php

For our study I simply want to point out that whether it was grape juice or wine with 3% alcohol content, or 6% content... the important thing to remember was that this was a great miracle.

> Vs. 11 – This beginning of His signs Jesus did in Cana
> of Galilee, and manifested His glory, and His disciples
> believed in Him.

John notes that this was His first sign. The Greek word for
miracle is "sign." The point is that a miracle is not done to amaze
but rather to point to someone or something or to reveal
something. In this case, the sign points to Jesus as someone
with supernatural power. The sign manifests His glory, His glory
as the God/Man.

John mentions that these disciples believed in Him because of
this sign; a brief show of one of the three strands of his
narrative.

> Vs. 12 – After this He went down to Capernaum, He
> and His mother and His brothers and His disciples; and
> they stayed there a few days.

We see from this verse that the feast was probably a family
affair because even Jesus' brothers were at the event. They,
however, were not privy to the miracle because John separates
them from the disciples and there is no word from Mary either.

Jesus returns to His home that was in Capernaum. (Some think
He may have lived with Peter.)

5.
THE CLEANSING OF THE TEMPLE

JOHN 2:13-25

After His baptism, Jesus returns to His home area and displays a sign of His miraculous powers to a small number of people. This event is part of the first strand of narrative where John describes Jesus doing things only God can do.

In the next section he continues with this strand demonstrating not in a miraculous act, but rather in an act of zeal and authority, Jesus' divine nature. This next scene is described as the cleansing of the Temple.

Cleansing of the temple

Now that Jesus has taken a first step into public ministry at Cana, He will go to Jerusalem for a very public and dynamic demonstration of His zeal and authority.

> Vs. 13-14 – The Passover of the Jews was near, and Jesus went up to Jerusalem. And He found in the temple those who were selling oxen and sheep and doves, and the money changers seated at their tables.

Even though Jerusalem is south of Galilee, a person was said to go "up" to Jerusalem, that was the Holy City. Jews from everywhere gathered in Jerusalem for the feast of Passover. The temple's center housed the Holy of Holies where only the High Priest could enter on a yearly basis. This building was segregated by a series of walls and courtyards that separated the priests from the people, the men from the women and the Jews from the Gentile converts.

The court of the Gentiles was symbolically the entrance court where all nations could gather and pray together to the God of all the nations. It was the largest of the courts and was separated from the courts where only the Jewish people and priests could go.

Porticos (Solomon's)

The Porticos or Great Colonnades were the location where Jesus taught when He taught at the Temple. It also became a meeting place for early Christians (Acts 3:22, 5:12). The Royal Porch of Herod (south side) was where Jesus sat among the doctors of Law at age 12 (Luke 2:46).

Temple area

All of the temple area was considered holy, but it increased in holiness as you approached the center area where the Holy of Holies was situated. These areas were separated according to who was permitted to enter.

Gates

There were eight entrances into the temple area, each with their significance.

For example, the Pilgrim Gate led to the court of the Gentiles for those visiting during festivals. There was a large pool of water where pilgrims washed before entering the temple area. The Pilgrim Road led from the pool of Siloam to the steps leading to the gate of Pilgrims (1/3 of a mile). It is where Peter preached his first sermon (Acts 2:38). People who were baptized then could have been baptized in this pool. Josephus, a Jewish historian, claims that one to four million pilgrims visited Jerusalem and the temple each year.

The Eastern Gate (Golden Gate) was the main entrance to the temple area. It was the approach through the Mount of Olives and facing the garden of Gethsemane across the small Kidron Valley. Through this gate Jesus entered on a donkey.

According to Jewish tradition, the Messiah was supposed to enter through this gate:

> Rejoice greatly, O daughter of Zion!
> Shout in triumph, O daughter of Jerusalem!
> Behold, your king is coming to you;
> He is just and endowed with salvation,
> Humble, and mounted on a donkey,
> Even on a colt, the foal of a donkey.
> - Zechariah 9:9

Ezekiel says that after the Messiah passes through the gate it will be shut:

> Then He brought me back by the way of the outer gate
> of the sanctuary, which faces the east; and it was shut.
> The Lord said to me, "This gate shall be shut; it shall
> not be opened, and no one shall enter by it, for the Lord
> God of Israel has entered by it; therefore it shall be
> shut. As for the prince, he shall sit in it as prince to eat
> bread before the Lord; he shall enter by way of the
> porch of the gate and shall go out by the same way."
> - Ezekiel 44:1-3

Interestingly, when the Muslims conquered Jerusalem in 1530 AD, they blocked up this gate with stones and planted a cemetery in front of it as their way of preventing the Jewish

Messiah from entering in (thinking that no Jew would step into a foreign cemetery). This part of Jerusalem is still controlled by Muslims; the gate is still blocked, the cemetery still there and a mosque stands where the Holy of Holies used to be.

Courts

Women's Court: Women could not mix with men in the temple area and had their own area but could go no further in. It was in this court that the court "treasury" was, having twelve trumpet shaped containers for voluntary offerings. Jesus was sitting "opposite the treasury" when He saw the widow put into the treasury her only two coins (Luke 12:41-44).

Court of Israel: This was the place where Jewish men gathered who were neither priests nor Levites. This is where Jewish laymen gathered for prayer, etc.

Court of Priests: Only priests could enter here. In this area was the altar of burnt offering where animal sacrifices were made (45' long and 22' high).

Holy Place – 3 areas

The Porch: This was an entrance way with a gold covered back wall and where a golden lamp hung. There were two tables (gold and marble) that held the showbread which was eaten only by priests. There was a veil at the entrance.

The Hall: In the hall stood the golden altar, golden table, frankincense cups, and a golden lamp stand. Priests offered incense here. (I.e. Zachariah, once in a lifetime for ordinary priest – Luke 1:8-23).

The Veil: A double veil separated the Holy of Holies from the Hall. Only the High Priest could access the Holy of Holies only once per year on the Day of Atonement. The Holy of Holies had no furnishings. What it originally contained were the tablets of the 10 Commandments, jar of manna and Aaron's rod, within the

Ark of the Covenant which was destroyed when the Babylonians destroyed Solomon's original temple in 587 BC.

Court of the Gentiles

Converts to Judaism as well as Gentiles could gather here, but go no further under penalty of death. Jews could not execute the death penalty under Roman law except in this case for this one violation (even Roman citizens). This is what Paul the Apostle was nearly killed over in Acts 21:27-32 when he was accused of willfully bringing a Gentile into the Court of the Israelites. This is where the money changers and merchants had set up shop and Jesus came to run them out (more later).

Antonia Fortress

Named after Herod's friend (Mark Antony) it housed a garrison of 600 Roman soldiers and had an underground passageway that connected the garrison to the court of the Gentiles. The Romans had abolished the role of king in Israel and allowed the High Priests to continue by appointment and approval of Roman leadership. The robes of the High Priest were kept in the towers and permitted usage only on special holidays (to restrict the influence of High Priests).

This area is where Jesus was questioned by Pilate and tortured by Roman soldiers before being handed over to Jewish leaders.

Temple tax was collected before Passover from everyone 20 years and over. Those coming from afar had to have their money exchanged into shekels and also had to purchase animals for sacrifice at Passover.

Originally this commerce had taken place outside the temple walls, but with time the merchants had been allowed to set up in the Court of the Gentiles. This rendered the area designated for the Gentiles unclean and therefore useless as a place of worship for them; it was the only place they could worship in the temple complex.

Even though it was the Court of Gentiles, it was still part of the temple and defiling this place defiled all of it; not to mention the hypocrisy and prejudice this represented (money changers paid a portion of profits to the priests so they could do business).

> Vs. 15-17 – And He made a scourge of cords, and drove them all out of the temple, with the sheep and the oxen; and He poured out the coins of the money changers and overturned their tables; and to those who were selling the doves He said, "Take these things away; stop making My Father's house a place of business." His disciples remembered that it was written, "Zeal for Your house will consume me."

Jesus forces these merchants and their goods out of the temple area.

People often see Jesus as the friend of children and suffering Savior, but in this scene we see Him demonstrating not only His righteous anger in defending what is proper but also His physical power. No one stood in His way or stood up to Him. Thirty years old with a couple of decades working as a carpenter and stone mason meant that He was no physical weakling. He was not afraid of removing those elements that were spoiling the purity of the temple.

In this scene we see Jesus show His humanity as His religious zeal moved Him to a righteous indignation and anger towards those who were in the wrong. This is a very human reaction to injustice and impurity.

> Vs. 18-22 – The Jews then said to Him, "What sign do You show us as your authority for doing these things?" Jesus answered them, "Destroy this temple, and in three days I will raise it up."

The Jews then said, "It took forty-six years to build this temple, and will You raise it up in three days?" But He was speaking of the temple of His body. So when He was raised from the dead, His disciples remembered that He said this; and they believed the Scripture and the word which Jesus had spoken.

The Jews had established certain customs in their religious lives with the disclaimer or epitaph that said "Until Elias Comes." They did this because they believed that when the prophet Elias/Elijah returned as a forerunner of the Messiah, he would either confirm or change the religious customs they had established. So after Jesus' cleansing of the temple area, the Jewish leaders do not arrest Jesus, instead they ask to see if He has any sign to confirm that He has a right to do this; after all He might be the prophet!

Jesus knows their hearts. They do not really want to believe. For people who do not want to believe, no amount of proof is sufficient.

So Jesus reveals (in a veiled manner) the sign that will furnish undeniable proof of His identity, however, in the end it will be the proof that will convict them for their disbelief. He will ultimately die because of their rejection and disbelief. His resurrection will become not only the proof of His legitimate claim as the Messiah, it will also be the proof that their unbelief was wrong.

Of course, the prophecy made here about the destruction of His body and its resurrection, as well as the destruction of the city and temple, were fulfilled first through His death, burial and resurrection only 3 years hence. Next, in 70 AD, the Roman army laid siege to the city and eventually killed most of the inhabitants and then took the city apart stone by stone.

If you travel by the city today, you can still see the huge stones in rubble at the base of the walls built by the crusaders; the very stones that the Romans tore apart in the 1st century. They burned what would burn; they carried off what precious metal and cloth they could; they disassembled the walls and temple of the Holy City.

They destroyed the genealogical records stored in the temple area by which the Jews could trace their original tribes. This was a deathblow because without the records there was no way to know for sure what land was yours or determine who could serve as priest.

Today a mosque called the Dome of the Rock stands on the spot where the temple and Holy of Holies once stood.

The Jews still believe that one day the temple and the Holy of Holies will be rebuilt. They pray for this at the Wailing Wall (Western wall) which is the only remaining section of wall from that time. It is 100 yards from the original spot where the Holy of Holies once stood. This is why it is considered a sacred place.

> Vs. 23-25 – Now when He was in Jerusalem at the Passover, during the feast, many believed in His name, observing His signs which He was doing. But Jesus, on His part, was not entrusting Himself to them, for He knew all men, and because He did not need anyone to testify concerning man, for He Himself knew what was in man.

John mentions, but does not describe, the miracles Jesus does during this time. Many believed because of the miracles but were not ready to receive His teaching. They were convinced He was special, but Jesus did not want to become their "leader" because He knew that their hearts were not yet turned to God and ready to accept what He was sent to do.

6.
CHANGED BY FAITH

JOHN 3:1-16

We are working our way through the gospel of John always keeping our eyes open for the three main ideas that John is weaving into one single narrative.

We begin chapter three in John's gospel reading about Jesus' encounter with Nicodemus, an elder and teacher of the nation of Israel. We will see in their exchange that John is showing Jesus, the God/Man, teaching with authority and revealing what only God could reveal to this seeker. The essence of their dialogue is about change, the change necessary to enter the kingdom of God.

We often hear the expression "saved by faith," and it is true, but the reason we are saved by faith is because faith changes us, and the change wrought in us by faith is the transition from death to life.

Keep these ideas in mind as we study about Nicodemus' meeting with Jesus the God/Man.

> Vs. 1-2 – Now there was a man of the Pharisees, named Nicodemus, a ruler of the Jews; this man came to Jesus by night and said to Him, "Rabbi, we know that

> You have come from God as a teacher; for no one can do these signs that You do unless God is with him."

Nicodemus came after dark for fear of losing his position. He was a member of the Sanhedrin, the ruling religious body made up of 70 priests, Scribes and elders. He himself was a Pharisee (a sect or party of Scribes who were extremely conservative and zealous for the Law and Jewish traditions). Nicodemus believed that Jesus was a prophet and teacher. He also acknowledged that Jesus' miracles were a manifestation of God's power and authority. (Other prophets had done miracles, i.e. Elijah.)

> Vs. 3 – Jesus answered and said to him, "Truly, truly, I say to you, unless one is born again he cannot see the kingdom of God."

Nicodemus expressed his limited faith in coming to Jesus, admitting what he does believe about Him. Jesus, in response to this, begins to explain to him the principle of regeneration, for which He uses the term "born again." The Lord says that unless one is "born again" (changed, regenerated) he cannot see the kingdom of God.

The "kingdom of God" is created and present when the will of God is being done. In the Old Testament period the Jews perceived it as a glorious earthly kingdom where God would guarantee His people prosperity, protection and power in the world (this was their notion of heaven). With the revelation of the New Testament we have come to understand that the kingdom of God is God's will being pursued and carried out in every dimension. It perfectly exists in heaven and it partially exists here on earth in the form of the church. The promise of Christ is that the earthly kingdom of God, in the form of the church, will one day be perfected, when Jesus returns, and joined to the heavenly kingdom to form the perfect union between God and His kingdom.

When all things are subjected to Him, then the Son Himself also will be subjected to the One who subjected all things to Him, so that God may be all in all.
- I Corinthians 15:28

The point here is that Nicodemus was told that in order to enter into "heaven" or the "kingdom" he had to be re-born, changed, regenerated! This was difficult for him to grasp because the Jews in general believed that because they had been chosen by God, no change was necessary. And for a scholar, elder, leader like Nicodemus, the thinking was that his type was guaranteed entry. But Jesus says to Nicodemus, unless he is reborn he cannot enter in. The conclusion was that power, position, training and tradition counted for nothing in the process of being reborn.

Vs. 4 – Nicodemus said to Him, "How can a man be born when he is old? He cannot enter a second time into his mother's womb and be born, can he?"

Nicodemus acknowledges that it is impossible to repeat natural birth, so what is Jesus talking about? He understood that a change was necessary but could not grasp what kind of change and how it could be accomplished.

Look at Nicodemus' attitude: even though he was older and in a better social position than Jesus, he wanted to know the truth and so he humbled himself in order to find it. This teaches us an important lesson: we cannot go forward in spiritual knowledge and understanding unless we humble ourselves.

God is opposed to the proud but gives grace to the humble.
- James 4:6

To go forward means leaving some things behind. This is a basic lesson in the exercise of humility. Change requires that we reexamine what we have learned, what we think, what we believe, and leave behind those things which are false, shallow, inaccurate and sinful.

> Vs. 5 – Jesus answered, "Truly, truly, I say to you, unless one is born of water and the Spirit he cannot enter into the kingdom of God."

Nicodemus humbles himself and Jesus gives him more information concerning this change. The change occurs not by being a Jew, a Pharisee or a teacher: you do not enter the kingdom this way. You enter the kingdom by water and the Spirit. In this short explanation Jesus gives Nicodemus two necessary insights:

1. The power of regeneration (the One who makes the change happen) is the Holy Spirit of God.
2. The place where this regeneration happens is not in your mother's womb but in the waters of baptism.

Nicodemus would have been familiar with these two concepts:

1. As a scholar and Pharisee he knew and believed that the Spirit gave power to the judges, kings and prophets in order to transform their lives and service. "The Spirit of the Lord God is upon me…" (Isaiah 61:1)
2. As a contemporary of Jesus, he also knew that John the Baptist as well as Jesus preached that all should repent and be baptized in order to prepare for the kingdom to come.

In His reply to Nicodemus' request for more information, Jesus simply puts these two ideas together for him. The message to the leader of the nation was no different than the message to the common people: repent and be baptized.

> Vs. 6 – That which is born of the flesh is flesh, and that which is born of the Spirit is spirit.

Jesus continues to repeat the idea that the power source for change (the change necessary to enter the kingdom) comes from God, not man. Whatever comes from the flesh cannot be transformed into something spiritual and vice versa, whatever comes from God is spiritual and remains that way. In other words, man cannot by himself change himself and avoid condemnation in this way. Only God can change man; 10,000 years of history prove this.

> Vs. 7-8 – Do not be amazed that I said to you, 'You must be born again.' The wind blows where it wishes and you hear the sound of it, but do not know where it comes from and where it is going; so is everyone who is born of the Spirit.

Nicodemus is amazed: that he needs to change (he thought he was okay); that he cannot do it himself (he thought he had achieved righteousness through the Law).

Jesus replies that not only is the Spirit doing the work, but you cannot see the Spirit working to effect this change in you, however the change is there nevertheless. He compares the work of the Spirit to the wind: you do not see the wind, just its effect on other things; you do not see the Spirit, but you see results: faith in Christ, love of others, hatred and remorse for sin (clearest sign).

> Vs. 9 – Nicodemus said to Him, "How can these things be?"

Nicodemus asks, "How does the Spirit do this?" He wants more details; it is not enough that the Spirit does this, he wants to know how.

We do not hear from Nicodemus again until much later, but for now we see Jesus giving him more answers, more insights into the process of regeneration.

> Vs. 10-11 – Jesus answered and said to him, "Are you the teacher of Israel and do not understand these things? Truly, truly, I say to you, we speak of what we know and testify of what we have seen, and you do not accept our testimony."

Jesus points out that it is not intelligence that is lacking, it is faith. Jesus tells him that what He is teaching him, He does so from personal knowledge and experience. Not like the Jewish rabbis who debated each other on the strength of what other rabbis wrote about the Law. His miracles were proof that what He said was indeed the truth.

The problem Nicodemus was facing was that he believed the miracles but was having trouble believing in the one who did the miracles, Jesus. Jesus brings Nicodemus to the core of his problem of not being able to perceive the truth: it began with his disbelief in Jesus. There is no understanding of spiritual things without first believing in Jesus.

> Vs. 12-13 – If I told you earthly things and you do not believe, how will you believe if I tell you heavenly things? No one has ascended into heaven, but He who descended from heaven: the Son of Man.

The Lord explains to him the necessity of faith for understanding spiritual things: He says, "I am explaining things that I have actually seen and experienced (because I have seen them in heaven), and you do not believe Me." If you do not believe me concerning things which can be explained using earthly examples (waves, etc.) how will you ever understand when I speak to you of heavenly things, which I have seen, such as glorified bodies, angels, etc, for which there are no earthly equivalents; things that require faith to understand, not mere human intelligence?

Now in saying this Jesus gives Nicodemus a third piece of information: the fact that the power of the Spirit to change a person and thus save him is ignited by faith, not intelligence, position or power. Salvation is possible because there is a change, and change is possible because of faith.

In the last section of this passage Jesus reveals the last point upon which all the process of change, rebirth and regeneration rests: the only faith that will move the Spirit to change us is faith in Jesus Christ the Savior. To illustrate this Jesus uses a powerful image from the Old Testament.

> Vs. 14-15 – As Moses lifted up the serpent in the wilderness, even so must the Son of Man be lifted up; so that whoever believes will in Him have eternal life.

Jesus makes a parallel between this incident that happened while the Jews wandered in the desert with Moses, and His own death on the cross which was still in the future, and He shows how faith connects both events.

In Numbers 21:9, the Bible tells the story of the people rebelling against Moses and God while in the wilderness, and for which God sent poisonous snakes among them as punishment. Many were dying and so they went to Moses for help. He prayed to God and was told to fashion a bronze serpent and place it on a pole/standard, and that whoever looked at the serpent would be healed. All those who did this were healed.

Now the key element for Nicodemus to understand was that it was not the snake that saved people, or just looking at it, it was the faith they displayed in obeying God that healed them. The snake represented an offering for sin.

In the same way, the death of Christ on the cross (lifted up) by itself does not heal men of their sins, otherwise all people in the world would have their sins forgiven by this act. His offering in payment for sin, looked upon with faith by those infected by sin, moves God to forgive men and empower them through the Spirit to change and thereby save them.

Jesus puts all these ideas together in the 16th verse.

> Vs. 16 – For God so loved the world, that He gave His only begotten Son, that whoever believes in Him shall not perish, but have eternal life.

Summary

If you were the one who had gone instead of Nicodemus, here's what you would have learned:

No one goes to heaven unless a change takes place here on earth first.

We cannot enter into the presence of God unless we are changed from guilty to forgiven; disobedient to a willingness to obey; condemned to accepted as sons; spiritually dead to spiritually alive and fruitful.

If these changes have not occurred in your life, you shall not enter the kingdom of heaven.

The change takes place in a particular way.

1. It is powered by God. He is the power behind the change, not us.

2. The change is based on faith in Christ, not intelligence, self-will, power or position. If you do not believe, there is no change.

3. The change happens at baptism. Just as looking at the snake was an expression of faith ordained by God, baptism is now that perfect expression of faith that

results in our forgiveness and reception of the Holy Spirit. (Acts 2:38)

Jesus Christ is at the center of this change.

The Spirit that changes us is sent by Him – Matthew 3:11.

It is not faith in general that saves or transforms; it is faith in Him that has the power to regenerate us. He is at the center of our faith – John 14:6.

When we are baptized we are reenacting His death, burial and resurrection. We are saying we believe in His death, burial and resurrection by going through a similar experience ourselves in the waters of baptism. It is the perfect expression because it is an expression of faith in Christ in particular.

Epilogue

Nicodemus' life changed after that night. You only see a few glimpses of him but enough to observe the transformation of faith in him:

In John 7:50 he defends Jesus to the Sanhedrin, not as a disciple, but as a point of Law. A timid defense but a beginning nevertheless.

After Jesus' death, he and Joseph of Arimathea bury the Lord's body. Again by night, again a timid gesture, but this time counting himself as a disciple.

Tradition, not the Bible, has it that he was finally put out of the Sanhedrin, baptized by Peter and John and, at his death, buried in a common grave with other Christians.

Let us hope that Nicodemus experienced the change he sought after when he came to Jesus on that dark night.

Let us also hope that our faith is changing us, not our circumstances, not our self-will, as we look to Jesus for rebirth and eternal life.

7.

THE MYSTERY REVEALED

JOHN 3:17-21

We are studying the gospel of John and focusing on how Jesus Himself is portrayed in John.

We see Him described as the God/Man, the One with both a physical and a divine nature. We also see the recurring themes of belief and disbelief among those who came into contact with the Lord. John skillfully weaves these three main themes together into one narrative.

We have also examined the dialogue between Jesus and a leader of Israel called Nicodemus. In their conversation Nicodemus tried to understand as Jesus revealed to Him the requirements needed to enter into the kingdom of God. Nicodemus accepted that the miracles Jesus did were from God, but had a hard time accepting that Jesus Himself was divine and the object of faith.

In essence, Jesus the God/Man was revealing to Nicodemus the "mystery" that had been kept secret for so long. This "mystery" as Paul refers to it in Romans 16:25, was the way to obtain eternal life. Jesus said that Nicodemus had to change and be reborn in water.

Of course it was hard for Nicodemus to understand because Jesus had not yet died on the cross and risen, but for now, in preparation for all of this, the change he needed to make was to humble himself in obedience to Jesus and be baptized to purify his soul. Later, as the gospel would be preached and the details of the kingdom explained, Nicodemus would be able to grasp more fully the meaning and value of what Jesus was offering him.

As I said previously, John 3:16 summarizes God's plan and purpose for sending Jesus. I would now like to review this plan of salvation, compare it to other plans and examine Jesus' feelings about the plan and why, for the most part, it was rejected.

God's plan: salvation by faith

When we study other major religions in the world we see that they also have plans for salvation. Major religions have traditionally been divided into 4 main groups which are listed below with general dates of their origin.

Near Eastern religions (Middle East/West/North)

Near Eastern religions and their subdivisions are the ones that we are most familiar with. These include:

1. **Judaism** (1400 BC) – Their concept of salvation is based on obedience to the Law of Moses and cultural identity.

2. **Zoroastrianism** (600 BC) – Salvation was based on the doing of good and certain worship rituals, especially with fire.

3. **Islam** (600 AD) – Salvation based on completing the 5 Pillars: a) confession ("There is only one God and Mohammad is his prophet."); b) alms (giving 2 ½% - "Zakat"); c) daily prayer ("God is great"); d) fasting (during the holy days – Ramadan); e) pilgrimage to Mecca, the holy city. JIHAD (holy war) guarantees salvation.

4. **Christianity** (40 AD) – When you study comparative religion, Christianity is categorized as a Near Eastern religion. We will discuss its plan or concept of salvation later. Salvation is by faith.

Eastern religions (mainly India)

Most eastern religions resemble one another. There are many but three are the source. They aim for the same goal but follow different ways.

1. **Hinduism** (oldest organized religion that still exists) – Concept of salvation for Hindus is the continual improvement of self in various ways for a number of lifetimes until one reaches "MOKSHA." A merging with deity; not a personal being but rather a "force of nature into which you merge unconsciously." Like a drop of water falling into the ocean.

2. **Jainism** (500 BC) – Salvation comes by total renunciation of the flesh and its pleasures (sex, personal relationships, personal possessions). This is how one reaches "MOKSHA."

3. **Sikhism** (1400 AD) – Love of God, doing good is the way to "MOKSHA."

Far Eastern religions (Asian)

1. **Confucianism** (500 BC) – Developing personal virtues, especially in leaders. No formal worship or deity. Social maturity was salvation for society.

2. **Shinto** (Japan) – They had no concept of salvation except to keep the Japanese nation supreme. Veneration of past family was main worship ritual.

3. **Buddhism** (500 BC) – Abandoning physical desire to possess things enables a person to be free. Freedom from the desire to possess is salvation. The method is to

renounce all; when you cease to be, then you become. NIRVANAH.

4. **Taoism** (600 BC) – To be in harmony with one's surroundings, because you have no power to change who or what you are. Salvation comes from balancing the Ying and Yang; by fitting into your surroundings. No afterlife (consciousness).

Miscellaneous religions

Some do not fit any category but are widely practiced.

1. **Animism** – Not a formal or organized religion. Common beliefs among primitive peoples, from various regions. Salvation in animistic religions (Voodoo for example) is found by appeasing the spirits with gifts and finding ways to be safe from them.

2. **Naturalism** (1700 AD) – Not a religion but a belief system. Finding happiness and contentment in this world by self-actualization because there is no God.

Each of the twelve main religions I have briefly described has its concept of salvation. Although they have different approaches, these eleven religions have only three ways they put forward for an individual to obtain salvation:

1. By doing religious exercises.

2. By doing good works.

3. By doing a combination of meditation and asceticism.

When it came to salvation, they only offered two possible scenarios for what that salvation was:

1. Physical paradise (now or later)

2. Absorption into a greater power, unconsciously

The majority of people on the earth have sought these two objectives by pursuing these three ways while practicing one of these eleven major religions.

When we look at Jesus' discussion with Nicodemus, we see another view of salvation pursued in a radically different way.

God's religion and salvation

For comparative religion courses in college, they place Christianity as the fourth major religion in the Near Eastern section. It is put here because historically and geographically it is similar to the other three, but that is where the similarity ends.

Christianity is a religion. However, by virtue of its fulfilled prophecy, witnessed miracles, written revelation and impact on the world, it is in a class all by itself. No other religion even comes close.

In John 3:14-16, Jesus reveals God's plan of salvation and man's response to it, this is why I have devoted so much time to it.

In vs. 14-15 Jesus summarizes the essence of God's plan to save man by tying together an event from the past with an event that was to take place in the future.

> Vs. 14-15 – As Moses lifted up the serpent in the wilderness, even so must the Son of Man be lifted up; so that whoever believes will in Him have eternal life.

In this, Jesus explains to Nicodemus that the plan God had for change (salvation), He previewed in the Old Testament and would accomplish through Him in the near future. The episode with the snake in the desert was a preview of His method of salvation.

> Then they set out from Mount Hor by the way of the Red Sea, to go around the land of Edom; and the people became impatient because of the journey. The people spoke against God and Moses, "Why have you brought us up out of Egypt to die in the wilderness? For there is no food and no water, and we loathe this miserable food." The Lord sent fiery serpents among the people and they bit the people, so that many people of Israel died. So the people came to Moses and said, "We have sinned, because we have spoken against the Lord and you; intercede with the Lord, that He may remove the serpents from us." And Moses interceded for the people. Then the Lord said to Moses, "Make a fiery serpent, and set it on a standard; and it shall come about, that everyone who is bitten, when he looks at it, he will live." And Moses made a bronze serpent and set it on the standard; and it came about, that if a serpent bit any man, when he looked to the bronze serpent, he lived.
> - Numbers 21:4-9

In this story we are able to see spiritual principles at work:

1. Disobedience is sin.
2. The penalty for sin is suffering and death.
3. The salvation from sin and death is achieved when God provides atonement or payment for sin and man believes and trusts that God's atonement removes his sins and thus saves him.

In the Old Testament story, the disobedience and murmuring of the people was sinful. The penalty was inflicted by the poisonous snakes sent by God. The atonement was represented by the bronze figure on the pole. The response of faith and trust was expressed as the people looked upon the bronze snake attached to the pole.

In John 3:15, Jesus looks ahead to His crucifixion and establishes this as God's final atonement or payment for all sins. The sins are every act of disobedience by all. The penalty is not just poisonous snakes but the eternal death of hell. The atonement of God is Jesus' perfect life offered as a sacrifice on the cross at Calvary. The response of faith and trust in Jesus is now expressed in repentance and baptism, as explained earlier to Nicodemus.

The salvation and the way to it is summarized in vs. 16.

> Vs. 16 – For God so loved the world, that He gave His only begotten Son, that whoever believes in Him shall not perish, but have eternal life.

We see that God's salvation is not a continuous cycle of life that ends in oblivion, nor a paradise of physical pleasure. It is an individual, personal, never ending experience of life with a new body on a level and in a dimension that can only partly be described with terms such as peace, joy, purity, power, love, wisdom, etc.

The way to God's salvation is not mediation, mysticism or philosophy; not the doing of religious exercises; not the performance of good deeds; not the denial of the body. Some of these things have value, but only in the context of Christian living.

No, the way to this salvation is through faith in Jesus Christ expressed at first through repentance and baptism, and then lived out through the love of others because of Him.

The reason God set this plan in motion is because He so loved the world. God's justice sends forth judgment and punishment for sin. God's love sends forth Christ to absorb the punishment and offer forgiveness based on faith.

The reason these other religious systems fail is because none of them provide mankind with what it needs, atonement for sin.

Jesus reveals to Nicodemus the plan of salvation (Christ dies for the sins of men); and the way or response to salvation: faith in Christ expressed in repentance and baptism. He also reveals the reason for salvation: God's great love.

Man's response to God's plan

In His dialogue with Nicodemus, Jesus also reveals how mankind in general would actually respond to God's plan, God's gift.

> Vs. 17 – For God did not send the Son into the world to judge the world, but that the world might be saved through Him.

If Jesus did come as judge, the entire world would be condemned. If He came for this judgment and punishment it would already have been handed out. Jesus says that He came as Savior not judge, so the world has an opportunity at true salvation.

> Vs. 18 – He who believes in Him is not judged; he who does not believe has been judged already, because he has not believed in the name of the only begotten Son of God.

In a rhetorical fashion Jesus poses the question: If Jesus did not come to judge, then why are men still condemned? The answer is that judgment is based on belief or disbelief. This is the dividing point for judgment: some believe, others do not. There is no need to wait in anticipation for the last day for the results of judgment, Jesus clearly states the terms: those who believe are saved and those who disbelieve are already judged.

At the end of the world there will not be any suspense, those who believed will take their place with God and those who disbelieved will be taken away. The charge that will condemn will be that they did not believe in the name (His true essence) which He explains is the "only begotten Son" (the only one who has this God/Man nature). This is the "essence" of Jesus.

In the next three verses He explains why this judgment is correct, to silence those who may take exception to His pronouncement (perhaps even Nicodemus).

> Vs. 19 – This is the judgment, that the Light has come into the world, and men loved the darkness rather than the Light, for their deeds were evil.

The word light refers back to Jesus and the truth that He brings, the plan He reveals from God concerning man's salvation. When people come in contact with this light some choose the darkness because they love sin and evil more than they love the truth. It is not that they cannot understand, it is that they desire one thing over the other.

This is the main reason why people do not want to talk about religion or the gospel: they love the darkness they are in (whatever it is) more than the possibility of light in their lives. This is why many will not convert or why certain Christians do not grow: they love their sins more than they love Christ.

> Vs. 20 – For everyone who does evil hates the Light, and does not come to the Light for fear that his deeds will be exposed.

Not only do people choose darkness over light, once they do so they hate the light. People who hear and reject the gospel are usually its worse enemies. They speak against the church, the preacher, the Bible; against what they know is right. They run away from the light because they want to remain where they are without being bothered.

> Vs. 21– But he who practices the truth comes to the Light, so that his deeds may be manifested as having been wrought in God.

In the final verse, Jesus compares two people: one comes to the light but his love of sin brings him back to the darkness where he would rather be, avoiding the light. The other practices the truth. He has accepted the truth, has let the light shine on him and follows the light.

The one that comes to the light is not afraid of it because it does two things for him. It shows where his sins are and how to get rid of them. It also reveals all the good things that God will work in a person including eternal life (i.e. for Nicodemus: faith equaled rebirth).

Other religions promise part of this and produce some of this while a person lives, but the gospel guarantees an eternity of it experienced personally and provides a resurrected savior to bolster our faith and hope.

God's justice is right: those who accept the light He sent will live in that light forever, those who reject it do so because of their own evil and consequentially are condemned to forever live in the darkness they so love.

8.
JOHN'S FINAL WITNESS

JOHN 3:22-36

As we study John's gospel we are keeping our eyes open for the three strands or themes that John interweaves into one single narrative. These are: Jesus demonstrating both His divine and human nature in various ways, people reacting to Him with faith, others reacting to Him with disbelief.

In the following passage John the Apostle records the last witness of faith in Jesus by John the Baptist and we will have some information on the various understandings of baptism that the people of those days had.

Baptism – 3:22-26

In verse 21 of chapter three we have the last of Jesus' conversation with Nicodemus. We do not hear of Nicodemus again until later when he will defend Jesus before the Sanhedrin and assist Joseph of Arimathea in burying the Lord.

> Vs. 22 – After these things Jesus and His disciples came into the land of Judea, and there He was spending time with them and baptizing.

John picks up the story with Jesus heading into Judea in order to preach and baptize along with His disciples, leaving the city behind. A little later in chapter 4:2 John clarifies that Jesus Himself did not do the baptizing but rather His disciples carried out this function. He did the preaching, they baptized those who responded.

The Bible mentions baptism quite often and I would like to pause here and look at this issue a little more closely so we can understand the various references to baptism John will make as we go on.

Baptism – the word

The word itself is not an English word but rather an anglicized version of the Greek word *BAPTIZO*. This word came from a root word which meant to make wet or to overwhelm. It was also used to describe something that was covered or immersed in water (i.e. a ship sinking or being overwhelmed by water).

In the New Testament it was mainly used to describe the religious rite of water purification where the individual was covered or immersed in water indicating a spiritual purification or cleansing.

Because of its special nature, when it came to translating the word it was simply kept in its Greek form and given an English suffix or ending (*BAPTIZO* became BAPTIZE).

Baptism – the practice

There were many types of baptisms in the Jewish religious experience, so the people in those days were familiar with the many references made about baptism:

1. Baptism and washing of priests (John 2:6)

Priests practiced water purification of objects. Proselytes to Judaism had to be circumcised, baptized and offer sacrifice.

2. John the Baptist's baptism

Immersion in water for forgiveness of sins and preparation for the kingdom to come. An expression of faith that this time was at hand.

3. Baptism of suffering (Mark 10:38)

Here the word refers to the idea of being overwhelmed, covered with suffering and not with water. Jesus is said to be immersed in suffering.

4. Baptism of fire (Matthew 3:11; I Corinthians 3:13)

This was a reference to testing and judgment. In I Corinthians Paul says that the work of the saved will be tested by fire, judged as it were. For the unsaved the fire of judgment is punishment and suffering (immersed in suffering).

5. Baptism with or in the Holy Spirit (John 1:33)

This is a reference to Jesus giving the Spirit to others. This is also a fulfillment of an Old Testament promise. Peter quotes the prophet Joel in saying that when the Messiah would come, this promise would be fulfilled (Acts 2:17).

So how exactly did Jesus fulfill this baptism with the Holy Spirit, this covering or immersing of His disciples with the Holy Spirit? He did it in different ways depending on the time period:

A. During the time before His coming

In the Old Testament only a few were baptized or immersed with the Holy Spirit. Patriarchs, leaders and prophets were empowered to minister to God's people in special ways, but this was rare and only a few were so blessed.

B. During the time of Jesus' ministry

Jesus Himself was filled with the Holy Spirit at His baptism and by His presence He blessed others with the manifestations of the Holy Spirit. His miracles showed the Spirit's power; His teachings revealed the Spirit's word.

C. After Jesus' resurrection

After His resurrection Jesus gave the Holy Spirit in three ways:

1. He gave the Holy Spirit to His Apostles and they gave it to some disciples to empower them to do miracles and thereby confirm that their preaching was true (Acts 2:1-4).

2. He gave to everyone who believed in Him and obeyed the gospel in repentance and baptism the Holy Spirit to dwell within them (Acts 2:38). (Note: The difference between indwelling and empowerment. Having one did not give the other.)

3. He poured forth the Holy Spirit on the entire world by providing the Holy Spirit's Word in the Bible, available for all (II Timothy 3:16).

And so when we speak of the baptism with or in the Holy Spirit, we are speaking of Jesus giving the Spirit to others in these different ways during these different time periods.

6. New Testament baptism or the baptism of Jesus (Mark 16:16)

Of all the baptisms mentioned, this is the one that we still do and must do today.

The baptism of Jesus was authorized by Him in Matthew 28:18-20. It was required by everyone who believed in His resurrection (Acts 2:38). Among other things, it was and is performed for the forgiveness of sins and the reception of the Holy Spirit. This is the only baptism now required; the only baptism left (Ephesians 4:5).

Jesus' baptism eliminates and supersedes all others:

- No need for Jewish purification rites, the blood of Christ purifies and we come into contact with that blood at baptism (Romans 6:3).

- John's baptism has been fulfilled, the kingdom has come.

- The baptism of suffering has been accomplished; Christ has died and is now risen.

- The baptism of fire is an expression for judgment and not a command to be obeyed.

- The baptism with the Holy Spirit has been given to the Apostles and made available to everyone in and through the gospel.

The only baptism left to be preached and practiced is the baptism commanded by Jesus, practiced by the Apostles, recorded in the Word: baptism in water by immersion for the forgiveness of sins and indwelling of the Spirit.

And so, in our brief review, we have looked at the various meanings of baptism that both the Jews and Christians had at that time. We have also looked at Jesus' commands concerning the baptism He wants His disciples to receive, the manner of it and what occurs spiritually when we receive it.

We can close this sub-file and get back to our main passage where John says that Jesus and His disciples were preaching and baptizing in the area where John the Baptist and his disciples were doing the same.

Question: Which baptism was Jesus preaching at this time?

Answer: The baptism of John the Baptist (to prepare for the coming) because He had not completed the work of salvation yet. Only after His death and resurrection did Jesus command to baptize in His name for the reception of the Holy Spirit. At this time He is still preaching John's baptism.

> Vs. 23-26 – John also was baptizing in Aenon near Salim, because there was much water there; and people were coming and were being baptized— for John had not yet been thrown into prison. Therefore there arose a discussion on the part of John's disciples with a Jew about purification. And they came to John and said to him, "Rabbi, He who was with you beyond the Jordan, to whom you have testified, behold, He is baptizing and all are coming to Him."

If one saw how dry and rocky most of the land is there, they would realize how special a place with "much" water was for a person whose ministry was largely to baptize or immerse.

We also note that there begins to be some confusion among John the Baptist's disciples. Note that it was a "Jew" who was the center of the dispute. The term Jew was used to describe Jesus' enemies and so it was a person who was not sympathetic to either John or Jesus. John's disciples note that a comment was made as to which baptism was superior (probably by the Jew and probably with the desire to sow discord). So they go to John to settle the matter. We can read of their disappointment at seeing their numbers growing smaller. They were with John but had they really understood his message? Many times immature disciples confuse faithfulness with "party spirit."

Note again the two strands of belief (those who were coming to be baptized) and disbelief (the Jew who caused the dispute) are woven as a constant backdrop into the main narrative. John will answer his disciples' question and in doing so give his final witness of faith.

John's witness about himself – vs. 27-28

Vs. 27 – John answered and said, "A man can receive nothing unless it has been given him from heaven.

First, John makes a general statement saying that all one has comes from God. In his case he is referring to his ministry. The gifts and opportunities to serve come from God and He can take them away as well. This should make us pay attention and be good stewards and not be proud because it all comes from Him and it can all be taken away.

Vs. 28 – You yourselves are my witnesses that I said, 'I am not the Christ,' but, 'I have been sent ahead of Him.'

Here John makes a specific statement concerning his own unique role. He repeats and confirms what his role was, to be a forerunner, one who would prepare the way for the Christ. His ministry was the culmination of all the prophecy and history of the Jewish nation contained in the Old Testament. John knew this and carried out the task given to him by God.

John's witness about his ministry – vs. 29-30

Vs. 29-30 – He who has the bride is the bridegroom; but the friend of the bridegroom, who stands and hears him, rejoices greatly because of the bridegroom's voice. So this joy of mine has been made full. He must increase, but I must decrease.

He is satisfied that he has both understood correctly and accomplished his ministry. He compares it to the role of "best man" at a wedding who is very busy before the big day, but once the wedding day arrives his role diminishes.

We see John's humble attitude in accepting his decreasing role and Jesus' constantly increasing and primary role. Humility is not speaking softly or having no opinion, humility is allowing God's will to be done in your life instead of your own.

We also note his joy at seeing God's will fulfilled in Jesus' coming. John testifies that what is happening (he is decreasing and Jesus is increasing) was in God's plan and he is happy that this is happening.

John's witness concerning Christ – vs. 31-36

John is still talking to his disciples and ends his comments with a final testimony about Jesus. In this he will answer three questions about Jesus that have not been asked but hang in the air as his ministry decreases and the Lord's increases.

1. Why he must decrease and Jesus increase

> Vs. 31 – He who comes from above is above all, he who is of the earth is from the earth and speaks of the earth. He who comes from heaven is above all.

The reason will become quite evident. John is from below, human, like all men. Jesus is from above, the God/Man, the greatest of all. It is only natural that this be the progress of events.

2. How will the people react to Jesus

> Vs. 32 – What He has seen and heard, of that He testifies; and no one receives His testimony.

Jesus will speak God's truth, but men, for the most part, will not believe. And considering Jesus' teaching, His pure life, His miracles and resurrection, disbelieving was a grave sin. John's point is that condemnation is deserved seeing that such a great witness was given.

3. Did everyone disbelieve?

> Vs. 33-36 – He who has received His testimony has set his seal to this, that God is true. For He whom God has sent speaks the words of God; for He gives the Spirit without measure. The Father loves the Son and has given all things into His hand. He who believes in the Son has eternal life; but he who does not obey the Son will not see life, but the wrath of God abides on him."

John concludes by saying that not everyone disbelieved. Those who did believe in Jesus' words however, were literally saying: God really is!

The word true in the Greek means "manifest, unconcealed." And they know this about God from Jesus Christ, because He comes and speaks from God. The only way to acknowledge God is to acknowledge Jesus Christ, to deny Christ is to deny God. One's eternal destiny was decided by how they responded to Christ.

John the Baptist believed this about Christ and the witness he is making to his disciples is done so they will believe and follow Jesus also. In doing this he is completely and joyfully fulfilling his ministry.

Epilogue

> Chapter 4, vs. 1-3 – Therefore when the Lord knew that the Pharisees had heard that Jesus was making and baptizing more disciples than John (although Jesus Himself was not baptizing, but His disciples were), He left Judea and went away again into Galilee.

We know that verse numbers and chapter headings were added much later after the original gospels were written and so there are some awkward divisions.

Chapter 4:1-3 is really a bridge between what happened in Judea with John's disciples and Jesus' leaving the area to return to His home area in the north, around the sea of Galilee.

Note that what moves Him to change locations is the news that the Pharisees have taken a greater interest in Him as His ministry has grown.

They were to become His fiercest critics and enemies, but not wanting a confrontation so soon, Jesus leaves for the friendlier and quieter surroundings of His home in Galilee.

This ends a section where we observe many descriptions of people who believe (John and many of his disciples) as well as those who disbelieve (some of John's disciples, the Jew and the Pharisees). In our next lesson we will get back to seeing Jesus, through His teachings and miracles, demonstrate once again His God/Man nature.

9.
THE WOMAN AT THE WELL

JOHN 4:1-42

We are continuing our study of the gospel of John and focusing on the three themes John pursues in his gospel narrative: Jesus showing both His human and divine natures, and people either accepting or rejecting His witness.

In chapter 4 we see Jesus leaving the populated areas of Jerusalem and Judea to return northward to His hometown and area around the Sea of Galilee. On this particular journey John recounts Jesus' encounter with a certain woman at a well and in so doing will touch each theme contained in his gospel.

The journey

> Vs. 1-4 – Therefore when the Lord knew that the Pharisees had heard that Jesus was making and baptizing more disciples than John (although Jesus Himself was not baptizing, but His disciples were), He left Judea and went away again into Galilee. And He had to pass through Samaria.

We saw in the last chapter the idea that Jesus did not want to confront the Pharisees so early in His ministry (to avoid public strife and guarantee future safe access to the city). When He sees that they are tracking Him, He leaves the capital city area to return to the friendlier and more remote area of Galilee.

In order to make the journey, He had to pass through what used to be the Northern Kingdom but was now called the region of Samaria.

The Samaritans were the half-breed or mixed race descendants of the Jews who had originally inhabited the Northern Kingdom. They had been defeated in 722 BC by the Assyrians and scattered among pagan nations. Eventually they had drifted back to populate the areas where the old Northern Kingdom once stood. They were no longer full-blooded Jews having intermarried with foreign nations, but still claimed Abraham as their ancestor as the Jews did. Because they lived in the old region of the Northern Kingdom with Samaria as its capital, they and their region were referred to as Samaritans and Samaria.

Vs. 5-6 – So He came to a city of Samaria called Sychar, near the parcel of ground that Jacob gave to his son Joseph; and Jacob's well was there. So Jesus, being wearied from His journey, was sitting thus by the well. It was about the sixth hour.

Samaria was once the capital of the Northern Kingdom, but by this time had been reduced considerably. The well is still there today, still providing water; one can visit it (inside a church building built over it). It was located near the place where Joseph, one of the twelve sons of Jacob, was said to have had his bones buried after the Jews left Egypt and carried his remains with them.

Note that John describes Jesus as being tired from the journey He was on. He was hot, tired, dusty and thirsty. Doesn't that sound like a human being's response to a long walk in the hot sun? This place was about 31 miles (50 km) north of Jerusalem.

Jesus was probably on the second day of His journey north. It was noon, the hottest time in a very warm climate. He arrives at this cool spot and sits to rest before moving on.

In order to understand more fully the amazing encounter Jesus has with the woman he meets here, it is helpful to know how the Jews felt about the Samaritans. In a word, they hated them because they were of mixed blood and therefore considered an impure race. They hated them because the Samaritans worshipped at Bethel, a place of worship in the North, established by the northern king Jeroboam long before, in order to keep the people from going to Jerusalem to worship and thus eroding his power base in the North. In addition to this, they accepted only the first 5 books of the Hebrew Scriptures as authentic and rejected the prophets.

Of course, the hatred was mutual because the Jews had rejected the Samaritans' offer of help to rebuild the temple after the southern Jews returned from their exile in Babylon. For this rejection and their superior attitude, the Jews had earned the reciprocal hatred of the Samaritans.

And so Jesus ventures into this town and meets a Samaritan woman who herself was coming to draw water on that hot noon day.

Jesus and the Samaritan woman

Note that the woman is drawing water at noon, an unusual time because the normal time for this would be at evening. Note also that she was alone, a fact that will have meaning as we learn more about her.

> Vs. 7-8 – There came a woman of Samaria to draw water. Jesus said to her, "Give Me a drink." For His disciples had gone away into the city to buy food.

It would be normal for a human being in this situation to ask for a drink. The amazing and ironic thing is that the fountain of life Himself asks for mere water. He was traveling with His followers who had left Him there to buy food in the nearby town.

> Vs. 9 – Therefore the Samaritan woman said to Him, "How is it that You, being a Jew, ask me for a drink since I am a Samaritan woman?" (For Jews have no dealings with Samaritans.)

She rebuffs Him because of the social barriers that separate them: man/woman barrier and Jew/Samaritan barrier.

> Vs. 10 – Jesus answered and said to her, "If you knew the gift of God, and who it is who says to you, 'Give Me a drink,' you would have asked Him, and He would have given you living water."

Jesus responds now as the Son of God, not the weary and thirsty traveler. He answers her by telling her that what He asks for is very small in comparison to what He (as the Son of God) is able to give her.

He offers "living water" a concept that goes far beyond social custom or old rivalries; a spiritual gift described by using spiritual words. Actually the term was used by Jeremiah in the Old Testament in warning the Southern Kingdom of its imminent destruction because of their sinful idolatry (Jeremiah 2:13). Jeremiah referred to God, who was the source of life, truth and light: the living water who would punish them for their sins.

Jesus tells her that if she knew who He was, He would give her the "living water" the spiritual life she needed. Of course, Jesus is saying that knowing Him and knowing the Truth, and obtaining the "living water" were all one and the same and wrapped around Himself.

> Vs. 11-12 – She said to Him, "Sir, You have nothing to draw with and the well is deep; where then do You get that living water? You are not greater than our father Jacob, are You, who gave us the well, and drank of it himself and his sons and his cattle?"

Note how she responds, how her response is similar to Nicodemus. When confronted with the reality of Jesus' person Nicodemus questioned the "literalness" or "meaning" of Jesus' spiritual words, "born again." He thought in literal terms, actually returning to the womb to be born a second time!

The Samaritan woman examines Jesus' words in the same literal way was well. For example, I do not think you are referring to this water in the well because you have no pot to use, and it is deep. So what do you mean by "living water"? Are you even greater than Jacob, the one who originally gave us the well itself? In other words he gave us the well that sustains our lives and animals; can you give us something greater than this?

> Vs. 13-14 – Jesus answered and said to her, "Everyone who drinks of this water will thirst again; but whoever drinks of the water that I will give him shall never thirst; but the water that I will give him will become in him a well of water springing up to eternal life."

Jesus now points out the difference between natural water and the living water that He is offering her.

1. Natural water satisfies temporarily, it is earthly, natural, and temporal.
2. Living water satisfies completely and without end.
3. Whoever drinks natural water will eventually die, it only keeps him alive for so long. Whoever drinks the spiritual living water will never die.

We know, of course, that Jesus Himself is that living water and that we drink Him in by believing and obeying His Word.

> Vs. 15 – The woman said to Him, "Sir, give me this water, so I will not be thirsty nor come all the way here to draw."

The woman has shifted from disbelief and doubt to curiosity, so she asks Him two questions:

1. Could she have this water?

2. If she could, would it mean that she would not have to come out each day at this time to fetch water? (I will explain the significance of this in a minute.)

> Vs. 16-18 – He said to her, "Go, call your husband and come here." The woman answered and said, "I have no husband." Jesus said to her, "You have correctly said, 'I have no husband'; for you have had five husbands, and the one whom you now have is not your husband; this you have said truly."

Jesus responds to her changed attitude by delving into her personal life. She responds honestly and Jesus reacts to her openness by revealing more of His own true nature and showing His intimate knowledge of her past, especially her sinful past. This may be why she was alone at noon to draw water; she may have been shunned by the other women of the village because of her background.

Note that Jesus offers her the "living water" or "new birth," but like all others she needs to begin with faith and repentance.

> Vs. 19-20 – The woman said to Him, "Sir, I perceive that You are a prophet. Our fathers worshiped in this

mountain, and you people say that in Jerusalem is the
place where men ought to worship."

The woman goes from curiosity to a preliminary faith; she sees
Jesus as a prophet of sorts (not fully correct but moving in the
right direction). Based on what Jesus has demonstrated, she
goes on to ask Him a question concerning a major dispute
between the Samaritans and the Jews: where is the right place
to worship, Bethel or Jerusalem?

Her thinking is that she has been revealed to be a sinner, where
then should she go to be cleansed? People would go to the
temple to be cleansed of sin, to offer sacrifice for their offenses.
She wants to know where is the right place, Bethel or
Jerusalem. Her conscience has been moved and it is now
important for her to know; there is a hunger for righteousness.
Her meeting with Jesus has sparked this. She has drunk the
living water and it already is having an effect on her.

> Vs. 21-24 – Jesus said to her, "Woman, believe Me, an
> hour is coming when neither in this mountain nor in
> Jerusalem will you worship the Father. You worship
> what you do not know; we worship what we know, for
> salvation is from the Jews. But an hour is coming, and
> now is, when the true worshipers will worship the
> Father in spirit and truth; for such people the Father
> seeks to be His worshipers. God is spirit, and those
> who worship Him must worship in spirit and truth."

Jesus responds directly to her question and elaborates on the
whole issue of worship that speaks not only to the dispute
between the Jews and Samaritans, but our own problems with
this issue today.

He says 3 things about worship:

1. The time is coming when it will not be important where
   the physical temple will be located. We know this is true

today because we are the temple in which God dwells (not a building) and it is unimportant where the meeting places are located (I Corinthians 3:16).

2. As far as the present day dispute between the Jews and Samaritans was concerned, Jesus tells her that the correct place to worship (at that time) would be Jerusalem. The Messiah was to come from one of the two tribes of the Southern Kingdom (Judah), not from the ten tribes of the Northern Kingdom.

3. It is not where you worship that counts. A person could be in the temple in Jerusalem but not worship properly if his heart was wrong.

If God were physical then the material would be very important (place, time, things used). But God is Spirit and it is the spiritual elements represented by the physical things that are important:

1. Singing is physical. A joyful heart, an understanding heart is spiritual.

2. Bread and wine are physical. Remembering Jesus in loving unity is spiritual and true.

3. Money is physical. Giving generously and joyfully is spiritual and true.

4. Words are physical. Preaching, teaching Jesus' words, this is spiritual and true.

We can do the right things, use the right words, but without the right and true spirit our worship is in vain and untrue as well as unspiritual.

Vs. 25-26 – The woman said to Him, "I know that Messiah is coming (He who is called Christ); when that One comes, He will declare all things to us." Jesus said to her, "I who speak to you am He."

The woman is on the verge of realizing the truth about Jesus and confesses her belief and hope concerning the Savior to come. The Samaritans believed that the Savior would be a prophet and an earthly ruler (like David was). Their name for him was the "Restorer" or TAHEB. She does not use this term, however, referring to the Savior with the Jewish term, MESSIAH.

Note also how she has gone from rejecting Jesus to voicing her hope in the Savior. She is not far from the truth.

Jesus helps her make the connection by declaring to her that He in fact is the Messiah. This is the climax of this dialogue and very unusual for Jesus to make this direct and dramatic declaration to a single person, let alone a woman from Samaria.

And in His answer He is making her take note that all the things that they hoped the Messiah would do, He has done for her:

- He has offered spiritual life, what the Messiah was supposed to bring.
- He has revealed where the true temple should be, what the Messiah would do.
- He reveals the heart of men, what the prophets said the Messiah would do.
- He knows and reveals what God really wants, true worship, what the Messiah would do.
- He reveals Himself as the Messiah, what the Messiah would do.

Dialogue with the Apostles

By now the Apostles return and comment on the strange scene before them, Jesus actually speaking to a Samaritan woman.

Vs. 27-30 – At this point His disciples came, and they were amazed that He had been speaking with a woman, yet no one said, "What do You seek?" or, "Why do You speak with her?" So the woman left her waterpot, and went into the city and said to the men, "Come, see a man who told me all the things that I have done; this is not the Christ, is it?" They went out of the city, and were coming to Him.

They voice their surprise at the scene before them. The woman, seeing the others arrive, leaves everything behind and, losing her shame, tells others who she believes Jesus to be. On the strength of her witness, the town gathers to see Jesus.

Vs. 31-38 – Meanwhile the disciples were urging Him, saying, "Rabbi, eat." But He said to them, "I have food to eat that you do not know about." So the disciples were saying to one another, "No one brought Him anything to eat, did he?" Jesus said to them, "My food is to do the will of Him who sent Me and to accomplish His work. Do you not say, 'There are yet four months, and then comes the harvest'? Behold, I say to you, lift up your eyes and look on the fields, that they are white for harvest. Already he who reaps is receiving wages and is gathering fruit for life eternal; so that he who sows and he who reaps may rejoice together. For in this case the saying is true, 'One sows and another reaps.' I sent you to reap that for which you have not labored; others have labored and you have entered into their labor."

In the meantime the Apostles want Jesus to focus on eating, missing the significance of the moment. The Lord uses the moment to teach them a lesson based on what has happened. Again He speaks to them on a spiritual plane and says the following:

1. His satisfaction (and theirs as well) comes from doing God's will, not from physical things. I.e. living water, bread from heaven, not well water and food.

2. They have to open their eyes and see how hungry and thirsty the people are for the spiritual food only they have to offer.

3. Doing God's will in giving the "living water" to others also brings great satisfaction.

4. Joy comes from doing God's will (whatever that is). Some sow, some reap, but both are rewarded for doing God's will.

Of course this is a preview and preparation for the Great Commission He will give them after His resurrection and before His ascension into heaven.

> Go into all the world and preach the good news to everyone.
> - Mark 16:15

The woman's witness

We do not see the woman again, but the living water springing up in her has now given a thirst to those with whom she has shared the story of her encounter with Jesus.

> Vs. 39 – From that city many of the Samaritans believed in Him because of the word of the woman who testified, "He told me all the things that I have done."

Many believed her account and pursued the Lord because of it. Her witness, not her knowledge, works or teaching ability is what affected others.

> Vs. 40-42 – So when the Samaritans came to Jesus, they were asking Him to stay with them; and He stayed there two days. Many more believed because of His

word; and they were saying to the woman, "It is no longer because of what you said that we believe, for we have heard for ourselves and know that this One is indeed the Savior of the world."

Her witness affected others in particular ways:

1. They came to see Jesus for themselves.
2. They were prepared to listen.
3. They believed what she said about Him after hearing Him for themselves.
4. They also acknowledged their faith in Him.

10.

JESUS' METHOD OF PERSONAL EVANGELISM

We are returning to mine yet more information from John 1:1-42 that describes Jesus' encounter with the woman at the well.

In our last chapter over this passage I pointed out how all three themes of John's book are brought out in this passage:

1. Jesus is tired and thirsty, and asks for a drink showing His human nature.

2. The Lord demonstrates His divine nature in revealing this woman's past.

3. We observe as she goes from disbelief to belief and how the village goes from disbelief to belief.

In this chapter we will examine the passage again, but this time to note the way that Jesus approaches the evangelizing of another person. Perhaps we can adapt this method to our own advantage today.

Personal evangelism

Everyone who has received the gift of salvation should have a desire to share that gift with others. We have received something precious because of the kindness and generosity of others. We ought to be ready to pass it on to others who have not yet heard or received the good news.

This process of sharing the gospel and bringing others to Christ is called "personal evangelism." Now when I'm teaching a Bible class, this is not personal evangelism, it is preaching and teaching in the assembly. When I write a blog post or add content to BibleTalk.tv, that is mass media evangelism and teaching. When, however, I sit down with one person and share my faith or teach the gospel, this is personal evangelism.

Now in the Bible I have explained that we find through commands, examples and inferences, the pattern for how to do certain things like communion or organizing the church, etc.

In John 4:1-42 we see a pattern or method Jesus used in the work of personal evangelism. The method He used, I call the "multiplication system." Let me try to explain how it works using this passage.

The multiplication system

First of all, a few rules of mathematics. We know that multiplication is a faster way of increase than simple addition.

A great example of this was demonstrated on TV a while back. Here is what they explained:

- If you took a simple checkerboard or chessboard and placed a single sugar cube on each square you would end up with 64 sugar cubes. That is addition.

- If, on the other hand, you simply multiplied by 2 the number of sugar cubes you put on each square… for example put one cube on square #1, then double that for square #2, then double that for square #3, and continued to double until you reached square #64.

- According to the Museum of Science and Industry in Chicago, if you multiplied the sugar cubes in this way you would have enough sugar to cover the State of Texas with 30 feet of sugar.

- Such is the power of multiplication.

Now pretend that those sugar cubes are people who are becoming Christians.

- If each Christian simply adds one Christian as a result of their conversion (a spouse, a child, a friend) you have the kind of growth the church has traditionally had (slow, small, steady).

- If, on the other hand, each Christian continually doubles himself and teaches others to double themselves, then the process of multiplication begins.

Our concept of evangelism is that we turn over to the ministers the responsibility of putting one sugar cube on every square or pew instead of reproducing ourselves and thus exponentially increasing the number of souls saved.

Jesus did not use the addition model, as we will see with the woman at the well, He demonstrates how to first make, and then multiply disciples.

Making and multiplying disciples

Now before multiplying, one must first make a disciple, and the passage in John reveals to us the process that Jesus used to accomplish this first and basic step of personal evangelism, and that is to convert one soul.

In this passage we are able to identify 7 steps in the making of a disciple of Jesus. A disciple is a follower, a learner, one who is committed to following, learning and obeying Christ and only Christ.

There are 7 steps to making one of these disciples:

Step #1 – Contact

The point of contact is anywhere when two people enter a conversation: any situation where two people connect in some way (sports, work, service, family, friends). Connecting with people.

Note that Jesus made contact by asking for a drink of water. Note also that He did not allow social, religious or barriers between genders at that time to stop Him from making contact with this woman. The rule about contact is that if the gospel is for all, then there should be no barrier we are not willing to cross in order to make contact.

Step #2 – Challenge

Challenge is when you step out from the normal course of polite conversation in order to open up a dialogue concerning spiritual rather than temporal things. This is difficult and where we fail most often. It is when the conversation turns to serious and important matters that challenge the non-believer to explore the true meaning of life or spiritual aspects of their lives that things get awkward.

Obviously it is difficult to do this at first, but with time these probes can be launched gently and without pride. Perhaps this can be a question about the Bible or religious background, church attendance, etc. Somewhere along the line, the time and opportunity present themselves for this and we need to recognize the moment and challenge our non-Christian friends or family to enter into a spiritually oriented discussion.

After having discussed the water He asked for, Jesus seized on the opportunity to talk to her about the "living" water. There is nothing to say we could not ask someone the same question at some point.

Step #3 – Confirmation

Once the challenge is made and the discussion entered into, it is up to the disciple to prove or confirm that he or she knows what they are talking about. It could be a demonstration of Christian kindness, a proof of Bible knowledge or an example of a good and pure Christian life. Once the disciple has engaged another in this spiritual dialogue, they need to be able to demonstrate the proof of what they are talking about in themselves somehow.

This is the second area where personal evangelism often fails. The unbeliever rejects the message because the messenger does not embody the message. It is just talk. For example, one Sunday there was a visitor looking for someone who had invited them to services but that person did not show for Bible class or worship. Do you think that guest will come back?

In His dealing with the woman, Jesus resists being offended by her initial rebuff and goes on to demonstrate His wisdom and knowledge of her life, her needs and her questions. He proved who He was.

Step #4 – The call

Usually after a personal study, a discussion or a sermon, there is a call to decide to accept as true what has been shared.

In the case of personal evangelism, the call is to follow Jesus. Even at the preliminary stage, the call is to follow the Lord, even if it is from the far off position of curiosity and finding out more. No one was ever saved without making a series of decisions. No one gets to heaven by someone else's decision or by accident. If you have not made a conscious decision to become a disciple of Jesus, then you are not a disciple!

Jesus tells the woman, "I am the Messiah," He called on her to believe this but could not force her, it was her decision to believe or not to believe. All He could do was call on her to choose.

We do this when we invite to church, ask for a Bible study, encourage hearing the gospel; every one of these is a "call" to follow Jesus.

Step #5 – Conversion

At some point the entire good news is conveyed, sufficient proof is provided through study and a good Christian example.

The amount of time differs from person to person, but eventually everyone must decide to follow Jesus or not. Eventually we bring them to the point of expressing their faith in obedience to Jesus' commands of repentance and baptism.

Sometimes we fail here by going to extremes:

1. We never ask or encourage the person to make up their mind, to make a commitment. We think that they will come to it by themselves. Even Paul the Apostle, when he was brought to this point, only moved when Ananias pushed him with these words, "And now why do you delay? Arise and be baptized and wash away your sins calling on His name." (Acts 22:16)

2. We also fail by asking too soon. We have only shared the basics, not developed a relationship, have not provided sufficient evidence. Faith grows at a slower pace than understanding. We may understand something without necessarily believing that it is true, right or good.

For example, democracy in Middle Eastern countries, they understand the concept but are not all convinced that it is better or true.

We rush to conversion and when people balk, we turn away from them instead of continuing to provide contact, challenge, proof, calling and encouragement to convert.

In the story of the woman we see her believing the proof Jesus gave her, confessing that faith by acknowledging her hope for a Jewish Messiah that would save her, a Samaritan. Today she would confess Jesus' name, repent of her sins and be baptized to demonstrate her conversion.

Step #6 – Consecration

This step is where the convert actually is trained for discipleship. The one who was formerly a non-believer, now becomes a believer and follower of Jesus. The convert, or new disciple, begins to act and sound like a disciple.

For example, he begins to have a prayer life; read and study the Word; identify and assemble with the other disciples; find ways to serve the Lord with his own skills.

The burden for this consecration of disciples rests with the leaders of the church. It is their job to make sure that there is a conscious effort by the congregation to integrate and equip the new disciple for effective and fruitful Christian living.

The woman, after her contact with Jesus, is immediately energized to share her brief but powerful encounter with Jesus among her family and community. Not everyone's consecration to service is as fast as the woman's, but not everyone is discipled by Jesus Himself.

Step #7 – Multiplication

In the addition model the woman would have gone home and maybe shared her experience with her partner so that he might know the Lord and become a disciple with her... another sugar cube on another square.

But this woman begins the multiplication model by sharing her experience with everyone in town who would listen. We do not see all the details, but in verse 28 she goes to the men of the city (ones she already had contact with) and she challenges them to consider what has happened to her. We then read that they believed because of her word and they brought others who then believed because of Jesus' word.

John does not spell it out, but at the end of the chapter the number of those who were converted and bringing others to Him was multiplied in much the same manner. One woman multiplies to several men who multiply into a great number, all in the space of a few days. That is the power of the multiplication system in personal evangelism.

Summary

If we used this model in our personal evangelism approach, we could plant churches everywhere they are needed in this state, in this nation and across the world in one generation. The question is: why are we not doing it, what is stopping us?

2 main reasons:

1. We are not consciously implementing this approach. Most churches use the addition approach, not the multiplication approach, usually because they do not know or are not trained.

2. When churches do try to use the multiplication approach they only use parts of it or it breaks down due to human weakness.

For example: We either do not ever go from contact to challenge leaving most of our communication with others at the non-spiritual level.

- We give up too quickly if the person does not respond to the challenge or the call.

- We drop people who do not convert the first time we present the gospel to them.

- We try to "qualify" our contacts by guessing which ones are sympathetic to the gospel and those who are not.

In the multiplying method of personal evangelism everyone is a potential contact. We are always looking for the opportunity to challenge our contacts. We are ready and able to provide proof of our faith and eager to repeatedly call on our contacts to follow Jesus in some way.

In multiplying disciples we are not afraid to go for closure in asking our contacts to be converted, to obey the gospel.

In multiplying ministry, the church is equipped to train and build up new converts and multiply their potential for new contacts, greater multiplication, etc.

The risk with all of this of course is that when the power of multiplying disciples takes hold, it is like riding a tidal wave. We are then once again like the Jerusalem church, doing incredible things, making incredible sacrifices, truly leaving the world behind to manage the harvest that God can and will give.

In the meantime, we stick to the addition model because we can control it, and growth at this rate does not disturb the status quo too much, leaving us in the boundaries of our comfort zone.

We leave our comfort zone one step at a time.

11.

TAKING GOD AT HIS WORD

JOHN 4:42-54

At the beginning of every chapter in this book I have repeated the idea that in this series John brings together 3 themes and interweaves them into his gospel: Jesus as the God/Man; reactions of faith; reactions of disbelief.

These are the themes that appear repeatedly, however, John's objective with his book is singular and stated in John 20:30-31:

> Therefore many other signs Jesus also performed in the presence of the disciples, which are not written in this book; but these have been written so that you may believe that Jesus is the Christ, the Son of God; and that believing you may have life in His name.

Whether the people in the book believed or not, and whether all of Jesus' words and miracles are recorded or not, the main objective of John's book is that those who read it will believe that Jesus is the divine Christ. That includes us today!

We are part of the group that either believes or disbelieves. The purpose of these profiles of believers and disbelievers is to enable us to see ourselves in them. The purpose of the accounts of

Jesus' ministry was to influence the reader to choose belief over disbelief. We need to keep in mind, as we study the book, that we are not simply disinterested students examining an ancient record of events. We are participants because John had us specifically in mind when he put together this account of Jesus' life.

Proof of divinity

Now that we are familiar with the main objective of John's gospel, I want to move on to briefly review Jesus' own approach to making a witness about Himself.

John describes the very human activities of Jesus as He walks and eats, is tired and thirsty. We see a normal human being interacting with others and the world around Him. We also see, however, Jesus' divine nature from time to time as John presents this in three ways:

1. The witness concerning Jesus

There are things said about Jesus that witness or point to His divine nature.

- John the Baptist with his own special birth and prophet's stature witnessed that He was the Lamb of God.

- The witness from heaven was made about Jesus at His baptism. The Father spoke and the Holy Spirit appeared confirming Jesus as the Son of God.

- And then there is Jesus' own witness about Himself. What He said to the Samaritan woman for example, "I am He" meaning He was the Messiah.

2. The teachings of Jesus

The teaching is like no other, with authority, and it provides revelation. We see this with Nicodemus, himself a respected teacher among the Jews, but totally eclipsed by Jesus' revelatory teaching.

We see it in the woman at the well who recognizes Him as at least a prophet when she first hears Him teach her.

Later on He will teach about His death and resurrection that is confirmed by a voice from heaven (John 12:27).

In all of these, the people come to the conclusion that He is the messiah simply from hearing Him teach. For example, the people of the Samaritan village:

> and they were saying to the woman, "It is no longer because of what you said that we believe, for we have heard for ourselves and know that this One is indeed the Savior of the world."
> - John 4:42

3. The miracles of Jesus

I mention miracles last because we are always quick to go to these first. We forget or overlook the fact that Jesus was also proven to be the divine Messiah by witness and teaching as well as miracles. Remember that many prophets and leaders had been instruments of God's power in the past, so doing a sign or miracle did not automatically confirm Jesus as the Messiah. The witnesses about Him, the teaching and prophecies He made along with the miracles closed the case concerning His true identity as the divine Son of God.

In this we see a cycle within a cycle. The larger cycle is Jesus' ministry and peoples' various reactions to it. The smaller cycle contains the various ways Jesus demonstrated His divinity within His ministry. Now that we have stepped back to look at the overview of the book and how it functions, let us go back to the text and finish chapter 4.

Jesus' return home – 4:43-45

These events are taking place early in Jesus' ministry. If we were to chronicle His life so far:

- He was born in Bethlehem and spent some time in Egypt before returning to settle in Nazareth in the north near the Sea of Galilee.

- He travelled to Jerusalem in the south each year with His family to celebrate the Passover.

- As a grown man of 30, He lived in Capernaum which is on the edge of the Sea of Galilee, the same town where Peter and his family lived.

- At that age He came to the area around Jerusalem to be baptized by John and begin His ministry.

- He spent 40 days in the Judean wilderness in a spiritual battle with Satan.

- He returned home and attended a wedding at Cana, a town not far from Capernaum. Here He performs his first miracle.

- He goes to Jerusalem, cleanses the temple, teaches, and speaks with Nicodemus.

- He preaches and his disciples baptize where John the Baptist is working.

- To avoid mounting opposition, He returns again to the northern region of Galilee by way of this Samaritan village.

- He speaks to the woman there and remains there for two days teaching these people.

Verse 43 picks up the story from here.

Vs. 43-45 – After the two days He went forth from there into Galilee. For Jesus Himself testified that a prophet has no honor in his own country. So when He came to Galilee, the Galileans received Him, having seen all the things that He did in Jerusalem at the feast; for they themselves also went to the feast.

Now that His reputation is growing and many are becoming His disciples, He once again returns to His hometown region. It is a fact of human nature that we rarely take seriously those who are from our hometown until they make it big somewhere else.

In Jesus' case, He had been to Jerusalem and while there performed miracles, taught the people and provided a witness concerning Himself. Now, because of His reputation there, even the people of His hometown are impressed. Apparently some had seen or heard of His reputation in Jerusalem and had come home to spread the news.

Jesus is not looking for personal glory or fame. He is, however, taking advantage of the situation so that He can preach to the people.

It is the same idea with TV, websites, VBS, newspaper articles and any form of advertising the church does. These things do not convert people; they are not designed to do this. These things make us stand out among the others; give us some familiarity with the community. People feel they know us because of that and are less afraid to visit. It also gives our members an edge when inviting someone to church because people feel they have already had contact with us through our different outreach efforts.

So Jesus returns to His hometown where He is a celebrity of sorts because of the stir He has caused in Jerusalem.

The people seek signs

Vs. 46-47 – Therefore He came again to Cana of Galilee where He had made the water wine. And there was a royal official whose son was sick at Capernaum. When he heard that Jesus had come out of Judea into Galilee, he went to Him and was imploring Him to come down and heal his son; for he was at the point of death.

John skips over the rest of the journey and picks up the story with Jesus back up north in the city of Cana, the site of His first miracle. Doubtless the people there have heard of His ministry in Jerusalem, but many of them were aware of the great sign He performed at the wedding.

A royal official is a servant of the king who, in this case, would have been Herod. The official was from Jesus' adult hometown, Capernaum, which was close by on the shores of the Sea of Galilee. Herod had many palaces, garrisons, and fortresses throughout the land and was continually building so it was not unusual to have his officials scattered at different posts throughout the land. This official is at the end of a painful episode as his son lies close to death (no cause is given). Reaching out to Jesus was risky for a man in his position to do, but he was a desperate father.

> Vs. 48 – So Jesus said to him, "Unless you people see signs and wonders, you simply will not believe."

Note how Jesus' answer seems at first harsh considering the circumstances. But there are reasons why He answers in the way He does:

1. The man's motivation

The man did not come for Jesus' witness or His teaching, he came in a desperate attempt to save his son. People who are in danger of death will try anything to save their lives, things they would scoff at in other times, they embrace when desperate. This man had a kind of faith, the faith you have in faith-healers and snake-oil salesmen, faith created out of desperation.

2. Incomplete faith

Jesus is commenting on the kind of faith that stood only on the witnessing of miracles. Unless He "wowed" them with signs, they would falter and no longer believe.

The faith of young Christians is often like that, unless prayers are immediately answered, unless they continually experience the excitement of new faith (like the "new car" smell), unless they feel the comfort of the Spirit at all times, they doubt, they become discouraged, they begin to go back to the world.

Mature faith perseveres on Jesus' word, Jesus' promise, Jesus' presence, regardless of the feelings we have or the circumstances we are in.

This is the kind of faith the Lord asks of the man (and of us): to take Him at His word.

The miracle

Vs. 49-52 – The royal official said to Him, "Sir, come down before my child dies." Jesus said to him, "Go; your son lives." The man believed the word that Jesus spoke to him and started off. As he was now going down, his slaves met him, saying that his son was living. So he inquired of them the hour when he began to get better. Then they said to him, "Yesterday at the seventh hour the fever left him."

Note that the man had asked Jesus to come with him in order to heal his son. Jesus then "challenges" the official to greater, more mature faith by taking Him at His word concerning the healing of his son.

If you remember our last chapter on the seven steps of Jesus' "multiplying method" of personal evangelism you will note the following:

Step 1 – Contact has been made with this man through Jesus' reputation and signs.

Step 2 – The challenge to believe only in the Word Jesus speaks to him has been given.

We note in the passage that after the man responds to the challenge, his faith is rewarded with the news that his boy has been saved and is recovering, exactly as Jesus said.

The system complete

> Vs. 53-54 – So the father knew that it was at that hour in which Jesus said to him, "Your son lives"; and he himself believed and his whole household. This is again a second sign that Jesus performed when He had come out of Judea into Galilee.

In these verses, we see the completion of Jesus' personal evangelism system. We see all seven steps in this account, just as we saw it in the account of the Samaritan woman:

1. **Contact** – The man knew Jesus by reputation and witness.

2. **Challenge** – He is called to step up to a more mature faith in taking Jesus at His word.

3. **Confirmation** – When the father does so by returning home, he learns of the miracle done.

4. **Call and Conversion** – These are compressed into one action as the father reacts to the proof with belief in Jesus.

5. **Conversion** – These are compressed into one action as the father reacts to the proof with belief in Jesus.

6. **Consecration** – He tells his household of the witness, word and miracle of Jesus.

7. **Multiplication** – The entire household believes in Jesus.

So what begins as a desperate man crying out to Jesus for help – "Do something!" – turns into the conscious and mature faith of not only this man but multiplied by his entire household.

Summary

Let us summarize some of the key things we have looked at in this chapter:

1. Jesus demonstrated His true nature as divine Messiah in three ways: witness from others and Himself; the power of His teachings; His miracles.

2. The point of John's book is to bring his readers to believe in Jesus as the divine Messiah.

3. Mature faith is that which takes God at His Word (Matthew 4:4). If He says, "I will take care of you," "I forgive you," "Do this or do not do this," a mature faith will act and persevere based only on God's Word. That is enough. Signs and miracles were given to make people pay attention, to lead them to Christ and His Word.

This man learned this lesson as every great servant of God from Adam to Paul and forward has learned, that you can only do great things for the Lord, you can only know the Lord, you can only become fruitful for the Lord if you learn to act on His Word, and His Word alone.

Our response is not based on how we feel, not on perceived signs, not on what is new, what is safe, what others say or do, but only on the Word of the Lord.

12.

SIX WAYS TO LOSE YOUR SOUL

JOHN 5:1-47

In the last chapter I explained the cyclical nature of this book.

- Large cycle: Jesus demonstrates His God/Man nature and people respond with belief or disbelief.

- Smaller cycle: The three ways Jesus' divinity is revealed - witness, teaching and miracles.

In this chapter we will see these cycles turning within each other again.

The miracle – 5:1-9

> Vs. 1-4 – After these things there was a feast of the Jews, and Jesus went up to Jerusalem. Now there is in Jerusalem by the sheep gate a pool, which is called in Hebrew Bethesda, having five porticoes. In these lay a multitude of those who were sick, blind, lame, and withered, [waiting for the moving of the waters; for an angel of the Lord went down at certain seasons into the pool and stirred up the water; whoever then first, after the stirring up of the water, stepped in was made well from whatever disease with which he was afflicted.]

After the miracle in the Galilean region Jesus returns once again to Jerusalem and has His first meeting with the opponents who will eventually have Him killed.

Jerusalem was surrounded by walls and entrances into the city called "gates." Near one of these was a pool surrounded by porches that served as a gathering place for the sick and lame. (Those pools or water reservoirs were for bathing and drinking.)

> Vs. 5-9 – A man was there who had been ill for thirty-eight years. When Jesus saw him lying there, and knew that he had already been a long time in that condition, He said to him, "Do you wish to get well?" The sick man answered Him, "Sir, I have no man to put me into the pool when the water is stirred up, but while I am coming, another steps down before me." Jesus said to him, "Get up, pick up your pallet and walk." Immediately the man became well, and picked up his pallet and began to walk.

Note that this man had no faith in Jesus; the miracle is performed as mercy but also as a demonstration of power and as a sign to those who were present. The objective was less about healing and more about how people would respond: belief or disbelief. John will describe the conflict that results from this miracle.

The conflict – vs. 9^B-15

> Vs. 9^B – Now it was the Sabbath on that day.

The day Jesus performed this miracle was the Sabbath. Sabbath comes from Genesis 2:1-3 and the word Sabbath means "to rest or to cease." Day 7, Saturday.

In Genesis God ceases from His cycle of creation and provides a divine example of rest, or cessation of work. If He did not, we would work ourselves to death.

In the Pentateuch, the first 5 books of the Bible, He describes how the day is to be used and not used (Exodus 13-17; 34:21). Many festivals were celebrated to praise God's mercy and greatness and culminated on the day of the Sabbath (Exodus 34:22).

With the construction of the temple and later on the establishment of synagogues in different cities, the Sabbath became associated with activities at the temple or the synagogues (place of meeting). Eventually the Sabbath came to mean no work and meeting at the temple or synagogue for prayer and teaching, and other forms of worship.

In the 4th century, before Christ, the rabbis or teachers began defining what the idea of "work" was and their definitions became burdensome and ridiculous. They prohibited 39 types of work. You could not walk more than one mile from your home or else it was "work" on the Sabbath. A scribe could not carry his pens on the Sabbath because this was "work."

> Vs. 10 – So the Jews were saying to the man who was cured, "It is the Sabbath, and it is not permissible for you to carry your pallet."

This explains why the Jews (Pharisees) were saying to the man that he was sinning because carrying his pallet on the Sabbath was considered "work." Note that they completely dismiss the miracle, the man's joy and freedom, the glory to God. All they want is that their concept of what is right be obeyed and were blind to the rest.

> Vs. 11 – But he answered them, "He who made me well was the one who said to me, 'Pick up your pallet and walk.'

Of course as far as the healed man is concerned, the only authority that counts for him is the power of the One who healed him. (I.e. Do not talk to me, talk to the one who healed me.)

> Vs. 12-13 – They asked him, "Who is the man who said to you, 'Pick up your pallet and walk'?" But the man who was healed did not know who it was, for Jesus had slipped away while there was a crowd in that place.

They want to know who Jesus is. In their blindness the only words they hear and the only thing they see is the man walking away with his pallet, the thing that goes against their rules about the Sabbath.

> Vs. 14-15 – Afterward Jesus found him in the temple and said to him, "Behold, you have become well; do not sin anymore, so that nothing worse happens to you." The man went away, and told the Jews that it was Jesus who had made him well.

Jesus dealt with poor physical health by healing the lame man, now He deals with His spiritual health as well. "Sin no more," carries with it the implication that sins are forgiven. He warns him to stay away from sin seeing what it has caused in his past (illness) and what it can cause in the future (hell).

And so the healing and witness as well as the teaching bring forth faith as well as new life. This man who was ravaged by illness and burdened by sin is freed from both and becomes productive (multiplication) by sharing his own witness with others.

The accusations – vs. 16-18

We see the man made well and producing a powerful witness on behalf of Jesus. This not only brings Jesus more contacts and more followers; it also provides ammunition for His attackers.

> Vs. 16 – For this reason the Jews were persecuting Jesus, because He was doing these things on the Sabbath.

The most obvious of their accusations is the one they leveled against the lame man. They accuse Jesus of "working" on the Sabbath and therefore defiling it and disobeying God.

> Vs. 17 – But He answered them, "My Father is working until now, and I Myself am working."

Jesus responds that if they are charging Him with this, they are also accusing God. His reasoning goes like this:

- God never stops working or doing good.
- What I have done is a manifestation of God's work on behalf of this man.
- If what I have done breaks God's law, then you are accusing God of breaking His own law because in reality, He is the one who has done this.

> Vs. 18 – For this reason therefore the Jews were seeking all the more to kill Him, because He not only was breaking the Sabbath, but also was calling God His own Father, making Himself equal with God.

The leaders are frustrated and angry, as well as recognizing that Jesus is claiming a special relationship or equality with God. In their frustration and anger, they launch an attack on Jesus and in the next section Jesus responds to them by warning them of the various ways they are in danger of losing their souls.

1. Disrespect

> Vs. 19-23 – Therefore Jesus answered and was saying to them, "Truly, truly, I say to you, the Son can do nothing of Himself, unless it is something He sees the Father doing; for whatever the Father does, these things the Son also does in like manner. For the Father loves the Son, and shows Him all things that He Himself is doing; and the Father will show Him greater works than these, so that you will marvel. For just as the Father raises the dead and gives them life, even so the Son also gives life to whom He wishes. For not even the Father judges anyone, but He has given all judgment to the Son, so that all will honor the Son even as they honor the Father. He who does not honor the Son does not honor the Father who sent Him.

They denounced Him for doing the very thing His divine nature was sent to do. They accused the sinless One of sin, the very thing that would eventually crucify Him. Jesus came to cleanse the world of sin, not add to the sins.

Jesus tells them that those who say they honor Him, but end up accusing Him of sin, do not really honor Him. In fact, they are guilty of disrespect. The word honor means "to place a value." We are in danger of losing our souls if we do not place the proper value (honor) on Jesus. Value His person (worship), value His Word (study and obey), value His work on the cross (proclaim good news). Many will lose their souls because they did not honor Christ.

2. Unprepared for judgment

> Vs. 24-30 – "Truly, truly, I say to you, he who hears My word, and believes Him who sent Me, has eternal life, and does not come into judgment, but has passed out of death into life. Truly, truly, I say to you, an hour is coming and now is, when the dead will hear the voice of the Son of God, and those who hear will live. For just as the Father has life in Himself, even so He gave to the Son also to have life in Himself; and He gave Him authority to execute judgment, because He is the Son of Man. Do not marvel at this; for an hour is coming, in which all who are in the tombs will hear His voice, and will come forth; those who did the good deeds to a resurrection of life, those who committed the evil deeds to a resurrection of judgment.
>
> "I can do nothing on My own initiative. As I hear, I judge; and My judgment is just, because I do not seek My own will, but the will of Him who sent Me.

Jesus is speaking of the judgment they are leveling against Him and continues by saying: speaking of judgment, anyone who listens to me will not be judged but will be saved. Where then does that leave you who accuse me? He tells them that they will see the day when He will arise and they will see the day when all (including them) will be judged by God through Him. That means that He will judge them. That means that they have been wrongly accusing their own judge!

We can lose our souls when we fail to realize that Jesus is not only our savior, but He will be our judge as well.

3. Stubbornness

Vs. 31-38 – "If I alone testify about Myself, My testimony is not true. There is another who testifies of Me, and I know that the testimony which He gives about Me is true.

You have sent to John, and he has testified to the truth. But the testimony which I receive is not from man, but I say these things so that you may be saved. He was the lamp that was burning and was shining and you were willing to rejoice for a while in his light. But the testimony which I have is greater than the testimony of John; for the works which the Father has given Me to accomplish—the very works that I do—testify about Me, that the Father has sent Me.
And the Father who sent Me, He has testified of Me. You have neither heard His voice at any time nor seen His form. You do not have His word abiding in you, for you do not believe Him whom He sent.

Jesus reviews with them their incredible stubbornness and hardheartedness. He says, you believe people who gladly boast about themselves, your earthly leaders. You believed John the prophet when he said that the time was near. But you refuse to believe Me whose message is greater than John's and whose miracles are irrefutable.

You refuse to listen to God because you do not like the message and will not permit it to come into your hearts. The implication is that your hardhearted disbelief in Me demonstrates that you never really believed in Him either.

We can lose our souls in the same way as we refuse to listen to God's Word. Every time the Word says do this; or go this way; or let go of that person or habit or attitude; and we refuse, offering reasons, rationale or plain old rebellion, we harden our hearts. Every time we resist the Word, resist the impulse to do better, to try to live or serve better, our heart becomes that much harder.

A hard and stubborn heart allows us to sin with little guilt or afterthought. When we arrive at this point, we are in danger of losing our soul because, like those Jews, we have been hardened through stubbornness.

4. Ignorance

> Vs. 39-40 – You search the Scriptures because you think that in them you have eternal life; it is these that testify about Me; and you are unwilling to come to Me so that you may have life.

Jesus rebukes them for being ones who had the privilege of knowing the Scriptures, being so-called experts in the Scriptures but missing the point the Scriptures make. They taught that the Scriptures led one to eternal life. The Scriptures also lead to Jesus, who gives eternal life. They did not make this connection. To miss this connection is to reveal one's true ignorance.

We should not be too quick to condemn these men because we also miss the connection at times: We are sometimes so busy planning the Bible studies, organizing the worship and activities that we forget that the purpose of it all is to grow in the knowledge and likeness of Christ. When we make "religion" our goal, when we act like fleshly people in order to advance our religious goals, or devour each other so we can set church policy, we have missed the point and show our ignorance.

A lot of people who know a lot about the Bible will lose their souls because they are ignorant about Jesus Christ, the main topic in the Bible.

5. Pride

> Vs. 41-44 – I do not receive glory from men; but I know
> you, that you do not have the love of God in yourselves.
> I have come in My Father's name, and you do not
> receive Me; if another comes in his own name, you will
> receive him. How can you believe, when you receive
> glory from one another and you do not seek the glory
> that is from the one and only God?

This one must have hurt. Jesus says to them, you are ready to honor kings, soldiers, even your own teachers but refuse to honor me because I do not honor you but reveal your sins. The reason they did not honor Him was because they were angry with Him. They were angry with Him because He did not approve of them and this was something their pride craved.

Many people will lose their souls because they would rather have the approval of the world, families, and friends than the approval that comes from God through obedience to Christ.

6. Disbelief

> Vs. 45-47 – Do not think that I will accuse you before
> the Father; the one who accuses you is Moses, in
> whom you have set your hope. For if you believed
> Moses, you would believe Me, for he wrote about Me.
> But if you do not believe his writings, how will you
> believe My words?"

Jesus tells them that He does not need to accuse them; He will only have to judge. There is no need for Him to accuse because their own words will accuse them. They say they believe God's Word in Moses, but God's Word in Moses tells all readers that they should believe in Christ Jesus. By disbelieving Christ, they demonstrate that they do not really believe in the Word or Moses to begin with. They stood condemned because their actions (disbelief and rejection of Jesus) demonstrated their true disbelief in God's Word.

A lot of people have a Bible or know about the Bible, even hear lessons out of it on a regular basis. But saving faith requires two basic responses to the Bible:

- Believing as true what God says in His Word
- Obeying God's Word

Jesus says,

> Those who believe and are baptized will be saved and those who disbelieve shall be condemned."
>
> - Mark 16:16

Some people are in danger of losing their soul because they know and understand what the Bible says but their disobedience to the Word shows that they do not really believe.

Summary

The Jewish leaders judged and accused Jesus of sin. Jesus replied that God had made Him to be judge of all men and that His witness, teachings and miracles are proof that this is true.

He demonstrates His power as judge by listing the reasons for their condemnation:

1. Disrespect for God by refusing to honor the Son.
2. Being unprepared for their own judgment.
3. Refusal to submit to God's Word.
4. Ignorance of God's true will or purpose.

5. Prideful love of this world.

6. Disbelief of the Word and manifestation of the Word in Christ.

This rebuke might give a person cause to think about things but not these men; this just made them angrier and more resolute to destroy Him.

13.

TWO PROMISES FROM JESUS

JOHN 6:1-40

We have seen a "cyclical" pattern of teaching in John's book.

- There is the cycle of Jesus revealing His divinity through a pattern of witness, teaching and miracles.
- There is a larger cycle of events that begin with Jesus revealing His divinity in some way, and people responding to Him with either belief or disbelief.
- And then, of course, we have noticed a familiar pattern of steps Jesus used in His personal evangelism.

Let us keep our eyes open for these particular features in John's gospel as we forge ahead in our study.

In our last chapter covering John chapter 5, we saw Jesus perform a healing miracle and the response of disbelief from Jewish religious leaders who were bent on destroying Him and His ministry. In rejecting this great evidence of His true nature we saw Jesus rebuking them and warning them on account of their dishonor for God, lack of preparation for the judgment, hardheartedness, ignorance, pride and disbelief.

In chapter 6, Jesus once again returns to Galilee and performs two great miracles. This time, however, He makes two promises to those who believe, instead of listing the dangers for those who disbelieve.

The first miracle – 6:1-15

Vs. 1-13 – After these things Jesus went away to the other side of the Sea of Galilee (or Tiberias). A large crowd followed Him, because they saw the signs which He was performing on those who were sick. Then Jesus went up on the mountain, and there He sat down with His disciples. Now the Passover, the feast of the Jews, was near. Therefore Jesus, lifting up His eyes and seeing that a large crowd was coming to Him, said to Philip, "Where are we to buy bread, so that these may eat?" This He was saying to test him, for He Himself knew what He was intending to do. Philip answered Him, "Two hundred denarii worth of bread is not sufficient for them, for everyone to receive a little." One of His disciples, Andrew, Simon Peter's brother, said to Him, "There is a lad here who has five barley loaves and two fish, but what are these for so many people?" Jesus said, "Have the people sit down." Now there was much grass in the place. So the men sat down, in number about five thousand. Jesus then took the loaves, and having given thanks, He distributed to those who were seated; likewise also of the fish as much as they wanted. When they were filled, He said to His disciples, "Gather up the leftover fragments so that nothing will be lost." So they gathered them up, and filled twelve baskets with fragments from the five barley loaves which were left over by those who had eaten.

Both Phillip and Andrew demonstrate that there is no possible way to feed the people with the resources at hand. They do not realize that with Jesus they have the source for meeting needs.

> For by Him all things were created both in the heavens
> and on earth, visible and invisible.
> - Colossians 1:16

The miracle is that from five loaves and two fish, Jesus feeds more than 5,000 people with 12 baskets left over. The lesson, of course, is that with Jesus as the source, there is always more than enough.

> Vs. 14-15 – Therefore when the people saw the sign
> which He had performed, they said, "This is truly the
> Prophet who is to come into the world."
>
> So Jesus, perceiving that they were intending to come
> and take Him by force to make Him king, withdrew
> again to the mountain by Himself alone.

Note the reaction of the crowd: they see Him as a savior, messiah of sorts. Not the one He is, but the one they want Him to be.

They want to force Him to become their king. Their view of the Messiah was that he would have great powers, save them from their earthly enemies and make them a great nation once again.

Jesus knows their hearts and does not want to be this type of king for them, and for good reasons:

1. Only God anointed kings and so the crowd's anointing would be meaningless.
2. They saw Him as a man, yes a "Super Man", but still only a man.
3. They wanted to put their plan for political redemption into action, Jesus was sent to put God's plan for spiritual redemption into action.

Jesus, needing to stop the momentum of their actions, leaves for solitary prayer. As God, He did not need prayer. As man, however, He needed to pray for the Father's will to be done despite this setback.

The second miracle – 6:16-36

1. The miracle itself

> Vs. 16-21 – Now when evening came, His disciples went down to the sea, and after getting into a boat, they started to cross the sea to Capernaum. It had already become dark, and Jesus had not yet come to them. The sea began to be stirred up because a strong wind was blowing. Then, when they had rowed about three or four miles, they saw Jesus walking on the sea and drawing near to the boat; and they were frightened. But He said to them, "It is I; do not be afraid." So they were willing to receive Him into the boat, and immediately the boat was at the land to which they were going.

This miracle is performed only for the Apostles and those of us who read their testimony. Both miracles, however, prepare the people, the Apostles, and all who read their witness for what is to come next.

2. Jesus declares His divinity (implicitly)

Notice in these events that the smaller cycle of Jesus declaring His divinity in a variety of ways will work within the larger cycle of people observing these things and reacting with belief or disbelief.

> Vs. 22-25 – The next day the crowd that stood on the other side of the sea saw that there was no other small boat there, except one, and that Jesus had not entered

with His disciples into the boat, but that His disciples had gone away alone. There came other small boats from Tiberias near to the place where they ate the bread after the Lord had given thanks. So when the crowd saw that Jesus was not there, nor His disciples, they themselves got into the small boats, and came to Capernaum seeking Jesus. When they found Him on the other side of the sea, they said to Him, "Rabbi, when did You get here?"

The multitude follows Jesus. It is not a huge lake, but much too large to walk around in just one evening (some 40 miles on foot). There was no boat to take Him across; they knew this, so the only conclusion (walking across on water somehow) involved the miraculous. They did not see it, but all signs pointed to this.

Vs. 26-27 – Jesus answered them and said, "Truly, truly, I say to you, you seek Me, not because you saw signs, but because you ate of the loaves and were filled. Do not work for the food which perishes, but for the food which endures to eternal life, which the Son of Man will give to you, for on Him the Father, God, has set His seal."

Jesus now confronts them about the miracle of the previous day:

- He reveals their true motives (physical satisfaction, free food).

- He reveals what their motives should be (spiritual satisfaction).

- God provides spiritual nourishment only through Christ and the proof (seal) that this is so is the miracle that filled your bellies.

With the miracle of the loaves and fishes, Jesus proves that He can provide the spiritual nourishment that only God can give.

3. Reaction of the crowd

> Vs. 28 – Therefore they said to Him, "What shall we do, so that we may work the works of God?"

The people misunderstand His statement thinking He can give them some sort of secret formula that will give them the power to make bread, etc. In this way they confuse spiritual food with spiritual signs. They could not grasp what He was offering them: not food for an empty belly, but an opportunity to fill their souls by opening their eyes.

4. Jesus' response

> Vs. 29 – Jesus answered and said to them, "This is the work of God, that you believe in Him whom He has sent."

Jesus goes ahead by explaining the purpose of the miracle, which is to create faith in Him as God's Son. This miracle is an example of how God promotes faith: He does not eliminate choice, He simply provides proof. In the end, all men choose to believe, but God provides the proof necessary to influence that choice. If we choose to believe and continue to do so, we demonstrate God's work and influence in us. Our faith, not our great or miraculous works, is what demonstrates God's power working in us.

5. The crowd's response

> Vs. 30-31 – So they said to Him, "What then do You do for a sign, so that we may see, and believe You? What work do You perform? Our fathers ate the manna in the

> wilderness; as it is written, 'He gave them bread out of heaven to eat.'

In essence they demand another miracle to convince them to believe. "Moses provided manna for 40 years, do the same or better, then we will believe." They want miracles in the style of Moses, better than Moses!

This is just another way of refusing to acknowledge who Jesus really was, based on the witness of miracles, teachings and declarations He has already made to them. When you do not want to believe, no amount of proof will change your mind.

Jesus refuses to be their "human" king because He is their divine king and they need to understand this. He does not deal with them on their terms but on His terms and salvation is based on their recognition of this.

6. Jesus' response

> Vs. 32-33 – Jesus then said to them, "Truly, truly, I say to you, it is not Moses who has given you the bread out of heaven, but it is My Father who gives you the true bread out of heaven. For the bread of God is that which comes down out of heaven, and gives life to the world."

The Lord corrects their misunderstanding of both Moses and manna. Moses never gave the true bread from heaven (spiritual life); only God can give this. Manna never came from "heaven"; it was simply on the ground in the morning when they arose. Manna had three purposes: feed the physical appetite, witness God's power, provide a type or preview for the true bread that would come from heaven and give spiritual life.

He continues to witness His divine nature by teaching them concepts that only God could know.

7. The crowd responds

> Vs. 34 – Then they said to Him, "Lord, always give us this bread."

Note that they address Him as Lord (Sir) not Lord (Savior). They see that what He is offering is desirable, but still do not understand what it really is; and do not believe in Him. Before, they wanted power to make bread in a miraculous way. Now they think the "true bread" is some kind of super-manna where if you eat of it you will not ever be hungry anymore; just a better way to satisfy their physical hunger evermore.

8. Jesus declares His divinity (explicitly)

> Vs. 35 – Jesus said to them, "I am the bread of life; he who comes to Me will not hunger, and he who believes in Me will never thirst."

Jesus stops speaking to them in parable-like terms and clearly declares His divine nature by linking Himself to the divine images He has been describing.

Throughout this chapter He has declared this same idea in different ways:

- He is the Messiah come into the world (vs. 14)
- He is the Son of Man (vs. 27)
- He is the One on whom the Father has set His seal (vs. 27)
- He is the One sent by the Father (vs. 29)
- He is the Son of God (vs. 32)
- He is the One who gives life to the world (vs. 33)
- He is the Bread of Life (vs. 35)

First by miracles, then by teaching, now by clear declarations, Jesus is trying to show them who He really is.

9. The crowd's response

> Vs. 36 – But I said to you that you have seen Me, and yet do not believe.

Jesus flatly states that after all of this their response is simple: disbelief. Their response is the same as the Pharisees at Jerusalem, they do not believe.

Jesus' two promises

Before Jesus explained the condemnation awaiting those who did not believe. And even though these in Galilee also respond with disbelief, He makes two promises to those who do believe, then and now:

1. Those who come to Him will be accepted.

> Vs. 37 – All that the Father gives Me will come to Me, and the one who comes to Me I will certainly not cast out.

All those who come through the cross of Christ will not be refused, regardless of sins, nationality, intelligence or social position. No matter where you are or who you are, there is no need for fear: God will accept you through Christ.

2. Those who do believe have eternal life.

> Vs. 38-40 – For I have come down from heaven, not to do My own will, but the will of Him who sent Me. This is the will of Him who sent Me, that of all that He has given Me I lose nothing, but raise it up on the last day. For this is the will of My Father, that everyone who beholds the Son and believes in Him will have eternal life, and I Myself will raise him up on the last day."

What God desires is that none who believe in Jesus will be lost. Those who trust Christ trust that He will save them despite their weakness.

Notice that first comes the eternal life, then comes the resurrection. You already possess eternal life through faith before you die and are resurrected. It is why you are resurrected to glory.

Summary

Jesus performs two great miracles. He declares that He is the Savior, the Son of God, the Giver of eternal life.

His audience does not believe, even though He has done the miracles and made His declaration. They search only for the physical blessings that miracles give.

To those who believe He makes two promises:

- All who come to Him, He will accept.
- All who believe in Him can rest assured that they have eternal life beginning now, their own resurrection will merely confirm it.

Exhortation

Do not be discouraged by your own lack of faith at times; and the total disbelief of others. Even eyewitnesses rejected Christ. Even after eating the bread miraculously made. It is normal to doubt; normal for the majority to reject: even Christ said that the way to life was narrow and few were on it.

When in doubt, remember the promises of whom you have believed. Realize you have eternal life now. Take heart that Jesus promised that He would not lose any, trust Him.

14.

BELIEF IS A MUST

JOHN 6:41-59

Since we are starting in the middle of a Bible chapter we need to set the scene of what has taken place so far.

1. Jesus has returned from Jerusalem and is in the northern region of Galilee in His adult hometown of Capernaum on the shore of the Sea of Galilee.

2. During this time He has performed two miracles: one public, the feeding of the 5,000; one private, walking on water to meet the Apostles in their boat.

3. These two miracles set into motion a dialogue between the people and the Lord as they met in the synagogue in Capernaum.

4. At first the people want Him to be their king but Jesus refuses, knowing that their desire is only based on physical and not spiritual reasons.

5. After His refusal, Jesus takes the opportunity to declare His true identity that has no relationship to an earthly king. In various ways He reveals His divine nature to them:

    • He is the Messiah (vs. 14)
    • He is the Son of Man (vs. 27)
    • He has the Father's seal (vs. 27)
    • He is sent by the Father (vs. 29)
    • He is the Son of God (vs. 32)

- He gives life to the world (vs. 33)
- He is the Bread of Life (vs. 35)

6. These declarations, along with the miracles, are rejected by the people. They want more proof, more miracles.

7. Jesus refuses to give them more proof, instead He makes two promises to those who choose to believe in Him based on the proof He has already given:

   a. They, whoever they are, will be accepted by God.
   b. They will have eternal life.

This is pretty much where we left off, but this is not the end of the dialogue Jesus is having with these people at Capernaum. Jesus has made two promises to the ones who believe, but in doing so He is also stating without words something to those who persist in disbelief:

- If believing brings one acceptance from God and eternal life with Him, then the opposite will also happen.
- The opposite being that if you do not believe, God will reject you and your eternity will be without Him.

Dialogue between Jesus and the crowd (continued)

1. The crowd's reaction to His claims and promises

> Vs. 41-42 – Therefore the Jews were grumbling about Him, because He said, "I am the bread that came down out of heaven." They were saying, "Is not this Jesus, the son of Joseph, whose father and mother we know?

> How does He now say, 'I have come down out of
> heaven'?"

Note that they do not talk about the promises, but finally begin to grasp what He is saying: that He comes from heaven.

Their reaction is to compare what they have seen and heard from Him to what they know about Him. They know He is a man (He never denies this) and do not want to go any further than this. Notice that they do not discuss the miracle or the promises, they simply allow their disbelief to grow into anger.

2. Jesus responds to their anger

> Vs. 43 – Jesus answered and said to them, "Do not
> grumble among yourselves.

They have lost their focus and are now grumbling and rising in anger, they are not paying attention to Him. He gets their attention back by telling them to stop.

> Vs. 44 – No one can come to Me unless the Father who
> sent Me draws him; and I will raise him up on the last
> day.

Their problem is that they are trying to figure out in a logical, physical way how Jesus came from heaven and they cannot so they are frustrated and angry about this. Jesus tells them that logic or rationalization cannot figure this thing out; you can only believe it (come to Jesus) through the method that the Father has prescribed and that is through faith. This is what He means by the Father "drawing" them.

The Father is the one who did the miracle through Jesus so that they would believe, draw near, accept Jesus and His claims. Believing does not mean you always understand "how" things are done. Believing means you accept as true the person or thing God points to through a teaching, revelation or miracle.

You do not come to Jesus by "logic," you are drawn to Him by God through His Word. Those who come in this way will receive these promises and more.

> Vs. 45 – It is written in the prophets, 'And they shall all be taught of God.' Everyone who has heard and learned from the Father, comes to Me.

Jesus goes to the Scriptures themselves to convince them that what He proposes is not a new method. That being drawn by a person, believing in His word, this is nothing new. The prophets write about this. The quote He refers to is from the prophet Isaiah who was referring to God's blessings on His special people. And these people were special because they believed the Word they had been taught.

The connection is implicitly stated, but it hangs there for everyone to see. If you are the special people of this age, you would believe the words I speak because they come from God. The miracle I have done proves it.

Belief in Jesus Christ is the way to separate those who belong to God from those who do not. This causes a lot of hard feelings but this is what Jesus taught. This is offensive to other religious groups and non-religious people, but it is what Jesus Himself taught.

I can understand non-Christians having trouble with this and calling us all kinds of names because of it, this is normal. What I do not understand is Christians who falsely teach that God accepts all sincere religions! If you want to be a universalist, that is fine, but do not pervert basic Christian doctrine in the process.

Jesus taught that only His disciples were accepted by God and received eternal life, and those who rejected this hated Him for saying this. We cannot expect to be treated much differently and must not change the Lord's Word in order to be accepted by those who reject us because of our faith!

> Vs. 46 – Not that anyone has seen the Father, except the One who is from God; He has seen the Father.

There is no one who has seen and been taught directly by God, in His holy presence. This privilege belongs to only one person, and by implication Jesus is referring to Himself. He has already said He is the one who comes from heaven.

The Lord re-summarizes His argument here by inferring that since they have not seen God, they should therefore believe the words of one who has and in so doing, demonstrate that they are truly God's people.

> Vs. 47-50 – Truly, truly, I say to you, he who believes has eternal life. I am the bread of life. Your fathers ate the manna in the wilderness, and they died. This is the bread which comes down out of heaven, so that one may eat of it and not die.

In continuing His response to them He repeats the promises and claims that He has made previously:

1. That the one who believes in Him has eternal life.

2. That He is the Bread of Life.

3. That He is superior to Moses, and what He offers is superior to what their forefathers received through Moses. Through Moses, God offered the people physical food to satisfy their hunger and prolong their lives for a short period of time. Through Jesus, God offers spiritual food which will nourish the soul and which will ultimately lead to eternal life.

> Vs. 51 – I am the living bread that came down out of heaven; if anyone eats of this bread, he will live forever; and the bread also which I will give for the life of the world is My flesh."

Once again Jesus calls on them to believe! Before, He had asked them to believe that He was divine and from God, by using symbolic language (Bread of Life, coming down from heaven). Now He explains how the spiritual food that produces eternal life is given. One must eat the bread of heaven (it has to get inside of you). This is a symbolic way of saying, "you must take me inside of you through faith." He also explains, in veiled terms, just how He will gain life for the world. He will do this by giving His body, His life, for the world. Of course, He is referring to the cross He will die on.

At this point they cannot begin to understand the significance of what He is saying, but if they believed God's word in the prophets about a suffering savior (Isaiah 53:1-ff) redeeming God's people, they would have seen this as yet another clue as to Jesus' true identity.

For now we see that Jesus has already laid out the basic elements of the gospel message:

1. Belief that Jesus is the divine Son of God.

2. Trust that His sacrifice saves us.

3. Obedience to His teachings.

3. Response of the Jews

> Vs. 52 – Then the Jews began to argue with one another, saying, "How can this man give us His flesh to eat?"

Remember, this is a conversation between Jesus and the people in the synagogue at Capernaum. In their response we see that they miss the spiritual significance in what He has said. They are judging everything He says from the perspective that He is only a man.

Of course, if Jesus is only a man, they are right and would be foolish to follow Him. But if the miracle is true and He is who He says He is, they are being foolish for rejecting the Son of God.

4. Jesus calls on them to convert

In this section the Lord declares openly the terms of salvation. He calls on them to decide.

> Vs. 53-55 – So Jesus said to them, "Truly, truly, I say to you, unless you eat the flesh of the Son of Man and drink His blood, you have no life in yourselves. He who eats My flesh and drinks My blood has eternal life, and I will raise him up on the last day. For My flesh is true food, and My blood is true drink.

Belief in Jesus equals eternal life and resurrection. One has no life unless one does this. Jesus is emphatic about this.

Note that He does not become exasperated or discouraged by their disbelief, He merely becomes more emphatic (clearer) about the way to eternal life.

The symbolic language merely repeats the same message. You must eat my flesh and drink my blood (believe) because my flesh and blood is true food (the only way).

> Vs. 56-59 – He who eats My flesh and drinks My blood abides in Me, and I in him. As the living Father sent Me, and I live because of the Father, so he who eats Me, he also will live because of Me. This is the bread which came down out of heaven; not as the fathers ate and

died; he who eats this bread will live forever." These things He said in the synagogue as He taught in Capernaum.

In these verses Jesus explains the dynamics of faith and how it produces life. The one who believes in Me becomes, by virtue of faith, part of Me and I become part of him and subsequently he receives all the life that I share with the Father because I also am united to the Father.

The key here is not to try to be like Jesus by trying to understand how all of this can be so. As if Jesus was a mere human being and becoming part of Him could be explained in a physical way.

Jesus is telling them to see this as an offer for a particular relationship with God through Jesus made possible by faith. By faith, we somehow become part of Jesus the Son of God. By faith, He becomes part of us. By faith, we are changed from physical, temporal beings into eternal, spiritual beings.

The faith we are talking about is expressed in a physical way, but it itself is not physical in nature.

Later on we learn that this faith has two physical expressions practiced by all who claim to believe:

A. Baptism – It is at this point in time that through faith we become united with Jesus and He is united to us. (Romans 6:3-6; Galatians 3:26-28). Baptism is a physical act, but at that moment we know by faith that His blood washes away our sins (Acts 2:38; 22:16; Revelation 1:5). There is no actual, physical cross or blood; our sins are not actually visible, but during the physical act of baptism we know that the invisible actions are taking place because we believe God's Word.

B. Communion – This is the other physical act that through faith connects us to Christ and every believer. The Word of God tells us that these spiritual, invisible things are taking place during this very visible and physical act. By faith we are united to the

Lord and to the church as we practice this ceremony each Sunday.

And so by direct declaration and prophecy of things to come concerning His cross, He is trying to reveal to them the relationship between faith, salvation and ultimately the key physical acts that accompany and express these things.

We will see that even with all of this effort, the majority of His hearers were not ready to believe.

Summary

There are some very important concepts here for us to learn.

1. You cannot know who Jesus is by human wisdom and knowledge alone; you can only know Him by faith.

2. Faith is the key to spiritual knowledge and wisdom. First you believe, and then your eyes are opened to see and know.

3. Genuine faith is expressed by converts through obedience in baptism. Genuine faith is expressed by Christians by faithful communion.

These are the basics of the Christian faith.

15.

JESUS KNOWS HIS OWN

JOHN 6:60-71

Most of chapter 6 in John's gospel is really a dialogue between Jesus and the crowd that followed Him. So far this is the sequence of events:

1. He performs two miracles (one public and one private) to confirm His claim to be divine.

2. The crowd asks for more proof, for a greater miracle.

3. He promises righteousness (i.e. acceptance before God) and eternal life to those who believe. He explains that He will obtain these by the offering of His life.

4. The crowd grows hostile at His "presumption" to offer them eternal life; after all, He is just a hometown boy.

5. Jesus declares that the promise of eternal life and righteousness has always been and is now offered on the basis of faith.

Previously I explained that faith is accepting as true what God says, does or is going to do based on the information He gives us. This means that sometimes we are asked to believe even if we do not understand how God does something or will do something.

A good example of this faith process is seen here as Jesus offers the people the opportunity to be united to God forever by faith in Him, and He performs two visible miracles to demonstrate His ability to fulfill these promises. However, He does not explain how these things will happen, only that they will for those who believe.

Dialogue between Jesus and His disciples

So far Jesus has been having a dialogue between Himself and the crowd in general. In the final verses of chapter 6, John will telescope in to a tighter scene between Jesus and His closer disciples and the conversation Jesus has with them concerning the miracles and the reaction of the crowd.

1. The reaction of the disciples

> Vs. 60 – Therefore many of His disciples, when they heard this said, "This is a difficult statement; who can listen to it?"

Jesus' disciples have only been witnesses to what has been taking place between Jesus and the crowds. However when Jesus actually claims to give righteousness and eternal life through Himself, they can contain themselves no longer and they begin to reconsider their positions.

A "difficult" or "hard" statement means stiff, dry, hard to accept or believe. The whole concept of Jesus' divinity, His ability to confer both righteousness and eternal life and resurrection through faith in Himself was just too much for them. They could not take anymore.

I want you to note the interesting process of sifting going on here. Sifting occurs when you continually refine something until you eliminate all the unwanted matter and are left with the purest element. For example, gold miners do this as they sift through all the minerals until just the few nuggets of gold are left, or researchers do this as they sift through a mountain of information to find just the most accurate and pertinent facts.

In the same way Jesus is doing this with the people who follow Him. He is continually sifting them looking for true disciples. First He sifts through the leaders in Jerusalem. Next He sifts through the crowd in His hometown of Capernaum. Here in this scene, He sifts through those who claim to be His disciples. Later on He will sift through His chosen Apostles. Even today He continues to sift through the world and the church separating the wheat from the chaff.

In this we see another recurring cycle where Jesus is continually sifting and refining His listeners through His Word, His miracles and His ministry. In the end, Jesus' sifting serves to separate those with faith from those who have no faith or those who are simply religious hypocrites.

2. Jesus' response to unbelieving disciples

Vs. 61-62 – But Jesus, conscious that His disciples grumbled at this, said to them, "Does this cause you to stumble? What then if you see the Son of Man ascending to where He was before?

In effect Jesus says to them, I tell you that I come from heaven and this makes you "stumble." The word "stumble" means to be killed in a trap. In other words, I say this to you and it traps and kills your faith in Me?

Of course this is the sifting process at work. The reason that His statements "trap" their faith is because their faith is in a man, not in the Son of God. His statement reveals the shallowness of their faith.

Because their faith is where it is, they cannot see how a mere man can actually give life, righteousness or resurrection. Of course it would be no problem for God to do this, but they do not yet believe in His divine nature. They have the same problem, they stumble at the same spot as the crowd did. Until now they were happy to claim Jesus as their own. He was popular, took on the leadership and even performed great signs like the prophets of old… "Jesus, He's our man! He's a winner!"

But now He makes this incredible claim and they are caught short because they are not ready to go this far in their belief in Him.

Jesus tells them that they have given up very quickly. He tells them, "What will you do with your unbelief if you see me returning to the place where I said I came from?" Of course the Apostles witnessed this after Jesus' resurrection when He ascended into heaven before their very eyes.

> Vs. 63 – It is the Spirit who gives life; the flesh profits nothing; the words that I have spoken to you are spirit and are life.

They cannot accept that He can actually give life because they believe that He is just a man. And He agrees with them. He is not a ghost, an appearance, just the reflection of a human being. He is a man! But, He says, it is the Spirit who gives life. Mere human flesh has no power to revive the dead or create life; only the Spirit can do this.

If I were only a man, Jesus says, I could not do any of these things. But, He claims, the Spirit does do these things through Me and the words that I speak. Therefore, this makes my words life-giving words, spiritual words if you take them in through faith. This is a reference back to eating the flesh and drinking the blood. Jesus becomes part of you as you take Him in by faith. The Spirit becomes part of you as you take Him inside of you by believing the words of Jesus.

Vs. 64-65 – But there are some of you who do not believe." For Jesus knew from the beginning who they were who did not believe, and who it was that would betray Him. And He was saying, "For this reason I have said to you, that no one can come to Me unless it has been granted him from the Father."

Jesus makes another divine witness of His person by claiming to know their hearts, thoughts and intentions. He tells them that He knows who follows Him and for what reason they do. This would mean that He not only knew who would betray Him but would also know when that thought would arise in his heart. Jesus was capable of knowing this and tells them that He is able.

Some people use this passage to promote the idea that God chooses and calls certain people and rejects others. This doctrine is called "Predestination."

But what Jesus is telling His listeners is that without God permitting the truth to be known, no one could know what the truth is.. that Jesus is God. The Father grants us to come to Him by revealing the truth through the miracles, teaching and witness of Jesus Christ, His Son. This is how God calls us, draws us, permits us to come to Him: by believing in His Son. Had He not done this, we would have not found Him on our own.

3. The response of the disciples

Vs. 66 – As a result of this many of His disciples withdrew and were not walking with Him anymore.

They did not go on. They would not be counted among His disciples anymore. Why? Jesus rejected them. He said that if they did not believe in Him now, they were never disciples to begin with; they were just along for the ride. Once they realized that Jesus knew that they were not disciples inwardly, they simply stopped pretending they were disciples outwardly. The result of sifting!

It does not say here, but what do you think happened to these who just quit? It seems that they went back to their old lives as fishermen, farmers, shepherds, homemakers, servants of the king, picking up where they left off before they began walking with Jesus. Is this not what we do when we stop following Jesus? We load up on hobbies, work, TV, other activities, to fill up the place that only faith and obedience to Christ can fill.

Dialogue between Jesus and the Apostles

1. Jesus questions the Apostles

> Vs. 67 – So Jesus said to the twelve, "You do not want to go away also, do you?"

Now it is the Apostles' turn to be sifted. The leaders are against Him, the crowd is hostile and the people in the synagogue are skeptical. He is losing His disciples, so now He challenges His chosen Apostles. He points out what is happening and says, "You see the crowds leaving, does this shake your faith?" The neighbors, friends, cousins, relatives, shaky disciples are leaving because the going was getting rough. Were they going to follow suit?

2. The Apostles' response to Jesus

Peter speaks up with a faith not yet fully matured, but a faith nevertheless.

> Vs. 68-69 – Simon Peter answered Him, "Lord, to whom shall we go? You have words of eternal life. We have believed and have come to know that You are the Holy One of God."

Note that Peter says NO, they would not leave for two very distinct reasons:

1. They have nowhere else to go where they can find "life giving" words. They could have gone back to the fishing business, back to the simple life along the Sea of Galilee. They had a place to go to but not one that offered them the life that Jesus offered. Only with Jesus did they have the "words of life."

2. They believed what Jesus said, even if they did not quite understand it all yet. They had seen the miracle and heard the words and were putting the two together. Peter articulates the thinking of the group by confessing that they are in the process of knowing Him not only as a man, but as the One Jesus claims to be, the Holy One.

Peter did not know anymore than the crowd about how things were done, how Jesus would give eternal life, but based on evidence provided, he was willing to believe and trust God for what he did not know.

Sometimes we want to know everything before we believe; Jesus calls on us to believe so that we can know.

3. Jesus' response to the Apostles' faith

> Vs. 70-71 – Jesus answered them, "Did I Myself not choose you, the twelve, and yet one of you is a devil?" Now He meant Judas the son of Simon Iscariot, for he, one of the twelve, was going to betray Him.

Peter had spoken for all of them and all of them, by their silence, showed their agreement with Peter. Their reward for this step of faith is yet another demonstration of Jesus' divine nature.

Jesus tells them that not only is He aware of His true disciples, He is also aware of His betrayer as well. He knows which ones have spoken the truth about their faith and which one has kept his disbelief secret.

John clarifies for the reader who the person was eventually known to be, showing that Jesus accurately revealed that He would be betrayed.

Summary

Let us quickly summarize this last section of dialogue:

- Jesus calls on the people to have faith in Him in order to receive eternal life.

- He declares that those who do not have faith are not really His disciples.

- Many who claimed to be His disciples leave Him at this point.

- Jesus calls on the Apostles for their reaction.

- Peter, in speaking for the 12, declares his belief in Jesus as the Messiah of God.

- Jesus accepts their acknowledgement of His person and gives further proof by claiming to discern the heart of a traitor among them, a claim later confirmed by Judas' betrayal.

Lessons

There are some important lessons we can draw from this personal exchange between Jesus and His disciples:

We cannot judge the heart.

Jesus showed us that only God can discern the motives of the heart. Our task is to share our faith, love others and serve where and when we can in Christ's name. We spend too much time trying to figure out motives of the heart and not enough time in loving service. God judges the hearts; we have other things to do.

You cannot fool God.

If God knows the heart, you cannot fake Him out. If Jesus knew about Judas then, He knows who the Judas' are now. Judas refused to believe, refused to repent. Let's not be like him, too proud or stubborn to repent and receive life eternal from Christ.

You must eat His flesh and drink His blood in order to have life.

Paul explains in Romans 10:17 that faith comes by hearing the words of Christ. This is how you receive and maintain spiritual life, by hearing the words of Christ continually.

Coming to Bible class, attending worship, making room for Wednesday night service, regular Bible reading, these are all wearying to the flesh because the flesh is weak and dying. Remember, it is your spirit that profits, not your flesh. The word you hear stimulates spiritual life and growth like love, joy, peace, patience, gentleness, self-control, etc. These things are not gained through the flesh, but rather through the Word affecting the spirit.

People fall away because they do not feed the spirit, they do not open their Bibles at home, they do not attend regularly; soon they doubt Christ and become like those who "no longer walk with Him."

Let us eat and drink regularly what is spiritual so we can maintain a healthy and growing spirit.

16.
JESUS IN JERUSALEM

JOHN 7:1-53

After 6 chapters of John's gospel you are surely beginning to see that much of his book is really a dialogue between Jesus and others in different locations:

- Jesus and the people in general
- Jesus and the crowds that continually followed Him
- Jesus and His disciples
- Jesus and His Apostles
- Jesus and individuals like Nicodemus or the Samaritan woman
- Jesus and His enemies, the Jewish leadership
- Jesus and disbelievers
- Jesus and those who come to Him for healing

John recounts these dialogues as they took place in Jerusalem, on the way to Jerusalem, or in the northern part of the country like Galilee and the towns around the lake.

We now begin chapter 7 and see a rare dialogue between Jesus and His own family concerning His ministry; then the dialogue between the people themselves concerning Jesus.

Dialogue between Jesus and His brothers

We know from other passages (Matthew 12:46-47; Mark 6:3) that Jesus had both brothers and sisters. Mark even names the brothers (James, Joses, Jude, Simon). John gives us a rare glimpse of what things were like for Jesus at home.

> Vs. 1-2 – After these things Jesus was walking in Galilee, for He was unwilling to walk in Judea because the Jews were seeking to kill Him. Now the feast of the Jews, the Feast of Booths, was near.

It had become dangerous for Him to be in Jerusalem, He had already been branded as a troublemaker and risked being arrested if He went to the capital city.

The feast of booths, sometimes called tabernacles, was celebrated in October. It was a time of celebration for the season's harvest of grain, fruit and wine. It was also a commemorative feast remembering the escape from Egypt. The men were required to attend and for the week-long festival thousands of booths or "tents" were erected outside the walls of the city of Jerusalem where the people would stay.

> Vs. 3-5 – Therefore His brothers said to Him, "Leave here and go into Judea, so that Your disciples also may see Your works which You are doing. For no one does anything in secret when he himself seeks to be known publicly. If You do these things, show Yourself to the world." For not even His brothers were believing in Him.

John recounts a very personal moment between Jesus and His earthly brothers. The key here, of course, is that the brothers did not believe in Jesus so their comments have to be taken in this light. Note also the cycle of belief and disbelief showing up here.

Even though these men (James, Jude, Joses and Simon) did not believe in Him as the Messiah, they were quick to point out how He should conduct His ministry. Their point makes sense: if you want to be known, why waste your time and energy around here, Galilee was scarcely populated and not important. Go where the action is: Jerusalem, especially while the crowds are there for the feast.

Note that they say, "If you do these things." They had not even bothered to go to any of His public meetings; they had not witnessed any of His miracles; they had only heard about Him.

They do not believe, will not make the effort to find out, but they give Him advice on how He should conduct His ministry. Perhaps they thought that if He turned out to be the great savior and king the Jews believed the Messiah would be, they would receive His good favor.

We learn later that they were converted after Jesus' resurrection. James became an elder and leader of the Jerusalem congregation, he also wrote the epistle of James. Historians tell us that he was thrown from the city walls and stoned to death as a Christian martyr. Jude went on to write the epistle of Jude.

> Vs. 6-9 – So Jesus said to them, "My time is not yet here, but your time is always opportune. The world cannot hate you, but it hates Me because I testify of it, that its deeds are evil. Go up to the feast yourselves; I do not go up to this feast because My time has not yet fully come." Having said these things to them, He stayed in Galilee.

Jesus explains that the "time" to do what they want Him to do (manifest or show Himself as the Messiah) is not at hand. They think that going among the crowds to do miracles is the way to do this. Jesus knows that dying on the cross and resurrecting, this is how He will manifest Himself and the "time" to do this is not yet at hand.

Their "time," however, is always ready because they have no set mission. They are free to go to the festival. They are free to return and go back to their jobs. They are free to believe.

They can do these things because they are not under restriction nor are they under attack. Jesus' movements are limited because He is hated by those whom He has accused of sin. His time is controlled by God because of His mission, but His brothers have no such restrictions.

He encourages them to go, but tells them that He will not go for the purposes they suggested. This does not mean He will not go, rather that He will not go with their plan or motives.

> Vs. 10-13 – But when His brothers had gone up to the feast, then He Himself also went up, not publicly, but as if, in secret. So the Jews were seeking Him at the feast and were saying, "Where is He?" There was much grumbling among the crowds concerning Him; some were saying, "He is a good man"; others were saying, "No, on the contrary, He leads the people astray." Yet no one was speaking openly of Him for fear of the Jews.

The scene now changes to Jerusalem where there is no lack of controversy over Jesus and His claims. John shows that the people were divided in their opinion of Him but were united in their common fear of the leadership and their opposition to Jesus.

With Jesus now gone to Jerusalem, not with a triumphal, miraculous entry as His brothers had suggested, but a secret one among the people, the scene is set for another dialogue.

Dialogue between Jesus and the crowd

In order to set the stage for this you have to go back to verse 7 where Jesus gives the real reason for His opposition: He reveals the sins of the people and they do not like it.

In His dialogue with the people and the leaders He will do this very thing, reveal the sin and hypocrisy of the crowd and the Jewish leaders. He does this by responding to their various charges.

1. They charge Him with being incompetent

> Vs. 14-15 – But when it was now the midst of the feast Jesus went up into the temple, and began to teach. The Jews then were astonished, saying, "How has this man become learned, having never been educated?"

They are impressed with His teaching but question His credentials. If He could not show proper credentials in having been trained in one of the rabbinical schools, how credible could His teaching be? The Jewish leaders ask the crowd this "rhetorical" question in an effort to discredit Jesus publicly.

> Vs. 16-19 – So Jesus answered them and said, "My teaching is not Mine, but His who sent Me. If anyone is willing to do His will, he will know of the teaching, whether it is of God or whether I speak from Myself. He who speaks from himself seeks his own glory; but He who is seeking the glory of the One who sent Him, He is true, and there is no unrighteousness in Him. "Did not

> Moses give you the Law, and yet none of you carries
> out the Law? Why do you seek to kill Me?"

Jesus comes right back at these leaders with 3 points:

1. The teaching He gives is not His own, it is the teaching of God who sent Him.

2. Anyone who claims to know God will do God's will and by this will be proven to be legitimate. *"You fail this test because you misinterpret God's will (given to you by Moses); and you are trying to kill Me."*

3. Those who speak by their own authority seek their own glory, those who speak with God's authority seek to glorify Him. The implication on this one is that it was evident who received the glory from His ministry and who received the glory and honor when the Jewish leaders taught and practiced their religion.

"Compare Me to them and you will see who is credible!"

2. They charge Him with being demon possessed

> Vs. 20 – The crowd answered, "You have a demon!
> Who seeks to kill You?"

This time it is the crowd who voices an opinion about Jesus' accusation of the Jewish leaders. In effect they are saying, "You are crazy, how can you say that our leaders are trying to kill you?"

Do not forget, most of these people are pilgrims in Jerusalem for the feast. They are not aware of all that has gone on, they have mostly heard of Jesus. They are having a hard time believing that their religious leaders would actually do this to Jesus.

Vs. 21-24 – Jesus answered them, "I did one deed, and you all marvel. For this reason Moses has given you circumcision (not because it is from Moses, but from the fathers), and on the Sabbath you circumcise a man. If a man receives circumcision on the Sabbath so that the Law of Moses will not be broken, are you angry with Me because I made an entire man well on the Sabbath? Do not judge according to appearance, but judge with righteous judgment."

The Lord does not even address their charge but shows by His unfailing insight that He is not crazy or possessed at all. He explains the charge that He had made against the leaders in His previous statement.

His reference to a miracle is the one where He healed the lame man on the Sabbath and was then accused of sinning because He healed on the Sabbath. This was also the cause of the great anger and violence directed toward Him by the Jewish leaders.

In effect He shows how His miracle is in perfect accord with Moses, even when done on the Sabbath. He says that the Law on circumcision, given by Moses but originated long before Moses through Abraham, commanded that each male child be circumcised on the 8th day after his birth. This was to be done even if the 8th day fell on a Sabbath. Since circumcision was the sign that this person was blessed by God by being included as part of the chosen people (not by birth but by obedience to circumcision), this ritual of blessing did not violate the Sabbath even when it was performed then.

In the same way, the healing of the man that was done on the Sabbath was not wrong because he was receiving a special blessing only God could give. Even if it was done on the Sabbath it was acceptable because, like circumcision, a person was being blessed by God. This was not a "work" of man, it was a blessing from God and He chose to give it on the Sabbath.

Jesus encourages them to judge correctly, to see the utter rightness of what happened, that it did not in any way violate

God's Law of Sabbath. The "appearance" was what the Jewish leaders were trying to make out of it, He is saying judge it for what it really is, God's will being done on the Sabbath.

3. They charge Him with being a pretender

> Vs. 25-27 – So some of the people of Jerusalem were saying, "Is this not the man whom they are seeking to kill? Look, He is speaking publicly, and they are saying nothing to Him. The rulers do not really know that this is the Christ, do they? However, we know where this man is from; but whenever the Christ may come, no one knows where He is from."

Jesus was speaking to the pilgrims, the out-of-towners, but now the very citizens of Jerusalem speak up testifying of their own, more authoritative, inside information about Jesus.

They have, they feel, more concrete reasons for denying Him and casting Him as a mere pretender:

A. The rulers, the leaders do not believe Him. He says they want to kill Him, but here He is speaking openly. He thinks too highly of Himself.

B. We know that the Scriptures teach that the Messiah will come from this area, our area, Bethlehem which is near Jerusalem in the district of Judea, not from some hick town in the north of Galilee.

They dismiss the pilgrims as being without proper information and Jesus as being from the wrong place. This is their reason for disbelieving. They, of course, have completely discounted His great miracle. Like the elephant in the room nobody wants to acknowledge.

4. Jesus declares their ignorance

> Vs. 28-29 – Then Jesus cried out in the temple, teaching and saying, "You both know Me and know where I am from; and I have not come of Myself, but He who sent Me is true, whom you do not know. I know Him, because I am from Him, and He sent Me."

There is a play on words here. In modern speech He would be saying, "So you think you know Me? So you think you know where I am from? You do not even know what you think you know. I am from God, I know this because I know Him and you do not know this because you do not know Him."

5. The citizens, the pilgrims, the leaders are divided

> Vs. 30-32 – So they were seeking to seize Him; and no man laid his hand on Him, because His hour had not yet come. But many of the crowd believed in Him; and they were saying, "When the Christ comes, He will not perform more signs than those which this man has, will He?"
>
> The Pharisees heard the crowd muttering these things about Him, and the chief priests and the Pharisees sent officers to seize Him.

They are upset and now even the citizens are siding with the leaders in wanting to seize Him, but their confusion prevents any action. This is because God will not allow any action against the Lord before the appointed time.

The crowds and pilgrims assess the situation and realize that they cannot dismiss the great miracle Jesus has done, no matter what the others think. The Pharisees, seeing the situation begin to unravel, join forces with their natural antagonists, the priests, in order to stop the momentum that is beginning to form behind Jesus. They give official orders to have Jesus arrested by the temple guard. They cannot go in and haul Him away fearing further trouble. They will seek an opportunity in the future.

6. Jesus responds to the leaders

> Vs. 33-34 – Therefore Jesus said, "For a little while longer I am with you, then I go to Him who sent Me. You will seek Me, and will not find Me; and where I am, you cannot come.

Knowing the end is near (6 months), Jesus looks ahead and declares that He will soon return to where He came from. He came from God, to God He will return. This is in response to the efforts of the Jews to find and seize Him. Soon He will be in a place they will not be able to follow. This is because as disbelievers they will not be able to come to the right hand of God.

> Vs. 35-36 – The Jews then said to one another, "Where does this man intend to go that we will not find Him? He is not intending to go to the Dispersion among the Greeks, and teach the Greeks, is He? What is this statement that He said, 'You will seek Me, and will not find Me; and where I am, you cannot come'?

Now they are really confused. They think He is afraid of capture and will perhaps escape to continue His preaching to Jews who live outside the country in other nations (diaspora). By their answer and speculation they prove that they do not understand at all the words He has spoken and they have quoted. Bottom line, they still do not get it!

7. Jesus makes a final plea

> Vs. 37-39 – Now on the last day, the great day of the feast, Jesus stood and cried out, saying, "If anyone is thirsty, let him come to Me and drink. He who believes in Me, as the Scripture said, 'From his innermost being will flow rivers of living water.'" But this He spoke of the Spirit, whom those who believed in Him were to receive; for the Spirit was not yet given, because Jesus was not yet glorified.

Before, Jesus made the plea to believe in Him in terms of eating His flesh and drinking His blood. Now He changes the imagery to offer yet another benefit of faith: the permanent indwelling of the Holy Spirit. Drinking of Him (believing in Him) will enable a person of never being thirsty again because the source to quench thirst will become part of the person, i.e. a river inside you.

In context Jesus promises that those who believe in Him will not suffer from the spiritual ignorance and blindness that these people demonstrate. This is because He will give them the Holy Spirit who reveals that God will become part of them.

In verse 39 John makes an editorial note for the reader to explain when this promise will be fulfilled (Acts 2:38) at Pentecost.

8. The people's reaction to Jesus' appearance in Jerusalem at the Feast of Booths

John summarizes this episode by describing the various reactions of the people who attended the feast that week in Jerusalem.

A. The crowds

> Vs. 40-44 – Some of the people therefore, when they heard these words, were saying, "This certainly is the Prophet." Others were saying, "This is the Christ."
>
> Still others were saying, "Surely the Christ is not going to come from Galilee, is He? Has not the Scripture said that the Christ comes from the descendants of David, and from Bethlehem, the village where David was?" So a division occurred in the crowd because of Him. Some of them wanted to seize Him, but no one laid hands on Him.

The crowds were divided, some believed because of the miracles, some doubted because of what the citizens said about His birth place.

B. The temple guards

> Vs. 45-46 – The officers then came to the chief priests and Pharisees, and they said to them, "Why did you not bring Him?" The officers answered, "Never has a man spoken the way this man speaks."

They failed to arrest Him being dazzled by His teaching and not finding any opening to seize Him.

C. The Pharisees and leaders

> Vs. 47-53 – The Pharisees then answered them, "You have not also been led astray, have you? No one of the rulers or Pharisees has believed in Him, has he? But this crowd which does not know the Law is accursed." Nicodemus (he who came to Him before, being one of them) said to them, "Our Law does not judge a man unless it first hears from him and knows what he is doing, does it?" They answered him, "You are not also

from Galilee, are you? Search, and see that no prophet
arises out of Galilee." Everyone went to his home.

The Pharisees were Jesus' fiercest enemies because it was
their teachings and hypocrisies that Jesus denounced. They
dismiss the guards and crowds as ignorant and uninformed.

Note the cycles are still going, belief and disbelief.

17.

THE PHARISEES' ATTACK

JOHN 8:1-59

In the previous chapter we saw Jesus among the people at the temple during the Feast of Booths. During His time in the temple He teaches the people and is, consequently, charged by them of various failings.

- They charge Him with being incompetent.

- They charge Him with being demon possessed.

- Jesus responds by declaring their ignorance and His response to them creates division between them, the leaders, the citizens and the people.

- In the end, Jesus makes a final plea to them to believe in Him and chapter seven finishes with the people reacting to Jesus' appearance in Jerusalem in a variety of ways.

- The crowd is divided, some believe and some disbelieve.

- The temple guards sent to arrest Him are dazzled by His teaching and cannot find an opportunity to seize Him.

- The Pharisees and the leaders dismiss the guards and the crowds as ignorant and begin to plot against Him.

Thus ends chapter 7 and brings us to the next scene where Jesus will return to the temple the following day to face the Pharisees once again.

1. The adulteress woman – 8:1-11

> Vs. 1 – But Jesus went to the Mount of Olives.

John says that Jesus went to the Mount of Olives, which is a hillside and valley, connected to the city itself. The Mount of Olives makes up and includes the garden of Gethsemane where Jesus went often to be alone to pray and did so on this occasion.

> Vs. 2 – Early in the morning He came again into the temple, and all the people were coming to Him; and He sat down and began to teach them.

Jesus begins again to teach the people who were in and around the temple and is doing this when He is interrupted by the Scribes and the Pharisees.

> Vs. 3-6 – The scribes and the Pharisees brought a woman caught in adultery, and having set her in the center of the court, they said to Him, "Teacher, this woman has been caught in adultery, in the very act. Now in the Law Moses commanded us to stone such women; what then do You say?" They were saying this, testing Him, so that they might have grounds for accusing Him. But Jesus stooped down and with His finger wrote on the ground.

The key here is in verse 6 where John says they were doing this in order to test Him so that they might have a way to accuse and condemn Him. The Pharisees and Scribes were trying to trap Him in two ways:

> A. If He said to let her go, they would accuse Him of being soft on adultery and thus not in compliance with the Law.

B. If, on the other hand, He said "Yes, let us stone her according to the Law of Moses," they would accuse Him of disobeying Roman law. The Jews had no permission to execute.

Of course, even the finding of the woman is questionable. It seems that even she was set up in order to be caught and create this particular opportunity to try to trap Jesus.

> Vs. 7-9 – But when they persisted in asking Him, He straightened up, and said to them, "He who is without sin among you, let him be the first to throw a stone at her." Again He stooped down and wrote on the ground. When they heard it, they began to go out one by one, beginning with the older ones, and He was left alone, and the woman, where she was, in the center of the court.

We do not know what Jesus wrote on the ground, we have no idea why He did that or what was written or drawn. There is a lot of speculation about what He did, but we just do not know. However, we do know where He is quoting from when He says, "He who is without sin among you, let him be the first to throw a stone at her." He is quoting this from Deuteronomy 17:7.

In this passage, Moses was giving instructions as to how a stoning for such a sin should be carried out. The idea was that the witnesses to the adultery were to be the first ones to cast the stones in the punishment and after they had thrown their stones, the people were to cast the stones to finish the job.

And so Jesus is referring them to this command in the Law of Moses, but He adds the idea that the one to cast the first stone should be the one who has not sinned himself, and not just a witness. Once He said this, He ignores them and allows them to mull this over. Of course, once they hear it, they are the ones that are in a catch 22. If they throw the stone, they acknowledge they are hypocrites and break Roman law; if they do not throw the stone, they acknowledge that they are sinners. For them, it is the acknowledgment of the lesser evil. Better to be recognized as a sinner than a hypocrite.

In His dialogue with the woman Jesus shows an alternative way of dealing with sinners. He offers forgiveness rather than condemnation and punishment. In this little scene we see the difference between the result of the Law that came through Moses which these men were trying to enact, and the grace of Christ that Jesus was bringing into the world. One condemned and punished for any infraction, the other offered forgiveness and restoration for those who acknowledged their wrong.

> Vs. 10-11 – Straightening up, Jesus said to her, "Woman, where are they? Did no one condemn you?" She said, "No one, Lord." And Jesus said, "I do not condemn you, either. Go. From now on sin no more."

In telling the woman that He did not condemn her and that she should go but not sin anymore, Jesus was showing the balance between grace and acknowledgment of sin and repentance. Yes, He had forgiven her, yes He did not condemn her, but this was not because He did not see any sin in her. He offered forgiveness with the condition that she repents.

We do not know what the woman did and how she acted after this event. We can only speculate that her contact with Jesus and His gracious conduct towards her motivated her to continue to strive to sin no more.

2. The Pharisees – 8:12-30

The event of the adulteress woman now sets the stage for the dialogue that will continue between Jesus and His fierce enemies, the Pharisees. Now that He has managed to escape their trap, He will begin with a statement that will draw them into more dialogue with Him.

Vs. 12 – Then Jesus again spoke to them, saying, "I am the Light of the world; he who follows Me will not walk in the darkness, but will have the Light of life."

Once again Jesus invites people to believe in Him. Now a person would normally say, I provide light for those who are in the darkness, but Jesus says, "I am the light." He claims that He is not just part of the light, but the whole of the light that shines not only in some part of the darkness but that illuminates all of the darkness.

You also see in this verse that He equates light with life. In other words, if a person has light, that same person has life. Or course, the light that He is talking about is the truth. The understanding that one has when one knows God. His point is, if you know the truth, then you have not just ordinary human life but you have spiritual life, which, in essence, is eternal life. Or course, Jesus is once again declaring His divinity and His association with God. Notice the cycle is beginning once again where Jesus is declaring His divine nature to those who would hear.

Vs. 13 – So the Pharisees said to Him, "You are testifying about Yourself; Your testimony is not true."

The Pharisees dismiss what He says and make no comment on it. They are more interested in discrediting Him than understanding what He says. They focus on what they see as a weakness. The fact that He has said something about Himself. They accuse Him of making a witness, or bragging about Himself, and claim that if He is doing this it compromises what He says about Himself. In other words, if you are bragging about yourself, then what you say is not true.

Vs. 14-18 – Jesus answered and said to them, "Even if I testify about Myself, My testimony is true, for I know where I came from and where I am going; but you do not know where I come from or where I am going. You judge according to the flesh; I am not judging anyone. But even if I do judge, My judgment is true; for I am not alone in it, but I and the Father who sent Me. Even in your law it has been written that the testimony of two men is true. I am He who testifies about Myself, and the Father who sent Me testifies about Me."

In this passage Jesus is answering from the perspective of His divine nature. He tells them that even though He makes a statement about Himself, that statement is nevertheless true because:

> A. He has complete knowledge about His entire past and His entire future and they do not.

> B. His assessment of His identity is not based on His own opinion alone but on the opinion of Himself and the opinion of the Father.

> C. That two agree on a thing is what the Law requires to establish validity. Therefore since Jesus and the Father agree on who He is and what He says, then their testimony is true.

We have to realize that Jesus' answer and justification for what He has just said comes from His divine knowledge and His insight as God and not man. That is why He says He does not judge from a fleshly perspective. A human being could not say the things that He says about Himself. However, since Jesus is also divine, He can say the things that He says because they are true and because God confirms them.

> Vs. 19a – So they were saying to Him, "Where is Your Father?"

Again the Pharisees respond with misunderstanding and confusion. They think that He is talking about His father, an earthly father, when Jesus is talking about the Heavenly Father. They want to know where the father He is talking about is so that they can verify the things that Jesus is saying.

> Vs. 19b – Jesus answered, "You know neither Me nor My Father; if you knew Me, you would know My Father also."

Jesus answers them plainly that in the way they treat Him, they demonstrate that they do not know His Father and cannot know Him.

> Vs. 20 – These words He spoke in the treasury, as He taught in the temple; and no one seized Him, because His hour had not yet come.

Again, John makes an editorial comment about the fact that they did not seize Him at this time because God would not permit it.

> Vs. 21 – Then He said again to them, "I go away, and you will seek Me, and will die in your sin; where I am going, you cannot come."

Jesus continues the dialogue by once again speaking from the divine perspective. Here He is talking about His death and His resurrection and the fact that they will not be able to understand what has taken place because they do not believe.

Seeking Him and trying to go where He is going refers to the fact that they try with human understanding to grasp what will take place and will fail. They will fail because they do not believe and they will die in their sins because they did not believe in Him. Jesus is condemning them for their lack of faith, but they do not understand even the condemnation that He gives them at this time.

> Vs. 22 – So the Jews were saying, "Surely He will not kill Himself, will He, since He says, 'Where I am going, you cannot come'?"

Here the Jews demonstrate that they truly do not understand what He is talking about. They think that His reference to death means that He will cause His own death.

> Vs. 23-24 – And He was saying to them, "You are from below, I am from above; you are of this world, I am not of this world. Therefore I said to you that you will die in your sins; for unless you believe that I am He, you will die in your sins."

Jesus once again reiterates that they are fleshly, they are from below and He is spiritual, from above. They are from this world; He is from another world. He summarizes the idea by telling them more plainly that they will die in their sins because they do not believe in Him.

We know from our perspective today that the reason they die in their sins is because only through faith can they have their sins forgiven. They do not understand this principle at this time and so they are confused.

> Vs. 25a – So they were saying to Him, "Who are You?"

We can tell by this verse that they are beginning to slowly open their eyes by the fact that they are actually asking a decent question. By asking, "Who are you?" the Jews demonstrate that they are beginning to sense that He is someone very special. So they ask the question, "Who are You" as a way of getting Him to be more clear as to His declarations about His person.

Vs. 25b-26 – Jesus said to them, "What have I been saying to you from the beginning? I have many things to speak and to judge concerning you, but He who sent Me is true; and the things which I heard from Him, these I speak to the world."

Jesus tells them that He has been trying to explain this to them from the very beginning. Jesus, in verse 26, reestablishes the idea that everything He is saying to them, whether it be something that He teaches them or something that brings judgment on them, comes from God; The God who is true. He also says that the things that He speaks are only those things He has been given to say by God. Of course, this is a very sweeping statement that establishes the idea that everything Jesus is saying comes directly from God. Yet, another time where Jesus is declaring His divinity: they ask "Who are You?" and He answers, "I am the One sent from God."

Vs. 27 – They did not realize that He had been speaking to them about the Father.

John makes another editorial comment by saying that the Jews finally grasp that He is speaking to them about God and that He is casting Himself in the position of God's Son and God's Spokesman. This does not necessarily mean that everyone believed what He said, but now they are a least understanding the point to His sayings.

Vs. 28-29 – So Jesus said, "When you lift up the Son of Man, then you will know that I am He, and I do nothing on My own initiative, but I speak these things as the Father taught Me. And He who sent Me is with Me; He has not left Me alone, for I always do the things that are pleasing to Him."

Again Jesus looks into the future to His crucifixion and resurrection and says that this will provide the proof they will need to believe the things He is saying to them now.

In verse 29 He simply repeats the idea that God is the one who sent Him; God is the one who is with Him; God will not leave Him alone now or in the future, and that all the things that He does are pleasing to God.

> Vs. 30 – As He spoke these things, many came to believe in Him.

John tells us that people who heard these words came to believe in Him. The combination of His challenging words, the declaration of His divinity, and the prophecy concerning the future work together to produce faith in the hearts of several of His hearers. We see from this the cycle repeating itself where Jesus declares His divinity in some manner and people either believe or disbelieve according to their will. In this passage, some of the Pharisees rejected what He said and some, as John tells us in verse 30, came to believe Him.

Jesus and His new disciples – 8:31-59

We have seen Jesus confront the Pharisees over the adultery issue with the woman and we have seen Him continue the dialogue with the Jews and the Pharisees as they discuss His identity. We also see the division of those who accept His word and believe Him and those who reject it.

In the next section Jesus will continue a dialogue, but this time with those who have believed what He has said about Himself. We are going to see that He continues to challenge those who say they believe in Him with further claims about His divinity. We will note that even those who have an initial belief in Him turn away when He challenges them to accept more fully who He really is and what He has come to do.

> Vs. 31-32 – So Jesus was saying to those Jews who had believed Him, "If you continue in My word, then you are truly disciples of Mine; and you will know the truth, and the truth will make you free."

In this verse someone has made some profession of belief, and Jesus in response says, *"If you are truly my disciples"* (meaning if what you say is true), then this will be proven because you will obey and continue to obey and believe what I say. The point He makes here is that if they continue believing and accepting His words, they will know the truth and the truth will free them from their ignorance and, eventually, from their sins.

> Vs. 33 – They answered Him, "We are Abraham's descendants and have never yet been enslaved to anyone; how is it that You say, 'You will become free'?"

Of course, they are offended by what He says concerning their freedom and the necessity of their obedience to His word. They claim to be Abraham's offspring, meaning they are descendants of Abraham and because of this have never been enslaved to any person. This, of course, is not true as history shows the Jews were often overrun and enslaved by a variety of opposing armies and nations. But these Jews like to think that their relationship to Abraham was the thing that made them right before God and they had religious freedom guaranteed because of this heritage. They reject Jesus' offer of freedom by saying, "We have always been free because we are Abraham's seed, we do not need you to free us spiritually."

> Vs. 34-38 – Jesus answered them, "Truly, truly, I say to you, everyone who commits sin is the slave of sin. The slave does not remain in the house forever; the son does remain forever. So if the Son makes you free, you will be free indeed. I know that you are Abraham's descendants; yet you seek to kill Me, because My word has no place in you. I speak the things which I have

> seen with My Father; therefore you also do the things
> which you heard from your father."

Jesus begins by explaining to them that their slavery is to sin
and that because of that, they will not remain in the house, or
the presence, of God forever. He however, because He has no
sin, will remain in the presence of God forever. His offer of
freedom is to free them from that sin and give them a portion of
what He has. He acknowledges that they are culturally related to
Abraham, but even this relationship does not protect them from
their slavery to sin. He repeats the fact that He speaks only the
things that He has seen in person with God and they act out the
urges from their father, the devil.

> Vs. 39a – They answered and said to Him, "Abraham is
> our father."

Now the crowd senses what He is accusing them of and they
come back with the idea that Abraham is their father. In other
words, they are saying they have no other father but Abraham.

> Vs. 39b-41a – Jesus said to them, "If you are
> Abraham's children, do the deeds of Abraham. But as it
> is, you are seeking to kill Me, a man who has told you
> the truth, which I heard from God; this Abraham did not
> do. You are doing the deeds of your father."

Jesus responds to their declaration by saying that if they were
Abraham's children they would not be doing what they intend to
do, that is to kill Him. Not only is Jesus accusing them of an evil
thing, but in doing so He demonstrates that He is reading their
minds. He finishes up the section by saying once again that
because of the thing they are trying to do, they prove that
Abraham is not their father because Abraham would never think
of trying to kill someone who is bringing the Word of God to
them.

> Vs. 41b – They said to Him, "We were not born of fornication; we have one Father: God."

Now the crowd steps up, if you wish, and declares not only are they children of Abraham, but God is their Father. The point they are making is that they are the children of God. The unspoken insult here is that they charge Him of being born of fornication. They are insinuating that His own birth was in question because of the conditions in which Mary conceived. They are saying to Him, "Well at least we are not illegitimate."

> Vs. 42-47 – Jesus said to them, "If God were your Father, you would love Me, for I proceeded forth and have come from God, for I have not even come on My own initiative, but He sent Me.
>
> Why do you not understand what I am saying? It is because you cannot hear My word. You are of your father the devil, and you want to do the desires of your father. He was a murderer from the beginning, and does not stand in the truth because there is no truth in him. Whenever he speaks a lie, he speaks from his own nature, for he is a liar and the father of lies. But because I speak the truth, you do not believe Me. Which one of you convicts Me of sin? If I speak truth, why do you not believe Me? He who is of God hears the words of God; for this reason you do not hear them, because you are not of God."

Jesus picks up on what they say about their father being God and turns it back on them by telling them that if they were from God, they would love Him because He was from God. However, because they reject Him and intend to kill Him for what He is saying, they prove that the source of their lives is not God but the devil himself whose nature is full of lies and aggression.

In the last verse or two, He summarizes His argument by saying simply that they do not believe what He says because they are not from God.

> Vs. 48 – The Jews answered and said to Him, "Do we not say rightly that You are a Samaritan and have a demon?"

The Jews obviously are angry and make two accusations:

1. He is a Samaritan, in other words, He does not belong to the nation of Israel.
2. He has a demon and is possessed by the forces of Satan.

Now they are simply angry and hurling insults and accusations against Him to keep Him quiet.

> Vs. 49-51 – Jesus answered, "I do not have a demon; but I honor My Father, and you dishonor Me. But I do not seek My glory; there is One who seeks and judges. Truly, truly, I say to you, if anyone keeps My word he will never see death."

In these verses, Jesus tells them that their accusations and insults dishonor Him, the One who is from God. But He also says that their dishonor does not discourage Him because He is not looking for His own honor, but rather the honor that should go to God. He finishes up by saying, "If anyone keeps His word, they will have eternal life." Once again He finishes the debate by challenging them to believe in Him.

> Vs. 52-53 – The Jews said to Him, "Now we know that You have a demon. Abraham died, and the prophets also; and You say, 'If anyone keeps My word, he will never taste of death.' Surely You are not greater than

our father Abraham, who died? The prophets died too; whom do You make Yourself out to be?"

The Jews pounce on His answer and use it to support their accusation that He has a devil. They say that if both Abraham and the prophets are dead, how can He claim that He can offer eternal life. They turn around and challenge Him by asking, "Are you greater than Abraham?" In the end, they are basically saying, who do you think you are?

Vs. 54-56 – Jesus answered, "If I glorify Myself, My glory is nothing; it is My Father who glorifies Me, of whom you say, 'He is our God'; and you have not come to know Him, but I know Him; and if I say that I do not know Him, I will be a liar like you, but I do know Him

and keep His word. Your father Abraham rejoiced to see My day, and he saw it and was glad."

Jesus picks up on their last question and answers them that if He is trying to glorify Himself, His glory does not mean anything, but if His glory comes from God, then He is truly glorified. Once again, He compares Himself to the crowd and tells them that it comes down to who really knows God. Does He know God or do they? The proof that He knows God is that He obeys God and He speaks only God's word and they do not. If this were not so, He would be a liar like them, but since it is so (that He does speak only God's word, that He only does what God gives Him to do), then He is the legitimate Son of God and not them.

He finishes up by saying that the person they claim to be their father, Abraham, was actually happy to know that one day Jesus would come and when through faith he saw it, it made him happy. Jesus is saying this in such a way to suggest that He Himself was there when Abraham understood the promise of the Messiah. This challenges the crowd one more time, and they give Jesus a response.

> Vs. 57 – So the Jews said to Him, "You are not yet fifty years old, and have You seen Abraham?"

Once again the Jews only accept the human nature of Jesus' character and not the divine. They simply see His physical age and claim that it is not possible for Him to have actually seen Abraham in person. Of course, this would be true if Jesus was only a man but since He is also the divine Son of God, He was present when Abraham lived and can make this claim.

> Vs. 58 – Jesus said to them, "Truly, truly, I say to you, before Abraham was born, I am."

In His answer to the Jews about seeing Abraham, Jesus not only says that He saw Abraham but the way that He expresses it is very remarkable. In saying *"Truly, truly, I say to you before Abraham was born, I am."* Jesus is referring back to the time when Moses was speaking to God and asking God who should he say sent him to Egypt?   God said to Moses, *"Thus you shall say to the sons of Israel, I AM has sent me to you."* (Exodus 3:13-14)

The Jews were very familiar with this passage and recognized that Jesus had referred to Himself, in the same way that Almighty God had referred to Himself. This, of course, was blasphemy in their ears for a mere man to declare and give himself the name of God. Of course, since Jesus was the Son of God, this was quite a legitimate name for Him to use. However, the Jews not believing this saw a blasphemy worthy of death.

> Vs. 59 – Therefore they picked up stones to throw at Him, but Jesus hid Himself and went out of the temple.

John then describes that the people tried to stone Him to death because of what He said. As a result, Jesus hid Himself and left the temple for safety sake. It is ironic that the chapter begins and ends with an attempt to stone someone to death.

Summary

So we see once again Jesus continuing His dialogue with a variety of people. We also see the continual cycle of the revelation of His person, along with the belief or disbelief of individuals.

In this chapter, we've noted three different examples of this cycle being carried out:

1. The Pharisees, trying to trap Him and being outwitted, leave in disbelief. The woman remaining behind goes away with forgiveness and a sense of faith in Christ.

2. Jesus speaking to the crowd, encouraging them to believe in Him and continuing with a dialogue about the source of His life. Once this dialogue is over, some of the people disbelieved but others came to initial belief.

3. Jesus has a dialogue with those who show interest and belief in Him. He challenges them to obey His word in order to be free from their sin. People stumble over this demand because of their pride. They feel that as descendants of Abraham they have no need of someone to deal with their sins. They believe that their cultural heritage is sufficient to make them right before God. Jesus teaches them that they need a Savior to free them from their sins no matter what their cultural and religious heritage is. These same people who believed in Him quickly turn against Him because they are unwilling to acknowledge their sin of pride. We find out at the end of the chapter that the very people who began to believe in Him quickly turned against Him and were prepared to kill Him because of what He said to them.

Lessons

There are still a couple of lessons that we can draw from this dialogue even though it repeats the cycle and pattern of discussion that Jesus has had with these people in the past.

1. Jesus came for forgiveness sake, not judgment.

In the story of the adulterous woman we see that Jesus' purpose in coming was to provide forgiveness for the people. Of course there will be a judgment to come, but the primary reason for Jesus' appearance was to open the gate to allow forgiveness and grace to come into a person's life. We need to remember this when we see others who have made mistakes or who have sinned. Our task is to lead people to forgiveness not to form a posse and/or a mob to carry out justice.

2. Obedience separates the men from the boys.

Regardless of what people say about their religious convictions or their Bible knowledge, it is their obedience to God's Word that determines their relationship to God. By doing what God wants us to do in worship, ministry, and relationships with other people that we prove that we are His people.

3. Jesus is always testing His disciples.

Even the people who said they believed in Him were subject to Jesus' tests. He challenged them to come to a higher level by depending on Him for their salvation.

This offended their pride and turned them against Him. Many times in our lives we are tested by the Lord in what we say, what we do or how we will respond to Him. We need to be conscious of this and remember that at any time He can test our faith. If we find ourselves falling away, neglecting Him, putting less emphasis on His Word, or growing cold in our love for Him, these are sure signs that we have fallen into disobedience. We have to be careful about becoming complacent because that is when the tests usually come.

18.

THE HEALING AND THE ATTACK

JOHN 9:1-41

This chapter and scene are divided into three sections:

1. Jesus heals the blind man – vs. 1-12

John describes another miracle that Jesus performs, this time the healing of a man born blind. This act will set the stage for a debate that will be carried on away from the presence of Jesus this time.

2. The debate – vs. 13-34

John will describe a debate that rages between the Pharisees and the people concerning the miracle that Jesus has done. He will also describe the questioning that the man and his family undergo at the hands of the Jewish leaders.

3. Jesus declares His deity – vs. 35-41

Jesus will once again confront the man he healed but this time reveals His person to him. The chapter will close out with a final debate between Jesus and the Pharisees over what He has done and what He has said.

Chapter 10 will also include a discussion between Jesus and these very same Pharisees and more declarations of His deity, and we will see the chapter end when Jesus will leave this area and continue His ministry in another geographic location.

The healing

The first part of chapter nine deals with the actual miracle that Jesus performed on the man who was born blind.

> Vs. 1-2 – As He passed by, He saw a man blind from birth. And His disciples asked Him, "Rabbi, who sinned, this man or his parents, that he would be born blind?"

The question by His disciple sets up a teaching opportunity for Jesus. The Jews of those days believed that there was a direct correlation between infirmity and sinfulness. The questions the disciples were asking stemmed from the fact that he was born blind. If he was already blind at birth, then who was responsible for this infirmity, the sins of his parents or was it his own sins?

> Vs. 3-5 – Jesus answered, "It was neither that this man sinned, nor his parents; but it was so that the works of God might be displayed in him. We must work the works of Him who sent Me as long as it is day; night is coming when no one can work. While I am in the world, I am the Light of the world."

Jesus does not answer this particular question because He would have explained to them that being born blind or becoming blind is a result of the fallen nature of man. Sickness, infirmity, accidents and death stem from the fallen nature of humanity which finds its source in the first sin of Adam. Jesus chooses not to explain this theological fact to His disciples but rather uses this opportunity to again focus their attention on His divinity. He tells them that in this particular case, the blindness is there to provide an opportunity to display the power of God.

They assume that He will be there for a long time and continue His ministry for a long time. Jesus understands that His ministry among them will be short lived and He must accomplish many things in a brief period of time. Note that He builds again on the theme of light and the fact that He is the light of the world. The miracle that He will perform will demonstrate that He is the light of the world and His words about this are indeed true.

> Vs. 6-7 – When He had said this, He spat on the ground, and made clay of the spittle, and applied the clay to his eyes, and said to him, "Go, wash in the pool of Siloam" (which is translated, Sent). So he went away and washed, and came back seeing.

A lot is said about the fact that Jesus made the clay mixture and applied it to the man's eyes and gave him instructions to go wash his eyes. He could have as easily said, "*Open your eyes and see*" and the miracle would have been completed in this way. Most scholars believe that the reason Jesus went through this process is probably because He wanted the man to participate in his own healing.

Having never seen, the man now is made aware that a miracle or an effort is being made to restore his sight. Putting the mud on his eyes has no medicinal purpose other than to give the man something to do as a response of faith. (In the same way, baptism has no medicinal effect.) And we see the man going to the particular pool to do exactly what Jesus said, and as a result his sight is regained.

The point here is that the miracle is done through the power of Jesus, but the man does make a response of faith in obeying Jesus' word to go wash the mud off his blind eyes in the particular pool of Siloam. As far as the man is concerned, there is no doubt who has performed the miracle because he has been touched by Jesus, he has heard Jesus speak to him, he has responded to Jesus in obeying His command to wash his eyes.

> Vs. 8-12 – Therefore the neighbors, and those who previously saw him as a beggar, were saying, "Is not this the one who used to sit and beg?" Others were saying, "This is he," still others were saying, "No, but he is like him." He kept saying, "I am the one." So they were saying to him, "How then were your eyes opened?" He answered, "The man who is called Jesus made clay, and anointed my eyes, and said to me, 'Go to Siloam and wash'; so I went away and washed, and I received sight." They said to him, "Where is He?" He said, "I do not know."

In this particular passage, John describes the reaction of the neighbors of the blind man to his miraculous healing. It is not a question of believing or disbelieving, they clearly see that he now has his sight, they simply are not sure who has performed the miracle. Obviously, a great miracle has been performed among them and they wish to make this known to their leaders, and so in the next section we will see the people bringing the blind man to the leaders of the nation.

Debate among the Pharisees

We will see here that this miracle will create controversy because it was performed on the Sabbath. John describes the debate among the Pharisees in terms of two witnesses that the blind man makes about Jesus when he is brought before them.

Witness #1

> Vs. 13-23 – They brought to the Pharisees the man who was formerly blind. Now it was a Sabbath on the

day when Jesus made the clay and opened his eyes. Then

the Pharisees also were asking him again how he received his sight. And he said to them, "He applied clay to my eyes, and I washed, and I see." Therefore some of the Pharisees were saying, "This man is not from God, because He does not keep the Sabbath." But others were saying, "How can a man who is a sinner perform such signs?" And there was a division among them. So they said to the blind man again, "What do you say about Him, since He opened your eyes?" And he said, "He is a prophet."

The Jews then did not believe it of him, that he had been blind and had received sight, until they called the parents of the very one who had received his sight, and questioned them, saying, "Is this your son, who you say was born blind? Then how does he now see?" His parents answered them and said, "We know that this is our son, and that he was born blind; but how he now sees, we do not know; or who opened his eyes, we do not know. Ask him; he is of age, he will speak for himself." His parents said this because they were afraid of the Jews; for the Jews had already agreed that if anyone confessed Him to be Christ, he was to be put out of the synagogue. For this reason his parents said, "He is of age; ask him."

In this passage the Pharisees question the blind man about his miraculous sight and he acknowledges that he was blind and was healed. There is great doubt about this and so the leaders of the Jews want to question his parents to see if this is some kind of a trick. His parents are brought forward but refuse to make a testimony because they are afraid of the Jews. In the end, they simply tell the leaders to question their son who is an adult and who can speak for himself.

Witness #2

> Vs. 24-34 – "So a second time they called the man who had been blind, and said to him, "Give glory to God; we know that this man is a sinner." He then answered, "Whether He is a sinner, I do not know; one thing I do know, that though I was blind, now I see." So they said to him, "What did He do to you? How did He open your eyes?" He answered them, "I told you already and you did not listen; why do you want to hear it again? You do not want to become His disciples too, do you?" They reviled him and said, "You are His disciple, but we are disciples of Moses. We know that God has spoken to Moses, but as for this man, we do not know where He is from." The man answered and said to them, "Well, here is an amazing thing, that you do not know where He is from, and yet He opened my eyes. We know that God does not hear sinners; but if anyone is God-fearing and does His will, He hears him. Since the beginning of time it has never been heard that anyone opened the eyes of a person born blind. If this man were not from God, He could do nothing." They answered him, "You were born entirely in sins, and are you teaching us?" So they put him out."

In the beginning, they suggest that he may be lying. When they say, "Give glory to God," they are saying "Tell the truth now." They want him to acknowledge that Jesus is a fake and a sinner because He has performed this miracle on the Sabbath in violation of their rules. In his second witness, the healed man is much bolder with the leadership in challenging them about the miracle that Jesus has performed for him. The leaders claim superiority because they are disciples of Moses and they claim to know the Law. The man responds that whether they know the Law or not, the fact that Jesus healed his blindness trumps all of their "so-called" knowledge. In the end, unable to resist his cold and clear logic, the Pharisees simply insult him and throw him out of the room.

Jesus affirms His deity

Until this point in the story this man has not yet actually seen Jesus. He has heard Him, has responded to Him by obeying, but once his eyes were opened, he did not actually see or know what Jesus looked like. In this final passage however, John describes the face-to-face meeting that the man does have with the one who healed him.

> Vs. 35-38 – Jesus heard that they had put him out, and finding him, He said, "Do you believe in the Son of Man?" He answered, "Who is He, Lord, that I may believe in Him?" Jesus said to him, "You have both seen Him, and He is the one who is talking with you." And he said, "Lord, I believe." And he worshiped Him.

In this passage, there is a dialogue between Jesus and the man. Notice that Jesus calls on the man to believe in Him and the healed man not only acknowledges his faith but John says he worshipped Jesus. The fact that he worshipped Him demonstrates that his faith was sincere.

> Vs. 39-41 – And Jesus said, "For judgment I came into this world, so that those who do not see may see, and that those who see may become blind." Those of the Pharisees who were with Him heard these things and said to Him, "We are not blind too, are we?" Jesus said to them, "If you were blind, you would have no sin; but since you say, 'We see,' your sin remains.

In these few verses, Jesus uses several play on words that summarize well the condition of those who believe and those who disbelieve.

A. He equates those who believe with those who are able to see. Whether they are physically able to see or not, the fact that they believe means that they are able to perceive the truth.

B. Those who disbelieve are compared to those who are blind. Whether they are able to see or not, the fact that they disbelieve demonstrates that they are truly spiritually blind because they cannot grasp the truth.

In the end, Jesus hurls an accusation at the Pharisees because they were complaining that His condemnations were directed towards them. Jesus tells them, *"At least if you acknowledged that you did not know the truth, then you would be innocent in this matter but because you boast that you are the guardians of the truth and yet deny me, then you are charged and found guilty of this sin of disbelief."*

In this final passage, we see Jesus not only declaring His divinity, but also attaching to His declaration the accusation that those who do not believe in His divinity are subject to condemnation. In this way Jesus is raising the stakes as far as the importance of believing in Him is concerned. For those who believe, there is great reward and now, for those who disbelieve, there is condemnation at hand.

Summary

Jesus will continue His dialogue with the Pharisees in the next chapter and will continue to assert His deity. For now, He leaves them with yet another uncontestable miracle that points to His divinity. And once again, the Pharisees are quibbling over the issue of when the miracle was performed rather than the power and the meaning of the act itself. The irony, of course, is that the person who was blind was able to clearly see the meaning of what had happened to him, and those who claimed to be the leaders and the visionaries of society were clearly blind to what was there before them.

19.

JESUS REBUKES THE JEWISH LEADERS

JOHN 10:1-42

Chapter 10 is the last chapter in a long section of material which began in chapter 7.

Here is the flow of events so far:

1. Jesus is challenged by His brothers to go and promote His ministry in Jerusalem during the feast of Booths.

2. The Lord dismisses their worldly approach and goes up to the feast without fanfare and teaches the people.

3. There is great division among the people over His claims and teachings.

4. The Pharisees try to trap Him by using a woman caught in adultery.

5. After this fails there is again a division among His hearers with some believing and others unwilling to accept His claims.

6. The ones who say they believe in Him quickly turn on Him when He calls on them to obey His words in order to be freed from their sins.

7. Jesus then heals a man born blind. This causes His main enemies, the Jewish leaders, to accuse Jesus of sinning because the miracle was done on the Sabbath.

8. In the end the leaders cannot deny or refute the great miracle done by Jesus. They cannot even persuade the healed man to witness against Jesus so they throw him out.

9. Once released from the Jews, we see Jesus revealing Himself to the blind man who acknowledges his faith by worshipping the Lord.

10. In the last scene Jesus denounces the Jews for their spiritual blindness in not accepting Him.

This will bring us to chapter 10 where Jesus will have one more volley of debates with the Pharisees before leaving Jerusalem and beginning the series of events that will lead to His death and resurrection.

Parable of the good shepherd – 10:1-21

Chapter 10 is a continuation of chapter 9. The original manuscripts did not have verse numbers or chapter divisions. These were added later for convenience sake. Sometimes the chapter division comes in the middle of a speech as it does in this case. In chapter 9 Jesus is condemning the Jewish leaders for their spiritual blindness in their unwillingness to see or believe in Him as the divine Messiah.

The parable of the good shepherd follows on the heels of this condemnation. The image of the shepherd and his sheep is the most used one to describe God and His people in the Bible. It appears over 500 times.

It is natural that Jesus uses this image to describe leadership in Israel, both good and bad. The "sheep fold" that Jesus will talk about here was a common form of shelter used by shepherds for themselves and their flocks. There were two kinds:

A. In an open field area the shepherd would gather stones and make a circular wall with a small entrance maybe 4 ft. high, as thick as the stones themselves and as large as needed for the sheep. When possible, he would put briars or thorns on the top of the walls to discourage foxes or other wild animals from jumping over the wall. The entrance would be no wider than necessary to let one sheep at a time into the sheepfold. Once the sheep were in and counted for the night, the shepherd would himself lie in the entrance way to the fold in order to provide protection.

B. Another type of sheepfold was built when there was a cave available. The shepherd would then build a wall surrounding the cave entrance and put a small entryway in the wall for the sheep. In bad weather they could all retreat into the cave for protection. It was in one of these cave "stables" near Bethlehem that Jesus was born. The "manger" He was laid in was a hollowed out stone used as a feeding through for animals.

Now that we have a physical description of what Jesus is talking about, let us look at the parable itself.

Vs. 1-2 – "Truly, truly, I say to you, he who does not enter by the door into the fold of the sheep, but climbs up some other way, he is a thief and a robber. But he who enters by the door is a shepherd of the sheep."

Some sheepfolds had a roughly made door used to secure the fold once the sheep were in. It was natural for the shepherd to use this door for his coming or going. If one were to climb over the wall, this would clearly indicate that he was an intruder, probably with the intent to steal. This was familiar imagery to the people who counted many generations of shepherds in their families.

> Vs. 3-5 – To him the doorkeeper opens, and the sheep hear his voice, and he calls his own sheep by name and leads them out. When he puts forth all his own, he goes ahead of them, and the sheep follow him because they know his voice. A stranger they simply will not follow, but will flee from him, because they do not know the voice of strangers."

Jesus now extends the imagery to include one more example of false leadership. At times several flocks of sheep were gathered together into a common fold and one person was left to tend the gate. When the shepherds arrived in the early morning to collect their sheep from among the many flocks within the enclosure, they would call out to them by name. The sheep, recognizing their own shepherd's voice would dutifully come out of the fold to follow him. It is an unsual fact that Jewish shepherds walked ahead of their flocks and not behind them as was the custom in other nations.

Jesus continues His parable by saying that the other sheep in the fold will not leave the fold to follow another shepherd's call or voice. The door was to keep intruders out; the sheep would not follow any voice, only the voice of their shepherd. Jesus emphasizes the point that sheep will not follow just anybody, only their own shepherd.

> Vs. 6 – This figure of speech Jesus spoke to them, but they did not understand what those things were which He had been saying to them.

John makes another editorial comment explaining that the people did not understand the parable. Of course they understood about sheep: that they were in sheepfolds; that they could pick out their master's voice, even when there were other voices calling at the same time. What they did not understand is what all of this meant for them, so Jesus explains the parable in the next few verses.

Explanation of the parable – vs. 7-21

Since they cannot open the meaning of the parable, Jesus clarifies what He means by the use of it.

> Vs. 7-10 – So Jesus said to them again, "Truly, truly, I say to you, I am the door of the sheep. All who came before Me are thieves and robbers, but the sheep did not hear them. I am the door; if anyone enters through Me, he will be saved, and will go in and out and find pasture. The thief comes only to steal and kill and destroy; I came that they may have life, and have it abundantly.

This is another one of Jesus' "I AM" statements where He declares His divinity in parable form. Jesus tells them that, as the door, the sheep coming through Him will find food and nourishment when they go out, and protection and comfort when they come in. Just like the shepherd was a human door that kept intruders out and preserved the lives of the sheep within, Jesus protected against false teachers and leaders, and provided saving grace for the sheep. The abundant life He gives in context is that He is the ultimate shepherd, protecting and giving eternal life to His flock.

> Vs. 11-13 – "I am the good shepherd; the good shepherd lays down His life for the sheep. He who is a hired hand, and not a shepherd, who is not the owner of the sheep, sees the wolf coming, and leaves the sheep and flees, and the wolf snatches them and scatters them. He flees because he is a hired hand and is not concerned about the sheep.

Here Jesus makes another "I AM" statement, this time calling Himself the good shepherd. In Old Testament times the only "good" shepherd was God. In essence He says that just like a good shepherd would risk his life to save His sheep, Jesus would not only "risk" His life, He would lay it down willingly for the flock.

In contrast to this, there is the "hireling." This is not an assistant shepherd or a contracted worker. In this case the hireling is someone who has gained control of the sheep in a negative way (since Jesus has talked about thieves earlier). This person is only interested in personal gain from the sheep and has no love for them. Consequently, when danger looms he quickly abandons the sheep to save himself.

> Vs. 14-18 – I am the good shepherd, and I know My own and My own know Me, even as the Father knows Me and I know the Father; and I lay down My life for the sheep. I have other sheep, which are not of this fold; I must bring them also, and they will hear My voice; and they will become one flock with one shepherd. For this reason the Father loves Me, because I lay down My life so that I may take it again. No one has taken it away from Me, but I lay it down on My own initiative. I have authority to lay it down, and I have authority to take it up again. This commandment I received from My Father."

The Lord now makes a third "I AM" statement repeating the fact that He is the good shepherd. This time He speaks in the first person and, as the good shepherd, declares the following:

1. In the way a shepherd knows his sheep and they know him, He knows who His true disciples are and they know exactly who He is. He knows the Father and the Father knows Him.

2. He will lay down His life for His followers. He has the authority to both lay it down and then pick it up again. This is what the Father has told Him to do. This is an allusion to His resurrection.

3. He will bring together another group of disciples and make one flock of all His followers, who will follow only

Him. This too is the will of the Father. Another allusion to the preaching to the Gentiles.

> Vs. 19-21 – A division occurred again among the Jews because of these words. Many of them were saying, "He has a demon and is insane. Why do you listen to Him?" Others were saying, "These are not the sayings of one demon-possessed. A demon cannot open the eyes of the blind, can he?"

Again John describes the reaction of the people to this latest declaration of His divinity. Note that the cycle of declaration followed by belief or disbelief continues to repeat itself.

Jesus declares His divinity without parable – vs. 22-42

The feast of Booths was in the fall and later in December the Jews celebrated the feast of the Dedication. This was a commemoration of the rededication of the temple after it had been desecrated by Antiochus Epiphanes. Antiochus was a northern king who sacrificed a pig on the altar of the temple during an invasion of the Holy City several hundred years before. They also called it the Feast of Lights because all the houses were lit up during celebrations. Today the Jews still celebrate this feast and it is called Hanukkah. Lighting of candles is the principal ceremony.

> Vs. 22-24 – At that time the Feast of the Dedication took place at Jerusalem; it was winter, and Jesus was walking in the temple in the portico of Solomon. The Jews then gathered around Him, and were saying to Him, "How long will You keep us in suspense? If You are the Christ, tell us plainly."

204 | MIKE MAZZALONGO

It has now been a few months since His clash with the Pharisees and Jesus finds Himself once again in the temple area during this feast. This time the Pharisees urge Him to make a clear declaration about His identity, no parables. Of course their objective is to have a solid charge to make against Him. They are not asking this question because of faith.

> Vs. 25-31 – Jesus answered them, "I told you, and you do not believe; the works that I do in My Father's name, these testify of Me. But you do not believe because you are not of My sheep. My sheep hear My voice, and I know them, and they follow Me; and I give eternal life to them, and they will never perish; and no one will snatch them out of My hand. My Father, who has given them to Me, is greater than all; and no one is able to snatch them out of the Father's hand. I and the Father are one." The Jews picked up stones again to stone Him.

Jesus responds with clarity, but a clarity they are not ready to accept. In answer to their question He says 3 things:

1. True believers accept the proof He has provided in the miracles the Father has given Him to do. They are not true believers (my sheep) because they rejected Him and the proof He offers.

    o   He knows and is known by His true followers and they have demonstrated that they are not true by what they have done in the past (regardless of the fake sincerity of their question). The question implies that He should do more to convince them. He claims that He has done enough to convince true believers.

2. It is His Father's will that He give eternal life to His followers. Nothing can prevent His followers from receiving this great gift. The implication is that nothing these Jewish leaders can do will stop the Father from doing this through Jesus.

3. Jesus and the Father are One. He is equal to, the same as, united to and shares the nature of God. Of course for the Jews who do not believe, this is blasphemy punishable by death.

> Vs. 32 – Jesus answered them, "I showed you many good works from the Father; for which of them are you stoning Me?"

Jesus points out the inconsistency of their actions. They have proof of His divinity but are acting against it anyways.

> Vs. 33 – The Jews answered Him, "For a good work we do not stone You, but for blasphemy; and because You, being a man, make Yourself out to be God."

In effect Jesus makes them declare clearly their disbelief in Him. Their stumbling block is that they cannot accept that God could be in the form of a man. This was too much to even consider.

> Vs. 34-38 – Jesus answered them, "Has it not been written in your Law, 'I said, you are gods'? If he called them gods, to whom the word of God came (and the Scripture cannot be broken), do you say of Him, whom the Father sanctified and sent into the world, 'You are blaspheming,' because I said, 'I am the Son of God'? If I do not do the works of My Father, do not believe Me; but if I do them, though you do not believe Me, believe the works, so that you may know and understand that the Father is in Me, and I in the Father."

Jesus says that it is not such a "stretch" to assign the title of divinity to humans, even in the Old Testament there were such references for those who served God as prophets (Psalm 8:17). If those who were sent by God as prophets were called gods in the Scripture, surely one who does the miracles of God and speaks for God can be called the Son of God. If you do not believe my teaching here, at least acknowledge the miracles, these do not lie.

> Vs. 39 – Therefore they were seeking again to seize Him, and He eluded their grasp.

Once again the Jews, quite unconvinced, try to arrest Him. Once again, because His time was not at hand, He manages to elude their attempts to capture Him.

> Vs. 40-42 – And He went away again beyond the Jordan to the place where John was first baptizing, and He was staying there. Many came to Him and were saying, "While John performed no sign, yet everything John said about this man was true." Many believed in Him there.

John summarizes the scene and the section by closing the cycle in the same familiar way. Jesus goes out of Jerusalem to continue preaching and baptizing. The people's rationale for following Him was: we believed John even without miracles; this man does miracles and fulfills all the things John said about Him. Because of this, some believed and despite all of this, some still disbelieved.

20.

THE RESURRECTION OF LAZARUS

JOHN 11:1-57

Chapter 11 begins a new section in John's gospel. Until now Jesus has been preaching and teaching to the people. He has been having ongoing debates with the Jewish leaders. He has, by His declarations and miracles, put forth the idea that He is the divine Son of God.

John has demonstrated that as a result of all these activities, a growing number have come to believe in Him and a far greater number have rejected Him in disbelief. This cycle has repeated itself enough times to become the major pattern in John's gospel.

In chapter 11 the time for Jesus' passion (a short-form way of referring to the final days of suffering and resurrection) is drawing near so John's book begins to compress time.

In the first 10 chapters John describes events that took place over a 30 to 33 month period. The last 11 chapters describe the words and events that take place in the last 2 or 3 months of Jesus' ministry on earth.

The first and very spectacular event John describes in detail is the death and resurrection of Lazarus, His friend and the brother of Mary and Martha of Bethany.

Except for His crucifixion, this will be the last public action that Jesus will do; from now on He will be exclusively in the company of His disciples. With this miracle, Jesus will end His public ministry, prove beyond a doubt His divine power and provide a preview of His own death and resurrection that is to come in the near future.

The death and resurrection of Lazarus

> Vs. 1-6 – Now a certain man was sick, Lazarus of Bethany, the village of Mary and her sister Martha. It was the Mary who anointed the Lord with ointment, and wiped His feet with her hair, whose brother Lazarus was sick. So the sisters sent word to Him, saying, "Lord, behold, he whom You love is sick." But when Jesus heard this, He said, "This sickness is not to end in death, but for the glory of God, so that the Son of God may be glorified by it." Now Jesus loved Martha and her sister and Lazarus. So when He heard that he was sick, He then stayed two days longer in the place where He was.

We have to understand that everything Jesus said and did had as its purpose the creation of faith in the hearts of the people. Soon He Himself would be killed. He knew this and His disciples had to be prepared to face His death without losing their faith. He was not worried about death. He already said that the Father gave Him the authority to both lay down His life and pick it up again (John 10:18). His disciples, however, needed help in experiencing the death of their leader without being totally crushed.

This miracle, therefore, was not only to create faith in new disciples; it was also to strengthen the faith of existing disciples in the face of death. As a matter of fact, this section has more to do with how the disciples react to Lazarus' death than to Lazarus himself.

John divides the story into four parts showing how four people reacted to Lazarus' death.

1. The Apostles

> Vs. 7-8 – Then after this He said to the disciples, "Let us go to Judea again." The disciples said to Him, "Rabbi, the Jews were just now seeking to stone You, and are You going there again?"

The Apostles noticed not so much the death of Lazarus but the threat of death to Jesus (and consequently to themselves) if they returned to the troubled area they just left. Their reaction in the face of all of this is fear.

> Vs. 9-10 – Jesus answered, "Are there not twelve hours in the day? If anyone walks in the day, he does not stumble, because he sees the light of this world. But if anyone walks in the night, he stumbles, because the light is not in him."

Jesus reassures them by explaining that their safety is not measured by the power of their enemy but rather by whose side they are on.

1. Jesus is the light, He guarantees the way, He creates day wherever He is. To be with Him is to be safe and not to stumble no matter how difficult the road.

2. The enemies of Jesus are the night, the darkness. Their plan will fail (in this case the Jews who want to kill Him before it is time) because they are on the wrong side and not because they are weak or without a plan.

Vs. 11-12 – This He said, and after that He said to them, "Our friend Lazarus has fallen asleep; but I go, so that I may awaken him out of sleep." The disciples then said to Him, "Lord, if he has fallen asleep, he will recover."

Jesus had said in the beginning "let us go," and seeing their fear He says, "I go to awaken him from sleep." The Apostles now think Lazarus is just asleep and try to discourage Jesus by saying "if he is sleeping he will be alright by himself, you do not have to go." They do not want His going to make them look bad (fearful). It is always easier to discourage someone who wants to go forward than swallowing our fear or pride and going with them.

Vs. 13-15 – Now Jesus had spoken of his death, but they thought that He was speaking of literal sleep. So Jesus then said to them plainly, "Lazarus is dead, and I am glad for your sakes that I was not there, so that you may believe; but let us go to him."

Jesus explains plainly that Lazarus is dead. He also expresses His joy at the fact that God has worked out the circumstances in such a way that Jesus will perform a great miracle before their eyes and thus encourage them to believe. Once more He encourages them to faith and courage by saying "let us go to him."

Vs. 16 – Therefore Thomas, who is called Didymus, said to his fellow disciples, "Let us also go, so that we may die with Him."

Thomas, after Jesus invites them all once more to come, finds his courage and encourages all to follow Jesus. In this exchange the Apostles went from fear to courage, but Jesus' miracle would bring them to the ultimate goal, faith.

2. Martha

> Vs. 17 – So when Jesus came, He found that he had
> already been in the tomb four days.

The body was in the tomb for four days. The Jews did not
embalm, they merely perfumed and cleaned the body and
wrapped it in cloth. The body begins to decompose after four
days in an airless, hot, stone tomb.

> Vs. 18-22 – Now Bethany was near Jerusalem, about
> two miles off; and many of the Jews had come to
> Martha and Mary, to console them concerning their
> brother. Martha therefore, when she heard that Jesus
> was coming, went to meet Him, but Mary stayed at the
> house. Martha then said to Jesus, "Lord, if You had
> been here, my brother would not have died."

Martha respects Jesus, sees Him as a great prophet and healer
and knows that He could have saved Him. She even expresses
this idea.

> Vs. 23 – Jesus said to her, "Your brother will rise
> again."

Jesus tells her what He is about to do.

> Vs. 24 – Martha said to Him, "I know that he will rise
> again in the resurrection on the last day."

She repeats what she has learned as a good Jew, that at the
end of the world the good and faithful Jews will all be raised from
the dead. She does not want to bother God... she is so

reasonable and controlled. Martha's response to death is resignation. She is resigned to the fact that death is there and somewhere in the future according to the religion she has learned, there will be a resurrection. At the moment, however, death is greater than resurrection. For her, death is real and resurrection is a doctrine. A true doctrine she believes, but something less real than the death she faces.

> Vs. 25-26 – Jesus said to her, "I am the resurrection and the life; he who believes in Me will live even if he dies, and everyone who lives and believes in Me will never die. Do you believe this?"

Jesus reveals to her the reality behind the doctrine. If there is a resurrection from the dead, the one who produces that resurrection is standing right in front of her! And He is real, not just a doctrine. If, by faith, you are united to the one who produces the resurrection, the resurrection will become a greater reality in your life than death.

Jesus says that union with Him through faith gives the believer two things:

1. Vs. 25: He will have life, true life, the kind of life that is not enslaved to the fear of death. The kind of life that has hope even in the face of death.

2. Vs. 26: The person united to Jesus will never die, be extinguished or separated from God. Death will only be a momentary shadow.

Jesus challenges Martha's inadequate view of the resurrection that produces resignation in her.

> Vs. 27 – She said to Him, "Yes, Lord; I have believed that You are the Christ, the Son of God, even He who comes into the world."

Martha goes from intelligent faith (resignation) to living faith. Note that she does not talk about the resurrection but rather it is her view of Jesus that changes. Note her response:

1. Yes – she says yes, not maybe or later.
2. Lord – she acknowledges His sovereignty.
3. Believe – she accepts as true what He says, who He is.
4. Christ – the anointed One of God (title).
5. Son of God – she accepts His divinity.
6. Comes into the world – the Messiah, the savior, my savior.

For Martha, Lazarus' death was the greatest of realities. Resurrection was a far away doctrine of her religion, bringing little comfort at the moment. Jesus redirects her attention so that it focuses not on the death, before her or the resurrection in the distant future, but on Himself. He was the only one who could give her true life now in spite of the daily terror of death and also give her absolute assurance now of everlasting life not just some vague promise in the future.

3. Mary

Vs. 28-31 – When she had said this, she went away and called Mary her sister, saying secretly, "The Teacher is here and is calling for you." And when she heard it, she got up quickly and was coming to Him.

Now Jesus had not yet come into the village, but was still in the place where Martha met Him. Then the Jews who were with her in the house, and consoling her, when they saw that Mary got up quickly and went out, they followed her, supposing that she was going to the tomb to weep there.

Martha goes and gets Mary and sends her to Jesus. Others follow.

> Vs. 32-33a – Therefore, when Mary came where Jesus was, she saw Him, and fell at His feet, saying to Him, "Lord, if You had been here, my brother would not have died." When Jesus therefore saw her weeping, and the Jews who came with her also weeping,

Mary's reaction to Jesus is similar to Martha's but her reaction to Lazarus' death was sorrow. She is not reasonable, she is crushed.

> Vs. 33b-37 – He was deeply moved in spirit and was troubled, and said, "Where have you laid him?" They said to Him, "Lord, come and see." Jesus wept. So the Jews were saying, "See how He loved him!" But some of them said, "Could not this man, who opened the eyes of the blind man, have kept this man also from dying?"

Notice Jesus' initial reaction to Mary was His own human emotion: moved, troubled (disturbed, uncomfortable emotionally), He wept. It was not the first time, He wept for Jerusalem because it rejected Him (Luke 13:34) and it would not be the last time (He wept in the garden before His death, Hebrews 5:7).

I think Jesus reacted in this way because this is a legitimate reaction a human person should have when facing death. 1) Moved with emotion at the trouble and sorrow of someone else. 2) Emotional and spiritual discomfort at facing the horrible results of sin and Satan. 3) Physical expression of sorrow.

I said that this was a legitimate human reaction shared by both Mary and Jesus, but Jesus was also God and so in the next few verses Jesus demonstrates how God reacts to death.

4. Jesus

> Vs. 38-40 – So Jesus, again being deeply moved within, came to the tomb. Now it was a cave, and a stone was lying against it. Jesus said, "Remove the stone." Martha, the sister of the deceased, said to Him, "Lord, by this time there will be a stench, for he has been dead four days." Jesus said to her, "Did I not say to you that if you believe, you will see the glory of God?"

Martha's faith weakens because once again she is faced with the reality (smell) of death being stronger than the reality of the resurrection. This is true of our everyday lives as well. Death always seems stronger and more real than resurrection.

Jesus reaffirms her faith, continues to encourage her to believe despite the doubt she experiences when facing the awful reality of death. This is also true of our lives. Jesus, through the Holy Spirit, the Word, the church, is always encouraging us to believe in the resurrection despite the great argument for the finality of death we see in our everyday lives.

> Vs. 41-42 – So they removed the stone. Then Jesus raised His eyes, and said, "Father, I thank You that You have heard Me. I knew that You always hear Me; but because of the people standing around I said it, so that they may believe that You sent Me."

Jesus prays aloud to show the people around Him that the miracle He is about to perform is from God and confirm in their eyes that He also is from God. He also wants to show how God reacts to death: not with fear like the Apostles; not with resignation like Martha; not with sorrow like Mary, but with power like One who has authority over death.

> Vs. 43-44 — When He had said these things, He cried out with a loud voice, "Lazarus, come forth." The man who had died came forth, bound hand and foot with wrappings, and his face was wrapped around with a cloth. Jesus said to them, "Unbind him, and let him go."

With one command Jesus demonstrates His power over death by calling Lazarus back to life. At this point the people were no longer reacting to death, they were reacting to Jesus Christ.

1. The Apostles now knew why they were on the right side and had no reason to fear: Jesus Christ had the power over death and the most fearful enemy was defeated.

2. Martha now saw how valid her faith was. Jesus was not just a promise or a doctrine: He was the power that guaranteed the promise and He demonstrated that power before her very eyes.

3. Mary could now go beyond sorrow to hope: she saw that death, although sad, was not final. This is what Jesus meant when He said "…he who believes in Me shall live even if he dies." (Shall live now and forever.)

> Vs. 45-46 — Therefore many of the Jews who came to Mary, and saw what He had done, believed in Him. But some of them went to the Pharisees and told them the things which Jesus had done.

Note once again that the result of this miracle follows the pattern of those that preceded it: some believe and some disbelieve. Even with the powerful proof before them, some still choose to reject the evidence and remain unbelieving of Jesus and His claims.

The conspiracy

John does add some further commentary, however, on the final impact that this miracle had on the unbelievers, especially those in the leadership roles of the Jews.

> Vs. 47-48 – Therefore the chief priests and the Pharisees convened a council, and were saying, "What are we doing? For this man is performing many signs. If we let Him go on like this, all men will believe in Him, and the Romans will come and take away both our place and our nation."

They acknowledge the miracle privately but completely miss its significance. To them it does not point to God being among them but rather someone who brings a threat to their position of leadership. In this dialogue John confirms about these men what Jesus had previously said about them in His accusatory parable about the good and bad shepherds.

> Vs. 49-53 – But one of them, Caiaphas, who was high priest that year, said to them, "You know nothing at all, nor do you take into account that it is expedient for you that one man die for the people, and that the whole nation not perish." Now he did not say this on his own initiative, but being high priest that year, he prophesied that Jesus was going to die for the nation, and not for the nation only, but in order that He might also gather together into one the children of God who are scattered abroad. So from that day on they planned together to kill Him.

Despite their evil intent, God still uses them for the purpose of Christ's work. Caiaphas argues that it is better that one man die than the entire nation be disrupted or even worse, destroyed. His argument is that if Jesus is left alive He may cause trouble to the extent that the nation would suffer at the hands of the

Romans. Better Jesus die than the nation. This argument he makes to win over the council to plot with him a way of destroying Jesus. John adds that even though the High Priest was saying this from an evil motive, God was actually making a prophet out of him, despite himself.

According to God's purpose Jesus was sent to die in order to save not only the nation of Israel, but all others "scattered abroad" including Jews living outside Israel and Gentiles.

John shows that even with all his power and cunning, the High Priest was not able to outmaneuver God and His final plan with Jesus.

> Vs. 54-57 – Now the Passover of the Jews was near, and many went up to Jerusalem out of the country before the Passover to purify themselves. So they were seeking for Jesus, and were saying to one another as they stood in the temple, "What do you think; that He will not come to the feast at all?" Now the chief priests and the Pharisees had given orders that if anyone knew where He was, he was to report it, so that they might seize Him.

Because the Lord knew of their plans and because He wanted to go to His death on His terms and not theirs, He leaves the city for a safer region (probably in the northern part of the Judean hills).

Jesus was usually found at the temple teaching during the important feasts when there were many people in Jerusalem. As the most important and well attended feast of Passover approached, the people began to wonder if He would show up as was His custom for the last several years.

With the last few verses, the stage is set for the final meeting between Jesus and His Apostles and His subsequent arrest by the Jewish leaders who have already decided to kill Him. All they lack is the opportunity and some charge.

21.

REACTION TO LAZARUS' RESURRECTION

JOHN 12:1-50

In our last chapter we saw Jesus perform His last public miracle. I mentioned then that in these final 10 chapters John will compress time and describe the events in the last few weeks of Jesus' life. These last few weeks mainly comprise of Jesus' final moments with His Apostles and close friends, a section many Bible commentators refer to as "the Passion."

Before John describes these, however, he will give us a view of how different individuals and groups react to Jesus' great miracle in raising Lazarus from the dead. John will show us five different reactions to Jesus' final miracle.

1. Mary, the sister of Lazarus and Martha

Vs. 1-3 – Jesus, therefore, six days before the Passover, came to Bethany where Lazarus was, whom Jesus had raised from the dead. So they made Him a supper there, and Martha was serving; but Lazarus was one of those reclining at the table with Him. Mary then took a pound of very costly perfume of pure nard, and anointed the feet of Jesus and wiped His feet with her hair; and the house was filled with the fragrance of the perfume.

It was Jesus' custom to stay with His friends in Bethany when He travelled to Jerusalem for feasts in order to preach and teach the people. His home was 80 miles north in Capernaum near the Sea of Galilee.

The Passover was the most important and best attended feast in the Jewish calendar, but Jesus was there for not only these reasons. He knew it was His appointed time and was there because of this.

Martha, true to her nature, was organizing the supper (this time with no complaint about her sister) and Lazarus, a walking miracle and witness, was at the table. In Matthew and Mark's accounts of this episode, they mention that Mary anointed the head of Jesus; John merely adds the fact that she also anointed His feet.

The wiping of His feet with her hair is significant in that a woman of that culture would not display her hair in public and certainly not to a group of men (there were only men at the supper because men and women did not recline to eat in mixed company). Her action demonstrated that she was laying her honor at her master's feet. The complete use of expensive ointment (nard is the plant from India that provides the essence for the perfume) and the way it was done was a perfect act of humility, devotion and honor to the Lord. Humility in that her head was at the Lord's feet. Devotion in that all the ointment was used. Honor in that Jesus was the total focus of this action (she did not anoint the others). Mary's reaction demonstrated her faith in Jesus, not as a friend or a teacher but as the divine Lord toward whom she directed her worship and love.

2. Judas Iscariot

> Vs. 4-8 – But Judas Iscariot, one of His disciples, who was intending to betray Him, said, "Why was this perfume not sold for three hundred denarii and given to poor people?" Now he said this, not because he was concerned about the poor, but because he was a thief,

and as he had the money box, he used to pilfer what was put into it. Therefore Jesus said, "Let her alone, so that she may keep it for the day of My burial. For you always have the poor with you, but you do not always have Me."

Judas could have objected on several grounds. That such a show was too lavish for a prophet of God, too showy for a simple rabbi from Galilee. He could have remarked that it was improper for a woman to be so forward in mixed company. These might have been legitimate complaints if Jesus were an ordinary man and rabbi. But Judas, revealing his nature, zeroes in on the value of the ointment and complains about the waste that the action caused. The perfume was worth several months of wages in those days. His accusation is that Jesus is wasting money on self-glorification instead of taking care of the poor.

John, in an editorial comment, reveals his true motivation, greed and the dishonesty that blinded him from seeing the truth before his very eyes. Judas sat with the resurrected Lazarus and still continued in his evil ways, even now accusing Jesus of sin and waste. Judas' reaction to Lazarus' resurrection was a hard heart. He swept away this chance to change his mind by continuing to reinforce his sinful ways.

Jesus does not let his accusation slip by however. He defends Mary's actions in consideration of several reasons. Her faith and devotion were well placed in Him. He is special and this was a worthy act. The poor are always there and this was not the only resource they had, they had helped in the past and would do so in the future but for now this was the best thing to do with this resource. His death was at hand and this action provided an opportunity to refer to it as well as prepare for it.

Jesus in His response provides a rebuke to Judas and a commendation to Mary.

3. The Jewish leaders

Vs. 9-11 – The large crowd of the Jews then learned that He was there; and they came, not for Jesus' sake only, but that they might also see Lazarus, whom He raised from the dead. But the chief priests planned to put Lazarus to death also; because on account of him many of the Jews were going away and were believing in Jesus.

The situation is now critical for the Jewish leaders because it is becoming evident that they are on the wrong side of the fence. Lazarus' resurrection has electrified the people and the word has spread. The leaders are in charge in principle but are quickly losing control of their authority over the people. Their plot to arrest and kill Jesus now includes Lazarus because he is causing as much of a stir as Jesus because of what has happened to him. The leaders react with the same disbelief and fear that they have consistently shown from the beginning except now they are resolved to take action, no turning back.

4. The multitudes

Vs. 12-19 – On the next day the large crowd who had come to the feast, when they heard that Jesus was coming to Jerusalem, took the branches of the palm trees and went out to meet Him, and began to shout, "Hosanna! Blessed is He who comes in the name of the Lord, even the King of Israel." Jesus, finding a young donkey, sat on it; as it is written, "Fear not, daughter of Zion; behold, your King is coming, seated on a donkey's colt." These things His disciples did not understand at the first; but when Jesus was glorified, then they remembered that these things were written of Him, and that they had done these things to Him.

So the people, who were with Him when He called

> Lazarus out of the tomb and raised him from the dead, continued to testify about Him. For this reason also the people went and met Him, because they heard that He had performed this sign. So the Pharisees said to one another, "You see that you are not doing any good; look, the world has gone after Him."

After the miracle in Bethany and the word of it spread, a large crowd formed around Jesus and accompanied Him to Jerusalem. They were blessing and praising His name and bringing Him into the city as a king, a victorious leader.

The words they use are phrases from different Psalms that indicate their belief in Him as the Messiah. The palm tree branches represented life and salvation to the Jews. Riding on a donkey was a direct fulfillment of the prophecy by Zechariah (Zechariah 9:9) concerning the manner that the Messiah would enter the city. Jesus came in meekness and grace riding on a lowly type of animal (a donkey), not a horse or chariot that worldly kings used.

John notes that after His resurrection the Apostles would realize the prophetic importance and rightness of this moment. John also notes that the miraculous raising of Lazarus is what galvanized His followers for this triumphant and enthusiastic entry into the Holy City for Passover.

John uses the comments of the Pharisees who watched helplessly. They say that the whole world (meaning their whole world) had gone over to Jesus (for the moment) and there was nothing they could do about it.

5. The Gentiles (Greeks)

> Vs. 20-26 – Now there were some Greeks among those who were going up to worship at the feast; these then came to Philip, who was from Bethsaida of Galilee, and began to ask him, saying, "Sir, we wish to see Jesus."

Philip came and told Andrew; Andrew and Philip came and told Jesus. And Jesus answered them, saying, "The hour has come for the Son of Man to be glorified. Truly, truly, I say to you, unless a grain of wheat falls into the earth and dies, it remains alone; but if it dies, it bears much fruit. He who loves his life loses it, and he who hates his life in this world will keep it to life eternal. If anyone serves Me, he must follow Me; and where I am, there My servant will be also; if anyone serves Me, the Father will honor him.

There was only one thing worse for the Jewish leaders than having the people go over to Jesus and losing their position. That was if non-Jews were also allowed to follow Jesus and both groups became one. This passage makes a faint illusion to this. It will only happen in the future once the gospel is preached beyond Judea and Paul brings the Gentiles into the church.

But Jesus sets the stage for this future event here. The Greeks were Gentile converts allowed to participate in the feasts and worship, but only from the outer court of the Gentiles. Jesus was probably in the court of men separated from them and they (knowing Phillip) requested that He come to them for a personal meeting. Phillip confers with Andrew (inner circle) perhaps because of the trouble Jesus speaking with Gentiles in the area of the temple might cause.

They finally pass on the request to Jesus who responds not by meeting with them but by making a general declaration that would affect them far into the future. He uses this request to declare two events:

1. The beginning of His Passion was at hand. His suffering, death and resurrection were going to happen soon, not next year or next decade but now. This showed in advance that He knew it, declared it and accepted it. He was the grain of wheat sown into the ground of death who would produce a great harvest of souls.

2. Those who would follow Him would need to make a difficult choice. This life, this world or the life and world to come, no

halfway measures, one or the other. And you lived accordingly.

These declarations were good news for the Greeks who had asked for a private meeting. Jesus said publicly, not privately, that anyone (not just Jews) who wanted to serve Him could do so by following Him.

The Greeks reacted with a desire for access to Jesus and the Lord offers them (and all who would follow Him, Jew or Greek) the opportunity to have full access to not only Himself but to the Father also on an eternal basis.

The Cycle Continues

John shifts gears at this point and reverts back to the familiar cycle where Jesus makes a declaration and there is a reaction of belief or disbelief.

> Vs. 27-43 – "Now My soul has become troubled; and what shall I say, 'Father, save Me from this hour'? But for this purpose I came to this hour. Father, glorify Your name." Then a voice came out of heaven: "I have both glorified it, and will glorify it again." So the crowd of people who stood by and heard it were saying that it had thundered; others were saying, "An angel has spoken to Him." Jesus answered and said, "This voice has not come for My sake, but for your sakes.
>
> Now judgment is upon this world; now the ruler of this world will be cast out. And I, if I am lifted up from the earth, will draw all men to Myself." But He was saying this to indicate the kind of death by which He was to die. The crowd then answered Him, "We have heard out of the Law that the Christ is to remain forever; and how can You say, 'The Son of Man must be lifted up'?
>
> Who is this Son of Man?" So Jesus said to them, "For a little while longer the Light is among you. Walk while

you have the Light, so that darkness will not overtake
you; he who walks in the darkness does not know
where he goes. While you have the Light, believe in the
Light, so that you may become sons of Light."

These things Jesus spoke, and He went away and hid
Himself from them. But though He had performed so
many signs before them, yet they were not believing in
Him. This was to fulfill the word of Isaiah the prophet
which he spoke: "Lord, who has believed our report?
And to whom has the arm of the Lord been revealed?"
For this reason they could not believe, for Isaiah said
again, "He has blinded their eyes and He hardened
their heart, so that they would not see with their eyes
and perceive with their heart, and be converted and I
heal them." These things Isaiah said because he saw
His glory, and he spoke of Him. Nevertheless many
even of the rulers believed in Him, but because of the
Pharisees they were not confessing Him, for fear that
they would be put out of the synagogue; for they loved
the approval of men rather than the approval of God.

Here we have four voices mingled in the dialogue.

1. Jesus declares that the hour (meaning the "time") of His
   death is at hand and by it He will both fulfill His reason for
   being here and be glorified (honored) by it. In other words,
   demonstrate who He really is. He also declares that by this
   death He will defeat Satan and take away his power to
   condemn mankind because of their sins. There will now be
   forgiveness of sin and fulfillment of the requirements of the
   Law through His cross.

   o He will also draw all mankind to Himself through this
     action because the preaching of the gospel to all the
     world will point all mankind to the cross for salvation.
     He encourages them to believe while the time for
     faith is ripe.

2. God the Father confirms what He has just declared by revealing Himself in a voice. He has done this before at Jesus' baptism and at the transfiguration, and does so again to the multitudes as a witness of Jesus' declarations.

3. The multitudes, the same ones who were praising Him as He entered the city, now begin to express their doubt. They do not like the idea of a tortured or dead Messiah; they interpret the Scripture to mean that the Messiah will never die. This is true, He is eternal and for this reason He is the only One who can offer His life as a sacrifice for sin, because He has the power to both lay down and take up His life again. The crowd does not understand this. They end up questioning and doubting who Jesus declares He really is. In other words they are saying "This is not the Son of Man (Messiah) we are looking for, one who dies. We do not want one like this."

4. John takes over at this point as the fourth voice and explains Jesus' response to the doubts of the multitude. He explains that their reaction to Him was exactly what the prophets predicted about how the people would react to the Messiah, even with the signs and miracles performed. Their centuries of stubbornness and disobedience have made them unable to see, even when the plain proof was there.

The section ends with the usual description by John of various individuals and groups who either believed or disbelieved and why (fear, greed, pride, etc.).

The warning

Vs. 44-50 – And Jesus cried out and said, "He who believes in Me, does not believe in Me but in Him who sent Me. He who sees Me sees the One who sent Me. I have come as Light into the world, so that everyone who believes in Me will not remain in darkness. If anyone hears My sayings and does not keep them, I do not judge him; for I did not come to judge the world, but to save the world. He who rejects Me and does not receive My sayings, has one who judges him; the word I spoke is what will judge him at the last day.

For I did not speak on My own initiative, but the Father Himself who sent Me has given Me a commandment as to what to say and what to speak. I know that His commandment is eternal life; therefore the things I speak, I speak just as the Father has told Me."

In this last section Jesus offers a warning to all those who have heard His words and seen His miracles. Basically His warning is twofold:

1. Reject Me and you reject God.

By declaring that all He says and does comes directly from God the Father, He puts the burden on His hearers. You reject one, you reject the other; you accept one, you accept the other.

2. The basis for judgment will be My words.

Light and darkness refers to truth, knowledge, salvation and good versus lies, ignorance, condemnation and evil. His words were God's words and believing and obeying them would be the basis for judgment and salvation.

This is Jesus' final public appearance and teaching so He uses it to draw a line in the sand as it were. You are with Me or against Me; you believe or you do not; you are in light or in darkness, saved or unsaved. Whatever category, the dividing line will be how you feel and what you believe about Jesus Christ. You have heard the words, seen the miracles, deal with it!

As it was then, so it continues today. We preach and teach about His words and miracles, His death, burial and resurrection, and all mankind has to choose whether they believe or not. We have the same decision with the same consequences today.

22.
THE LAST SUPPER

JOHN 13:1-30

In our study we have seen certain "patterns" emerge, cycles where a series of events continue to repeat themselves in order to drive home a point. The most prevalent cycle in John is that which sees Jesus declaring His divinity (by teaching or miracle) and His hearers either believing or disbelieving His claims.

There were several objectives that the repetition of this cycle seemed to aim for:

1. To make clear Jesus' claims and actions.

You may or may not believe it but there is no doubt that Jesus taught and demonstrated through His power that He was the Son of God. People can choose to disbelieve and reject this notion, but Jesus' message was clear: He believed and wanted us to believe that He was divine and the Messiah.

2. To provide proof for the claims.

John records several miracles in detail in order to support the claims of Jesus. Some may not have believed, but he writes as one who believed strongly the proof before Him.

3. To record the reaction of the people.

Jesus demonstrated that the disbelief among the Jews was widespread, not just a fluke or a narrow opinion. John describes the familiar scene of Jesus demonstrating great power and the leaders, and eventually the crowds that celebrated Him, turn against Him in disbelief and anger. This scene is repeated over and over again to reinforce the idea that some believed but most disbelieved, and this was the line where the great divide between saved and lost would be.

This brings us to our last lesson where I compared the reaction of various people to Lazarus' death and resurrection now made possible by God through Christ. In that lesson I showed you how different people had their faith strengthened by this great miracle and how others, like Judas and the religious leaders, hardened their heart in disbelief and thus repeated the cycle of faith or rejection one more time.

In this chapter John begins the narrative that will describe the final hours of Jesus' ministry here on earth, and how people reacted to Him with or without faith.

The Passover Meal – Background

Each year the Jews celebrated the feast of the Passover that commemorated the liberation of the Israelites from Egyptian slavery. The feast focused on the final powerful sign God used in freeing them: He sent an angel to destroy every firstborn in Egypt (both human and animal). He instructed the Jews to kill a lamb and sprinkle their doorposts with its blood, and then cook and eat the animal while indoors that night. When the Egyptians awoke to the death of all their firstborn the next day, even the Pharaoh's child, the Jews were set free. The Lord commanded them to keep a remembrance of this time by having the Passover meal each year.

There was a set order to the meal itself: a lamb was sacrificed at the temple on behalf of a family or group of family representatives. The meat was then prepared along with unleavened bread, bitter herbs and wine for the meal.

Each element had its own significance:

1. The lamb was the sacrifice offered in place of the firstborn.

2. The bitter herbs (like a salad) represented the harsh experience they had as slaves.

3. The unleavened bread signified the haste with which they left Egypt, no time to even make the bread rise.

4. The wine was added later, but came to represent the new and abundant land that God had eventually brought them to.

According to the Law, the Passover lasted seven days and the meal was prepared and eaten on the evening prior to the Passover Day. This would be Thursday evening. During the week the Jews would make sure that no yeast or fermenting agent would be present in their homes or food. Yeast was a symbol of decay and so was eliminated totally during this time. The bread was without yeast or leaven; the wine was mixed with water as was the custom.

During the meal, the father or presider (if no father was present) would direct the proceedings: he would first eat and the others would follow; he would offer a blessing as they shared the wine; when all was finished they would stand and sing the "Halel" (Psalm of praise).

It was this meal that Jesus gathered with His Apostles to share that John describes in chapter 13.

Jesus and the Passover – 13:1-30

John does not provide any details concerning the Lord 's Supper (this is already done adequately in Matthew, Mark, Luke and I Corinthians). John does, however, provide a lot of detail as to what was said and done that night that the others do not include. His description of that evening in the upper room will go on from chapter 13 to the end of chapter 17. Most of the information includes a long prayer and teaching section by Jesus for His Apostles on His final night with them before His death.

Before He begins this prayer, however, He will do two important things for His Apostles:

1. He washes the feet of the Apostles – vs. 1-20

> Vs. 1-5 – Now before the Feast of the Passover, Jesus knowing that His hour had come that He would depart out of this world to the Father, having loved His own who were in the world, He loved them to the end. During supper, the devil having already put into the heart of Judas Iscariot, the son of Simon, to betray Him, Jesus, knowing that the Father had given all things into His hands, and that He had come forth from God and was going back to God, got up from supper, and laid aside His garments; and taking a towel, He girded Himself. Then He poured water into the basin, and began to wash the disciples' feet and to wipe them with the towel with which He was girded.

Jesus was fully aware of who He was, why He was sent, that His time was near, and what kind of men His Apostles were. Knowing and accepting all of this, He still loved them and accepted what He was sent to do on their behalf. Even knowing that one of His Apostles would betray Him, even with that knowledge, He loved them nevertheless and humbled Himself to do the thing He was about to do.

In those days the host would set a jar of water, a bowl and towel near the doorway for the purpose of washing his guests' feet. It was their version of a doormat. Usually the task was given to a slave or the youngest boy in the household. Since they had borrowed the upper room and it was a private meal, no one had been assigned to take care of this detail.

Imagine, each Apostle coming in with dusty, dirty feet; no one greeting them or serving this need. Imagine as each new Apostle arrived, no one offering to do the courteous thing because it would be too demeaning. Imagine their chagrin when the Lord Himself gets up from the dinner and quietly begins to do the honors... the work of a slave, the task belonging to the one with least position and honor.

The other writers describe an argument among the Apostles concerning who was the greatest, because they probably did not like the seating arrangement. Jesus silences them with this action.

> Vs. 6-11 – So He came to Simon Peter. He said to Him, "Lord, do You wash my feet?" Jesus answered and said to him, "What I do you do not realize now, but you will understand hereafter." Peter said to Him, "Never shall You wash my feet!" Jesus answered him, "If I do not wash you, you have no part with Me." Simon Peter said to Him, "Lord, then wash not only my feet, but also my hands and my head." Jesus said to him, "He who has bathed needs only to wash his feet, but is completely clean; and you are clean, but not all of you." For He knew the one who was betraying Him; for this reason He said, "Not all of you are clean.

Of course Peter breaks the awkward silence with a show of protest. He does not understand all the implications of this action and what Jesus will say about it later, and what it will mean later. The implication hereafter is that they will realize that God washed their feet! Jesus presses him by saying that without this Peter cannot remain a part of Jesus. Peter reverses himself and goes to the other extreme: if washing my feet unites me to you, wash me all over to make sure. Jesus reassures him that only this is necessary for now and those who have a clean heart (meaning they sincerely believe and act from it) are completely clean (absolved) and have no need for further purification. Then He makes reference to the fact that there is a traitor among them: one who has received the foot washing but whose heart was unclean!

> Vs. 12-17 – So when He had washed their feet, and taken His garments and reclined at the table again, He said to them, "Do you know what I have done to you? You call Me Teacher and Lord; and you are right, for so I am. If I then, the Lord and the Teacher, washed your feet, you also ought to wash one another's feet. For I gave you an example that you also should do as I did to you. Truly, truly, I say to you, a slave is not greater than his master, nor is one who is sent greater than the one who sent him. If you know these things, you are blessed if you do them.

Later they will feel the impact of this gesture (that God humbled Himself before them). For now, He uses the foot washing as an example upon which they should base their attitude toward one another. If the Master can wash your feet, certainly you can do it for one another.

Today we have doormats, but the need to humble ourselves before one another is still the basic way we avoid strife and division caused by pride.

> Vs. 18-20 – I do not speak of all of you. I know the ones I have chosen; but it is that the Scripture may be fulfilled, 'He who eats My bread has lifted up his heel against Me.' From now on I am telling you before it comes to pass, so that when it does occur, you may believe that I am He. Truly, truly, I say to you, he who receives whomever I send receives Me; and he who receives Me receives Him who sent Me.

Here Jesus reveals to them not only that He will be betrayed by one of them but that the betrayal was prophesied long ago by David (Psalms 41:9). In addition to this He tells them that this will be another indicator of His divine nature: the ability to predict the future accurately. At this point the Lord does the second important thing for His Apostles.

2. He reveals the traitor – vs. 21-30

Until now, the Apostles have not grasped what Jesus has been saying to them. In the following verses the Lord not only makes it plain to the Apostles, but He also reveals to Judas that He knows what Judas is planning to do.

> Vs. 21-30 – When Jesus had said this, He became troubled in spirit, and testified and said, "Truly, truly, I say to you, that one of you will betray Me." The disciples began looking at one another, at a loss to know of which one He was speaking. There was reclining on Jesus' bosom one of His disciples, whom Jesus loved. So Simon Peter gestured to him, and said to him, "Tell us who it is of whom He is speaking." He, leaning back thus on Jesus' bosom, said to Him, "Lord, who is it?" Jesus then answered, "That is the one for whom I shall dip the morsel and give it to him."
>
> So when He had dipped the morsel, He took and gave it to Judas, the son of Simon Iscariot. After the morsel, Satan then entered into him. Therefore Jesus said to him, "What you do, do quickly." Now no one of those reclining at the table knew for what purpose He had said this to him. For some were supposing, because Judas had the money box, that Jesus was saying to him, "Buy the things we have need of for the feast"; or else, that he should give something to the poor. So after receiving the morsel he went out immediately; and it was night.

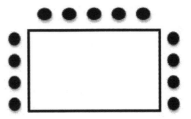

Imagine the scene:
Thirteen men reclining on cushions around a table. The host or organizer of the dinner sat at the head of the table so he could protect and serve the honored guest or preside. The honored guest would assign seats around the table, usually in order of status. There was complaining among the Apostles about who was important. It seems that John and Peter organized the dinner (Luke 21:7-8) and it seems that they had hoped to take the coveted spots next to Jesus. John, as host, in the first seat with Jesus to his left as the guest of honor, followed of course by Peter the leader and then the other Apostles doing the best they could. Probably Judas last, since they knew he was a thief and untrustworthy.

Things start as planned with John taking the first spot (we know this because he leaned his head on Jesus). Jesus in the honored position which no one contested. But John tells us three important facts: 1) When washing their feet, He came to Peter last. 2) When speaking to John, Peter had to gesture to him to get his attention. 3) Jesus spoke and handed the morsel directly to Judas. This means Judas was next to the Lord and Peter sat at the end of the table.

Perhaps when assigning seats Jesus placed Judas next to Himself because He knew what was to come. And Peter, in a pout, went to sit as far away as he could. This certainly explains his behavior when Jesus came to him with the water and towel to wash his feet. Much of the evidence points to this scenario.

In any case, Jesus forces Judas' hand without any of the others knowing what had taken place. The idea that "Satan entered him" is not to suggest that Judas was demon possessed and not responsible for his action. This reference indicates when Judas finally gave in fully to the temptation. Judas was no longer under the influence of Christ, he had completely given himself over to the sin he was about to commit, therefore Satan was now controlling him.

Summary

We will stop here because the next section begins Jesus' last prayer and exhortation for His Apostles before He is killed. Even though the Lord's Supper is not described here, this passage does provide lessons that are usually found in those passages where the Lord's Supper is found.

1. A servant is not above his master

If we choose to follow Jesus, we must follow Him in all His ways, not just some. If He was willing to wash feet before the communion, so must we. In other words, if He was willing to humble Himself, so should we; otherwise we do not belong at the table.

2. A servant should examine himself/herself

If Judas would have examined his heart full of disbelief and greed, he might not have fallen into the total control of Satan. When the Lord hands us the communion bread, let us make sure it is not an accusation of infidelity and hypocrisy, like the morsel He handed to Judas. Let us be sure our hearts are right before we sit to eat with the Lord and we are not sitting in Judas' seat. He was in a position of honor (next to the Lord) before men, but Jesus knew his heart.

23.
JESUS' FINAL TEACHING
PART 1

JOHN 13:31-14:31

In our previous chapter we began the section in John's gospel where Jesus is ministering exclusively to His Apostles as His death is imminent. We studied the events that took place as the Lord shared the final Passover meal with them. We saw that although the Lord's Supper is not mentioned here, John does provide a lot of information concerning the events that took place that night.

One major event was the unmasking of Judas as the traitor. This set into motion the sequence of events that ultimately led to Jesus' arrest. With the few remaining hours left before His suffering was to begin, Jesus focuses on providing His Apostles with the teaching and encouragement they are to need in order to make it through the next few days.

We have other teachings and words of encouragement from the Lord after His resurrection and even after His ascension into heaven (i.e. Paul, Acts 18:9-10), but this section in John's gospel is the last full and lengthy teaching He provides. This body of teaching and exhortation will go on for several chapters and is only interrupted occasionally by questions from the Apostles based on what Jesus is saying.

The section we will cover here includes the teaching of Jesus, the questions of four of the Apostles and the response of the Lord to their queries (4 dialogues).

Dialogue #1 – Jesus and Peter – 13:31-38

Vs. 31-33 – Therefore when he had gone out, Jesus said, "Now is the Son of Man glorified, and God is glorified in Him; if God is glorified in Him, God will also glorify Him in Himself, and will glorify Him immediately. Little children, I am with you a little while longer. You will seek Me; and as I said to the Jews, now I also say to you, 'Where I am going, you cannot come.'

With the departure of Judas, Jesus knew that the cycle of events that would eventually bring Him to the cross was beginning. He places His suffering and death in the same category as His miracles, His prophecies, His teachings, His resurrection and ascension; all of these things glorify Him (point to Him as God the Son).

Jesus declares that even the cross is a source of glory to Him. We know now that this is true because the cross provides redemption and salvation for all men, a truly glorious thing. It is important for Him to say this because there will be a temptation to view His cross as an object of shame and defeat. Not so, Jesus says.

The cross was God's plan, the Father sent the Son to the cross and the fact that the Son is ready to go will also glorify, honor and reveal the Father, His plan and His sacrifice to save man.

The Father and the Son will both be glorified (not dishonored as some Jews might think) by the cross. Jesus prepares them to correctly view what will soon ("immediately") take place. He also reminds them that this is one place where even they will not be able to follow Him: the cross is uniquely His and cannot be carried by anyone else, even them.

Vs. 34-35 – A new commandment I give to you, that you love one another, even as I have loved you, that you also love one another. By this all men will know that you are My disciples, if you have love for one another."

The commandment to love is not new, but the reason and manner is new. They are to love each other because of their faith in Jesus. They are to love each other in the way He loved them. They are to use their love for one another in the name of Christ as a witness for their faith.

For the Jews, their religious system and rituals separated them from other people. For Christians it will be their love for one another, not their worship style or religious systems that will distinguish them from others. And Jesus laying down His life on the cross for His disciples will be the standard for that love.

Vs. 36 – Simon Peter said to Him, "Lord, where are You going?" Jesus answered, "Where I go, you cannot follow Me now; but you will follow later."

Peter is curious about Jesus' destination, thinking it to be a place (maybe out of the country to preach to the Jewish Diaspora). Jesus repeats His previous statement in reference to the cross and adds that they will also follow His way to suffering, but later on, referring to their own martyrdom because of the gospel.

Vs. 37-38 – Peter said to Him, "Lord, why can I not follow You right now? I will lay down my life for You." Jesus answered, "Will you lay down your life for Me? Truly, truly, I say to you, a rooster will not crow until you deny Me three times."

Peter suspects that some kind of danger might lay ahead in further ministry with the Lord; after all, they had been threatened with death by the Jewish authorities before. He makes a rash statement; he wants to continue the momentum Jesus has produced at all costs, even future danger. He loves the Lord and wants to continue their present ministry.

Jesus, knowing the immediacy of His death and knowing how not ready Peter is to face this, declares how Peter will react when faced with the real possibility of torture and death. We sometimes fault Peter for his rash behavior. However, we act in the same way when we think we are spiritually strong but cave in at a little temptation or find excuses when called upon to give or help others.

Dialogue #2 – Jesus and Thomas – 14:1-6

> Vs. 1-4 – "Do not let your heart be troubled; believe in God, believe also in Me. In My Father's house are many dwelling places; if it were not so, I would have told you; for I go to prepare a place for you. If I go and prepare a place for you, I will come again and receive you to Myself, that where I am, there you may be also. And you know the way where I am going."

The evening has become quite depressing. Judas has left. Peter has been told that he will deny the Lord that very night. The Lord is talking about leaving them. So Jesus shifts gears and gives them words of encouragement. He sees their troubled hearts and tells them not to be down. He points them to the future He is preparing for them in heaven.

The figurative language of dwellings and house are used to comfort the Apostles with the notion that there is a place in heaven for each one of them regardless of their talents, disposition, strength or wealth. He assures them that He Himself will guarantee their entry.

> Vs. 5 – Thomas said to Him, "Lord, we do not know where You are going, how do we know the way?"

Thomas acknowledges that they still do not grasp that He is talking about His death, resurrection and ascension into heaven. If we do not know where you are going, how can we know the way to get there?

> Vs. 6 – Jesus said to him, "I am the way, and the truth, and the life; no one comes to the Father but through Me.

Jesus answers in a beautiful and perfectly concise manner: the way to heaven is Himself; the destination in heaven is Himself; the experience (life) of heaven is Himself. We see in this dialogue a challenge once again by Jesus to His disciples to believe, based on His prophecy and teaching.

Dialogue #3 – Philip – 14:7-15

> Vs. 7 – If you had known Me, you would have known My Father also; from now on you know Him, and have seen Him."

Jesus continues the thought brought on by Thomas' question and expands on it. There is some debate over the exact wording of this verse. Some scholars argue that it should read, "In the way you have known me, you will know the Father." Others claim that it should read as the NAS version (New American Standard) has it, "If you would have known Me, you would have known My Father." The difference is that one is a promise and one is a rebuke. Either way, Jesus finishes the verse by saying that whatever happened before, they now can look forward to knowing the Father, because they have seen Him in the flesh. This, of course, is another declaration by Jesus concerning His divine nature.

Vs. 8 – Philip said to Him, "Lord, show us the Father, and it is enough for us."

Philip only gets it in part. He thinks Jesus can show them a sign, a vision of the Father (i.e. the burning bush). Philip thinks that if Jesus can do this, it will be the "sign" that will confirm all He has said and they will be satisfied.

Vs. 9-15 – Jesus said to him, "Have I been so long with you, and yet you have not come to know Me, Philip? He who has seen Me has seen the Father; how can you say, 'Show us the Father'? Do you not believe that I am in the Father, and the Father is in Me? The words that I say to you I do not speak on My own initiative, but the Father abiding in Me does His works. Believe Me that I am in the Father and the Father is in Me; otherwise believe because of the works themselves.

Truly, truly, I say to you, he who believes in Me, the works that I do, he will do also; and greater works than these he will do; because I go to the Father. Whatever you ask in My name, that will I do, so that the Father may be glorified in the Son. If you ask Me anything in My name, I will do it "If you love Me, you will keep My commandments.

Jesus' initial question in response to Philip shows how pained He is by his lack of understanding, but He convinces him further. If you need proof that I am divine (the Father in Me, Me in the Father) just examine my works (miracles). That I declare my divinity is another proof that the Father is in Me. I would not say this if this was not the case (it would be sinful and worthy of death).

In addition to these, Jesus adds other proofs for His divine identity: the Apostles will do miracles in His name; He will answer their prayers.

He finishes by imposing a condition that only God can impose and did in the past, that their faith, love and devotion be measured by obedience.

Dialogue #4 – Judas (Thaddeus) – 14:16-24

> Vs. 16-21 – I will ask the Father, and He will give you another Helper, that He may be with you forever; that is the Spirit of truth, whom the world cannot receive, because it does not see Him or know Him, but you know Him because He abides with you and will be in you.
>
> "I will not leave you as orphans; I will come to you. After a little while the world will no longer see Me, but you will see Me; because I live, you will live also. In that day you will know that I am in My Father, and you in Me, and I in you. He who has My commandments and keeps them is the one who loves Me; and he who loves Me will be loved by My Father, and I will love him and will disclose Myself to him."

Jesus builds another idea upon the one He had just given in response to Philip. Philip wanted to have a clear vision, an experience of the Father, something that would "stay" with them into the troubled future Jesus was speaking of. Jesus promises that even if He leaves them, they will not be alone, they will not be without the spiritual comfort they have experienced with His presence among them.

Still referring to His association with the father, Jesus promises to ask the Father to send the Spirit not only to be among them, but be within them; not only for a little while, but forever. He has been with them through Christ, but will be in them when Christ leaves. They will recognize this Spirit because it will bring them the truth, the same truth originally given them by Jesus.

He points them to the future and once again speaks of His death, but now adds the idea of His resurrection and tells them that the sign of His resurrection will guarantee their own. This final miracle (resurrection) will be the proof Philip needs to believe in the divinity of Jesus. This proof will also confirm all He has said to them, even the prophecy concerning the sending of the Spirit and their own resurrection.

In the end He repeats again that Christian love is expressed in obedience to Christ's word and those who do will be rewarded by the "experience" that Philip searched for but could not find. This experience is "God's manifestation." God "manifests" Himself to the believer through the Holy Spirit, His Word and the loving lives of believers. All these elements were made possible through Jesus Christ.

> Vs. 22 – Judas (not Iscariot) said to Him, "Lord, what then has happened that You are going to disclose Yourself to us and not to the world?"

Jesus has focused His attention and promises on the Apostles themselves. Judas (not the traitor) brings up another point: if our task is to convert others, how come you are only revealing yourself to us? Why not the Jews? Judas (Thaddeus) wonders if there has been a change in plans.

> Vs. 23-24 – Jesus answered and said to him, "If anyone loves Me, he will keep My word; and My Father will love him, and We will come to him and make Our abode with
>
> him. He who does not love Me does not keep My words; and the word which you hear is not Mine, but the Father's who sent Me.

Jesus answers him that the revelation of the Father for everyone is based on the acceptance of the Son. If a person accepts the Son (by loving Him through obedience to His word), both the Father and the Son will be revealed to them. There is no change in plan, it is a clarification of how these spiritual things will work. This instruction is from God Himself.

The Lord assures not only Judas, but the other Apostles as well, that the thing which they desire (assurance and comfort from God) is within reach, even standing before them in person.

Summary – vs. 25-31

Jesus has answered their questions and will summarize His response to them about these matters.

> Vs. 25-27 – "These things I have spoken to you while abiding with you. But the Helper, the Holy Spirit, whom the Father will send in My name, He will teach you all things, and bring to your remembrance all that I said to you. Peace I leave with you; My peace I give to you; not as the world gives do I give to you. Do not let your heart be troubled, nor let it be fearful."

Jesus renews His promise of the Holy Spirit once again, but this time emphasizes the fact that the Holy Spirit will not only comfort them and speak the truth to them, He will also enable them to both remember and understand all the teachings of Christ. This will be comforting indeed.

This is the way His peace will be imparted to them. The world tries for peace with treaties or threats. Jesus gives them a knowledge and understanding of the truth, this brings peace.

When they will put together the teachings and promises of Christ with the resurrection of Christ, they will have peace concerning their lives here and their hope for eternal life; no need for fear or anxiety (trouble).

He reminds them of His prophecy:

> Vs. 28-31 – You heard that I said to you, 'I go away, and I will come to you.' If you loved Me, you would have rejoiced because I go to the Father, for the Father is greater than I. Now I have told you before it happens, so that when it happens, you may believe. I will not speak much more with you, for the ruler of the world is coming, and he has nothing in Me; but so that the world may know that I love the Father, I do exactly as the Father commanded Me. Get up, let us go from here."

Jesus assesses the situation as it ought to be: if they really loved Him they would be happy that He is leaving this earthly body to be with the Father. After all, once He is with the Father not only is His suffering over, He can send the Holy Spirit. When Jesus refers to the Father as greater than Himself, He means Himself as a man, especially one condemned to die.

He repeats His prophecy of the coming events so that they will remember clearly that He called it in advance of the actual events (death and resurrection). This is yet another invitation to believe, but one that points to the future: when you see all the things I predicted would happen actually happen, let this be another reason for you to believe.

He claims that His own end is near and Satan will do his work to destroy Him. But He wants them to know that He will accept the torture and death because the Father commanded Him to do this and He will obey to demonstrate His love, another example for them to follow, obedience proving love.

He finishes with the command to rise from the table, not leave the room. While they are still in the room He will continue to teach and encourage them.

24.
JESUS' FINAL TEACHING
PART 2

JOHN 15:1-27

In our study of John's gospel we have arrived at the place where Jesus is preparing His Apostles for His death and resurrection. He does this in several ways:

1. He washes their feet

This is done to impress upon them the need for humility and service after He is gone. They were already fighting among themselves in His presence, He wants them to remember this action and attitude when their pride gets out of hand in the future.

2. He purges them of the traitor

Judas was the weak link and so Jesus reveals his treachery and forces him out before the actual event. Had he stayed he could have led them to disbelief and total abandonment or turned them all in to the Jewish leaders after His death.

3. He prophesizes concerning His death and resurrection

So they will not be caught by surprise, He tells them in advance that He will be killed and eventually resurrect. When the deed is done He wants them to be assured that He is still in control: He predicted it.

4. He promises to take care of them

- He promises to send the Holy Spirit to comfort them in their sorrow and provide the support that usually came from Him.

- He promises to send the Spirit to help them remember and understand all the things He taught them.

- He promises that Satan's attack on Him will fail. (Don't worry, don't be afraid.)

- He promises that He and the Father will be with them as they love each other and obey His word.

These promises are all included in the first teaching or dialogue section we studied in the previous chapter. In this chapter (John chapter 15) we begin the second part of Jesus' long teaching section that takes place just before His death.

Jesus' final teaching and encouragement

In the previous section we learned that Jesus and the Apostles are in the upper room having shared the Passover, and although John does not mention it, the Lord's Supper is instituted as well. In this setting Jesus has been teaching and encouraging them. Before, His teaching was interrupted by questions from the Apostles, but having answered these, He now goes on for a long stretch without any comments from His disciples.

In chapter 15 He touches on three subjects not directly related to the cross, but rather how they should act because of the cross of Christ.

1. They should bear fruit – 15:1-11

Jesus has already taught them concerning obedience along with love, is the response of faith that He requires. In chapter 15 He explains in detail the blessings and the curses attached to one's obedience or disobedience.

> Vs. 1-2 – "I am the true vine, and My Father is the vinedresser. Every branch in Me that does not bear fruit, He takes away; and every branch that bears fruit, He prunes it so that it may bear more fruit.

These two first verses summarize the entire eleven verses that address this subject. This is an allegory (the use of imagery to make a point in concrete terms). For example: Jesus = real; vine = image; Father = real; vinedresser = image.

Jesus uses many of these "I AM" allegorical statements in order to make a concrete point:

- "I am the bread of life" (John 6:48)
- "I am the light of the world" (John 8:12)
- "I am the door" (John 10:7)
- "I am the good shepherd" (John 10:11)
- "I am the way, the truth and the light" (John 14:6)

Here the imagery is that of a vine and its fruit, a common sight in Israel. Jesus says that He is the true vine meaning the "real" vine, the original vine upon which all of the others are patterned in design and function. He also says that the Father does the work of pruning that vine. Jesus bears the fruit; the Father harvests the good and removes the unproductive. The disciples are the branches that are connected to the vine. The fruit is what the disciples produce because of their relationship to Jesus.

In Galatians Paul tells us that "fruit" produced in the disciples' lives through the Holy Spirit include love, joy, peace, patience, kindness, goodness, faithfulness, gentleness, self-control: "the fruit of the Spirit."

In the summary statement Jesus explains the following ideas:

1. He is the only vine that produces this kind of fruit. There are other vines but only He is the true vine.

2. You must be connected to Him in order to become a fruit-bearing branch of this kind.

3. God the Father is active in either pruning for growth or cutting away the dead wood.

4. You either produce fruit, in which case you are pruned in order to allow more growth; or you do not produce, then you are cut away altogether.

> Vs. 3-11 – You are already clean because of the word which I have spoken to you. Abide in Me, and I in you. As the branch cannot bear fruit of itself unless it abides in the vine, so neither can you unless you abide in Me. I am the vine, you are the branches; he who abides in Me and I in him, he bears much fruit, for apart from Me you can do nothing. If anyone does not abide in Me, he is thrown away as a branch and dries up; and they gather them, and cast them into the fire and they are burned. If you abide in Me, and My words abide in you, ask whatever you wish, and it will be done for you. My Father is glorified by this, that you bear much fruit, and so prove to be My disciples. Just as the Father has loved Me, I have also loved you; abide in My love. If you keep My commandments, you will abide in My love; just as I have kept My Father's commandments and abide in His love. These things I have spoken to you so that My joy may be in you, and that your joy may be made full.

After His opening statement the Apostles' first question might have been about their own situation, whether or not they were worthy of being branches attached to Jesus. The Lord reassures them that they are "clean", worthy, purified, a state they have reached because they have believed Jesus' word.

In other words, they are not branches because of their closeness to Jesus, they are branches because they believed

Jesus' word, and have obeyed it. This is what has made them clean.

Jesus emphasizes that if they wish to produce fruit, they must remain part of Him. Jesus then goes on to mention seven specific details concerning the relationship between the vine, the vine-dresser, and the branch:

1. You become a branch by believing and obeying the word of Christ.

2. You remain a branch and produce fruit by continuing to believe and obey the words of Christ.

3. The more you believe and obey, the more fruit you produce.

4. The less you believe and obey, the less you produce and the more you risk being cut away and destroyed.

5. The more you believe and obey, the greater power your prayers have in being answered.

6. The bearing of much fruit glorifies God.

7. The way to a joyful life is to bear much fruit through obedience to Christ's word and the love of others. This will mirror the relationship and joy that Jesus has with the Father. This is how we gain the "experience" of being part of the Godhead because we are in or attached to Christ.

After completing His description and teaching using the imagery of the vine, Jesus picks up on the last idea of "love" and builds another teaching section about what they need to do when He is gone.

2. They should love each other – vs. 12-17

Vs. 12-13 – "This is My commandment, that you love one another, just as I have loved you. Greater love has

> no one than this, that one lay down his life for his friends.

Jesus continues in the style He has used previously. He summarizes the idea and then explains it in detail. Jesus has given them the instruction to love each other several times and in different ways before (i.e. foot washing). The difference this time is that He establishes the ultimate level of love as the laying down of one's life for a friend.

They may not be called upon to do this but the willingness to do so will mark their love as the kind He had for them. We will die instinctively to protect our family, perhaps an ideal. To die for a friend is a willful act, a straight exchange of one life for another.

Although He mentions death and His death was not only for His friends, it was for His enemies also (which makes His love divine), Jesus does not dwell on this idea.

> Vs. 14-15 – You are My friends if you do what I command you. No longer do I call you slaves, for the slave does not know what his master is doing; but I have called you friends, for all things that I have heard from My Father I have made known to you.

Jesus focuses on the word "friends" and brings out the idea that they have become His friends. In reality they are His creation, His slaves, at very best His disciples, but Jesus raises them (and us) to the level of "friends" based on their faith and obedience.

They are friends because they are now privy to the secret, the mystery, the purpose of His coming (His death and resurrection) and how spiritual things work (i.e. bearing fruit, etc.).

> Vs. 16-17 – "You did not choose Me but I chose you, and appointed you that you would go and bear fruit,

> and that your fruit would remain, so that whatever you ask of the Father in My name He may give to you. This I command you, that you love one another."

Their friendship has conditions however. Every friendship does, no matter how laid back it may be. (I.e. keep in touch, be honest and fair, don't mention "touchy" subjects, etc.)

A friendship with Jesus has special conditions but is still a friendship because it yields all the things and more, that a friendship produces: companionship, encouragement, support, joy, communication, edification, etc. All this we receive and give in a relationship with Jesus.

Jesus qualifies the friendship and defines the conditions, this is so because He is God and we are not. For example, when in the military, my daughter was friends with another girl who was a sergeant. In this situation the higher ranking soldier placed limits and defined their friendship because of her higher rank and the orders she was under, but there was still a mutually satisfying friendship that respected these boundaries.

And so Jesus defines the friendship as one where He, as God, chooses us as friends and places the conditions on the friendship: produce fruit, answered prayer in His name, love of the brethren. His conditions for friendship are all those things that will contribute to the friendship: continued spiritual growth, continued dialogue in prayer, continued love in His body.

3. They should persevere in ministry – vs. 18-27

We need to remember that He is preparing them for His departure not only for the three days after the cross, but His eventual departure when He will return to the Father that will take place in forty three days. He must prepare them for what they will face after that departure as well.

> Vs. 18-20 – "If the world hates you, you know that it has hated Me before it hated you. If you were of the world,

> the world would love its own; but because you are not of the world, but I chose you out of the world, because of this the world hates you. Remember the word that I said to you, 'A slave is not greater than his master.' If they persecuted Me, they will also persecute you; if they kept My word, they will keep yours also.

Again Jesus summarizes the entire thought at the beginning of the passage. Essentially He warns them of 5 things:

1. **The world will hate them.** Just in case they thought that by bringing the good news of life eternal and peace, joy and love to the world the world would be happy to hear it.

2. **The world will reject them.** Be prepared for hatred and rejection because this is how they treated ME.

3. **The world will not recognize them.** The hatred and rejection of this world will be due to the fact that they sense you do not belong here (and you don't, you belong to the world to come).

4. **The world will persecute them.** What the world rejects, the world wants to destroy because it is threatening.

5. **The world will not obey the Word.** If they did not obey with the Lord present in all His glory, they will not obey when the same word is preached by mere men.

This is not the case in every instance, but it will be the general rule as the Apostles will begin preaching when He is gone, and He wants them ready for it.

> Vs. 21 – But all these things they will do to you for My name's sake, because they do not know the One who sent Me.

There is a reason why the world will hate, reject, persecute and disobey them and it will have nothing to do with them. This is how the world will react to the truth of the gospel because they have not accepted the Father in the past: the Gentiles are into complete paganism and idolatry; the Jews have hardened their hearts by refusing to accept the One sent by the Father. In either case the offense begins with an offense against the Father.

> Vs. 22-25 – If I had not come and spoken to them, they would not have sin, but now they have no excuse for their sin. He who hates Me hates My Father also. If I had not done among them the works which no one else did, they would not have sin; but now they have both seen and hated Me and My Father as well. But they have done this to fulfill the word that is written in their Law, 'They hated Me without a cause.'

Jesus goes on to say that this rejection of the Father is without excuse. It is without excuse for the Gentiles because, as Paul says, they have a witness of the Father through creation, through conscience and through the Jewish nation. It is without excuse for the Jews because Jesus was among them teaching and performing miracles for three years. It is without excuse because the Word provided warnings about this happening.

To hate Jesus is to hate the Father, and Jesus tells them that the opposition to them because of this even though it might be quite strong, is without basis or excuse.

> Vs. 26-27 – "When the Helper comes, whom I will send to you from the Father, that is the Spirit of truth who proceeds from the Father, He will testify about Me, and you will testify also, because you have been with Me from the beginning.

This warning may shake them and frighten them, but Jesus promises again that He will send the Holy Spirit to be with them. The Spirit will help them in their ministry (bear witness) so they can face all of this opposition without stumbling. There will be difficult and fearful moments when Jesus dies. There will be equally discouraging times when they will have to go out and preach the gospel. Jesus prepares them for these times by encouraging them to continue to bear fruit, continue to love each other and continue to serve in ministry.

Many times when we encounter rejection and discouragement in our faith we tend to retreat and lay low instead of doing what Jesus says we should continue in when there is trouble: be productive, be loving and kind, be useful in service.

25.

JESUS' FINAL TEACHING
PART 3

JOHN 16:1-33

In our study of the book of John we are covering Jesus' lengthy teaching section that occurs while the Lord is sharing the Passover meal on the night before His death.

So far He has washed their feet, revealed the traitor among them, prophesied concerning His death and resurrection, and promised to send them the Holy Spirit. He has also encouraged them to bear spiritual fruit in His absence, love each other as He has them and continue in ministry despite opposition.

In this section Jesus will continue encouraging the Apostles as He reviews with them what will take place in the near future, and this time the Apostles will grasp some of what He is saying.

The warning

Verses 1 to 4 in chapter 16 are merely a continuation of what Jesus was saying in the previous chapter, which we discussed in our last lesson.

> Vs. 1-4 – "These things I have spoken to you so that you may be kept from stumbling. They will make you outcasts from the synagogue, but an hour is coming for everyone who kills you to think that he is offering service to God. These things they will do because they have not known the Father or Me. But these things I have spoken to you, so that when their hour comes, you may remember that I told you of them. These things I did not say to you at the beginning, because I was with you.

The "things" He refers to are that they must bear fruit, love each other and persevere in ministry despite the fact that the world will hate them, reject them, not recognize them, persecute them, disobey the Word, and do all of this because it rejects the Son and the Father who sent Him.

So the warning is given because all these things will happen. Jesus says that He has warned them in advance of these things so they will not stumble (lose faith, begin to doubt, lose their way, fall down spiritually). If they know in advance, they will be prepared for the rough time ahead and not be discouraged to the point of quitting.

In verse 2, unlike the previous one, Jesus describes in more detail how the peoples' rejection of the Christ will affect them personally. Peter said earlier that He would follow Jesus anywhere, now Jesus reveals to Peter and the others the full extent of their suffering in the future. They will be rejected by their countrymen, excommunicated from their religious past, and cut off from their families and communities. They will be martyred, but their killing will be especially difficult for them to bear because they will be executed by those who claim to be doing the God they serve a favor. In other words they will not die as heroes in the eyes of the people.

In verse 3, Jesus repeats the idea that the reason for all of this is because they have rejected both the Father and the Son. Remember, Jesus tells them, it is not about you, it is about Me and the Father. In this they will later find comfort, that their suffering is connected to their faith in Christ.

In verse 4, He also repeats that He is giving them this warning so they will know and be prepared in advance for the hard times ahead. He says that while He was with them there was no need to tell them, but now that they will be alone without Him, they need this knowledge to protect their faith.

Now that His warning is complete, Jesus goes ahead to make four promises to His Apostles.

Four promises

Promise #1
The promise of the Holy Spirit – vs. 5-15

Jesus has mentioned the Spirit before but adds new details in this section concerning His coming.

1. The condition of His coming

> Vs. 5-7 – "But now I am going to Him who sent Me; and none of you asks Me, 'Where are You going?' But because I have said these things to you, sorrow has filled your heart. But I tell you the truth, it is to your advantage that I go away; for if I do not go away, the Helper will not come to you; but if I go, I will send Him to you.

Jesus reviews their reaction to the news of His departure. They are saddened and confused about where He is going. Jesus reassures them concerning His departure saying that His leaving will bring a great blessing to them. Of course, all they can see is that their leader is leaving and the problems this will cause them. What they cannot see, but what Jesus refers to here, is the mighty work He will accomplish with His cross and resurrection and the new power they will have when the Spirit will come to them.

The Holy Spirit can only begin His work in and for the Apostles after Jesus accomplishes His mission. This is why it is advantageous to them and why Jesus must go.

2. The work of the Spirit in the world

> Vs. 8-11 – And He, when He comes, will convict the world concerning sin and righteousness and judgment; concerning sin, because they do not believe in Me; and concerning righteousness, because I go to the Father and you no longer see Me; and concerning judgment, because the ruler of this world has been judged.

Jesus has previously told them that the Holy Spirit would provide them with the spiritual comfort that He (Jesus) Himself had provided them while with them. He also has told them that the Spirit would help them remember His teachings and enable them to remain in fellowship with Himself and the Father, even when not physically present with them.

This time Jesus focuses more on what the Holy Spirit will do (through them) in the world and what His impact on the world will be. Basically the Holy Spirit will convict (comes from a root word meaning to prove with evidence, to find a fault, to convict).

Jesus speaks of the Spirit's work as it is in total. In other words, what the Spirit will accomplish when all is said and done: the cross and resurrection; the Apostles' preaching and establishing of the church; the life of the church until the second coming of Jesus; the judging of the world; and in heaven, the glorification of the church.

Concerning the total of the Holy Spirit's work, Jesus says He will convict the world of three things (convict means to find and prove with evidence a certain fault):

A. Sin

He will show that the world is guilty of the most grievous sin, disbelief. He will spread the gospel everywhere and prove in the end that the majority in the world will have disbelieved.

B. Righteousness

He will show that the world will seek righteousness in other ways besides the only way God has provided it, through the cross of Christ. Jesus mentions the cross in an oblique way (go to the Father, you no longer see Me).

His departure through resurrection and ascension confirm the work and power of the cross to confer forgiveness and righteousness.

The Holy Spirit (by His work through the Apostles) will convict the world of having rejected the avenue to righteousness by the cross in favor of other ways to be right before God.

C. Judgment

The cross engenders belief, produces righteousness and also condemns and binds Satan forever (Hebrews 2:15).

The Holy Spirit will convict the world concerning the sure judgment to come by pointing to the judgment and condemnation of the ruler of this world who has already been judged. In other words, the Holy Spirit will prove there is a judgment and that it will be for sin by bringing the judgment of Satan to the attention of the world. If God had judged this mighty spiritual being for his disobedience, He can and will judge you.

3. The WAY the Spirit will work

In giving details concerning the Holy Spirit, Jesus has said that the Holy Spirit will be given only when His own ministry is completed and He returns to the Father. He has said that the Holy Spirit will work to convict or demonstrate the world's fault concerning sin (disbelief), righteousness (seeking it without

Christ) and judgment (that even with Satan's judgment before them, people still ignore it).

In this section the Lord spells out how the Spirit will do not only His work of convicting but also His work of comforting as well.

> Vs. 12 – I have many more things to say to you, but you cannot bear them now.

Jesus, knowing their limits, does not go into too much detail now. After the passion they will better be able to understand His words.

> Vs. 13 – But when He, the Spirit of truth, comes, He will guide you into all the truth; for He will not speak on His own initiative, but whatever He hears, He will speak; and He will disclose to you what is to come.

The details about what He has just said and the ability to understand it will be the result of His power working in them. Not only what Jesus has said and what it means, but what things are to come in the future. (Peter and John speak of future events and the end of the world in their epistles).

> Vs. 14 – He will glorify Me, for He will take of Mine and will disclose it to you.

Jesus will be glorified through the preaching of His word and the exercising of His power through the Apostles. This will be made possible through the Holy Spirit. This ongoing witness will be what the Spirit uses to convict the world. If no one witnessed the words, power and person of Jesus there could be no conviction, but the witness has been going on for 2000 years and will continue until He returns.

> Vs. 15 – All things that the Father has are Mine;
> therefore I said that He takes of Mine and will disclose it
> to you.

He reassures them now that what they will receive from the Holy Spirit will be directly and completely from Him and that all He has, He has been given by the Father and He has all that the Father has. In other words, this section and the first promise of sending the Holy Spirit ends with another declaration of Jesus' divinity. After all, who else could send the Holy Spirit and have all of what the Father has?

Promise #2
His death and resurrection are imminent
– vs. 16-22

Jesus leaves off His discussion of the Holy Spirit and refocuses them in the very present time of His imminent death and resurrection. Yes, He must first go before He can send the Spirit, and the time of His departure is now.

> Vs. 16 – A little while, and you will no longer see Me;
> and again a little while, and you will see Me.

Jesus makes reference to His death and resurrection saying that both will take place very soon.

> Vs. 17-18 – Some of His disciples then said to one
> another, "What is this thing He is telling us, 'A little
> while, and you will not see Me; and again a little while,
> and you will see Me'; and, 'because I go to the
> Father'?" So they were saying, "What is this that He
> says, 'A little while'? We do not know what He is talking
> about."

The Apostles are speaking among themselves now, not wishing to ask Jesus a direct question. They have had enough bad news and mystery for one night. They are especially curious about the immediacy of what is going to take place. What does He mean by "a little while"?

> Vs. 19-20 – Jesus knew that they wished to question Him, and He said to them, "Are you deliberating together about this, that I said, 'A little while, and you will not see Me, and again a little while, and you will see Me'? Truly, truly, I say to you, that you will weep and lament, but the world will rejoice; you will grieve, but your grief will be turned into joy.

Jesus tells them that what will happen to Him will cause them great sorrow and their adversaries great rejoicing. But their sorrow will be turned to joy. Again, Jesus is describing in advance the effects of His death and resurrection on the world of unbelievers and on them.

> Vs. 21-22 – Whenever a woman is in labor she has pain, because her hour has come; but when she gives birth to the child, she no longer remembers the anguish because of the joy that a child has been born into the world. Therefore you too have grief now; but I will see you again, and your heart will rejoice, and no one will take your joy away from you.

Jesus compares their experience of sorrow and pain followed by joy to that of a woman giving birth to a baby. There is fear, pain and sorrow during labor, but once the baby is born this sorrow is replaced with a joy that overwhelms the pain and sorrow to the point where (after a time) we are willing to go through it again.

Jesus promises that a time of sorrow and pain is coming soon but that it will quickly pass into a joy that will never be taken away.

Promise #3
Their prayers in His name will be answered
– vs. 23-24

Jesus, continuing His teaching, looks ahead to the time when His work on the cross will be complete; His resurrection and ascension also complete; and the Holy Spirit is sent, and He promises one other thing that will take place at that time.

> Vs. 23-24 – In that day you will not question Me about anything. Truly, truly, I say to you, if you ask the Father for anything in My name, He will give it to you. Until now you have asked for nothing in My name; ask and you will receive, so that your joy may be made full.

Until now He has prayed for them, but now He says that they are to pray to God themselves, in His name. And when they do, God will answer their requests.

We must realize that Jesus is speaking to the Apostles concerning the work of the Holy Spirit and their task as witnesses. What they ask, in this context, God will give: Apostles doing miracles, raising the dead, asking to give power to others, asking for wisdom and direction in ministry.

They will see Jesus no more after He is ascended, but their prayers constantly answered in His name will confirm His words and promises, and give them the joy of home (anticipation of their own reward in heaven).

Promise #4
Your faith will be shaken – vs. 25-33

> Vs. 25-28 – These things I have spoken to you in figurative language; an hour is coming when I will no longer speak to you in figurative language, but will tell you plainly of the Father. In that day you will ask in My

name, and I do not say to you that I will request of the
Father on your behalf; for the Father Himself loves you,
because you have loved Me and have believed that I
came forth from the Father. I came forth from the
Father and have come into the world; I am leaving the
world again and going to the Father.

Jesus explains to them that despite their confusion now, they will
understand what will happen and what to pray for more clearly
later. He also encourages them by telling them that because of
their initial belief, the Father loves them. He repeats, once again
in a general way, the sequence of events (He came from the
Father, He was in the world, He now returns to the Father).

Vs. 29-30 – His disciples said, "Lo, now You are
speaking plainly and are not using a figure of speech.
Now we know that You know all things, and have no
need for anyone to question You; by this we believe
that You came from God."

The Apostles, who were whispering their doubts and questions
among themselves before, now openly and loudly claim their
belief in Him. Even though He has spoken in figurative
language, the fact that He knows their questions before they ask
them, and that He has spoken with authority and more clarity
than anyone else, is sufficient for them to confess their belief in
Him. There may be more information and explaining to come
later on, but they have enough now to declare their faith. This is
the last time they will do this before His death.

Vs. 31-33 – Jesus answered them, "Do you now
believe? Behold, an hour is coming, and has already
come, for you to be scattered, each to his own home,
and to leave Me alone; and yet I am not alone, because
the Father is with Me. These things I have spoken to
you, so that in Me you may have peace. In the world

> you have tribulation, but take courage; I have overcome
> the world."

Jesus' answer is surprising in that at this moment when they are confessing their faith He prophesizes about their fall from faith caused by His arrest, torture and death. It is unusual that He uses this failure of faith as a way to build their faith in the future:

1. Do not worry, even though you leave Me, I will not be alone, the Father will be with Me.
2. Remember all of the things (including this prediction of your downfall) so you can believe (or renew your faith) when I am gone.

In the end He encourages them by telling them that even at the darkest hour when He is gone and they are burdened by their own guilt, remember that He has won the victory over sin and death.

Summary

Jesus promises them four things as He finishes His time with them in the upper room:

1. The Holy Spirit after He is gone.
2. The end of His mission soon.
3. The honoring of their prayers in heaven.
4. The downfall and renewing of their faith.

In our next chapter we will cover the last part of Jesus' long teaching section commonly referred to as the "High Priestly" prayer.

26.
JESUS' FINAL TEACHING
PART 4

JOHN 17:1-26

We are studying Jesus and how John portrays Him in his gospel.

Just a reminder that throughout this book John has followed a certain cycle in presenting Jesus as the divine Son of God:

1. First he details the miracles and teachings of Jesus throughout His ministry.

2. Next he records how Jesus challenges His audience and followers to believe in Him as the divine Christ.

3. Then he shows how the people react with belief or disbelief to the words, actions and claims of the Lord.

It has been no different in this last scene where Jesus teaches and encourages His Apostles one last time before His death. Even at this critical moment as He prepares them for His departure, He continues to challenge them to believe in Him, but this time He urges them to keep on believing because His suffering and death as well as their own rejection and persecution will put a lot of pressure on their faith.

He has warned them of the persecution to come and has promised them that the Holy Spirit will be sent to them to comfort, empower, and enable them to carry on the ministry He has charged them with.

Jesus has even given them an overview of what the Holy Spirit will accomplish through them and through their spiritual descendants who will carry forth the word of the gospel until He returns.

In a cryptic way He says that despite their crisis of faith and persecution, the Holy Spirit will convict the world of the sin of disbelief, of seeking to be right with God without the cross of Christ, of failing to prepare for judgment, even after the judgment and condemnation of Satan was made public through the revelation of Scripture. These things the Holy Spirit will accomplish through them and those that follow them in the faith.

Having completed His teaching and encouragement, Jesus, a presider at the Passover and their leader, takes this final opportunity to pray for His Apostles before He is arrested and led away to be killed.

When they leave the upper room and go to the Garden of Gethsemane, He will then pray for Himself and His own struggle, but for now He prays for them and John, an eyewitness, records the prayer said by the Lord.

The High Priestly prayer – 17:1-26

This section has been referred to as the "High Priestly" prayer by David Chytraeus (16th Century Lutheran scholar) because in it Jesus exercises His High Priestly office in taking on the sins of the people and offering up prayer and sacrifice for those sins.

The essential difference, of course, is that Jesus did not need to offer first a sacrifice for His own sins, as Jewish priests needed to do, because He was sinless. Jesus did not offer an animal as sacrifice but rather He was both priest and sacrifice in offering Himself up as an atonement for sin.

Jesus could relate to sinful men as priest because He too bore a human body. As the divine Son of God, however, His prayer was perfect and heard in the throne room of grace because of His perfect righteousness. If the prayer of a righteous man avails much (James 5:16b), then imagine what the prayer of a perfectly righteous God/man can do?

With all of this in mind, let us break this passage down.

For study purposes this chapter/prayer can be divided into three main sections:

- Vs. 1-5 – Prayer concerning Himself and the Father in heaven.
- Vs. 6-19 – Prayer concerning the Apostles at His side.
- Vs. 20-26 – Prayer concerning all future believers.

In this way Jesus prays for Himself and all mankind in these few verses.

1. Jesus' prayer for Himself – vs. 1-5

There are many kinds of prayer (thanks, praise, repentance, lamentation, etc.) but this prayer is one of supplication, of asking. Jesus asks God for various things for Himself, the Apostles and all future Christians.

> Vs. 1 – Jesus spoke these things; and lifting up His eyes to heaven, He said, "Father, the hour has come; glorify Your Son, that the Son may glorify You,

Having finished teaching His Apostles and giving them comfort, the Lord ends their time in the upper room and the Passover meal with a prayer as was custom. He has told them that the time for His departure was near and He repeats this as He opens His prayer.

274 | MIKE MAZZALONGO

The "hour" is not only the time for His death, but the time for all of the things He came to do. These are to be fulfilled in His death, resurrection and ascension.

He asks God to glorify, exalt, lift up the Son so that the Son may do the same for the Father. Jesus will be glorified at this time because it is the hour of His death and especially His resurrection.

- John 20:31 – Resurrection confirms all of His teachings as true. Resurrection confirms all of His claims as true.

- Colossians 1:16 – Resurrection confirms His position over all men and all angels.

The Father is glorified in resurrection.

- Romans 1:4 – Resurrection reveals His power.

- Romans 3:21-26 – Resurrection reveals His righteousness.

- Romans 5:8 – Resurrection reveals His love.

Jesus asks the Father to go through with His plan for His death and resurrection because this will result in glory for both the Father and the Son.

> Vs. 2-3 – even as You gave Him authority over all flesh, that to all whom You have given Him, He may give eternal life. This is eternal life, that they may know You, the only true God, and Jesus Christ whom You have sent.

This moment of glory is not a self-serving action for God. What will take place will be done to serve mankind. As a result of the death and resurrection, forgiveness will be available, and along with that forgiveness will come the righteousness that produces eternal life for the forgiven. The Father and Son will be glorified in their combined effort to grant human beings the gift of eternal life.

Jesus received the authority or power to offer this through His death and resurrection from the Father. He now asks the Father to complete the plan for the good of man.

Jesus also summarizes the experience of eternal life not simply as human life without end but a new kind of life experience, one where a person will have an ongoing knowledge or intimacy (to know) with the true God and His true Son. The Father and Son will be glorified and man will share in that glory as well by His association with them.

> Vs. 4-5 – I glorified You on the earth, having accomplished the work which You have given Me to do. Now, Father, glorify Me together with Yourself, with the glory which I had with You before the world was.

Jesus, once again repeats His request and this time makes a specific reference to His divine nature. He specifies that His glory is connected to His divine nature, before He took on human flesh. His glory will be seen without the interference and limiting handicap of a human nature. This refers ahead to His resurrection and manifestation in His glorified spiritual state before He returned to heaven.

2. Prayer for the Apostles – vs. 6-19

Jesus' prayer for the Apostles is in two sections: how He feels about them and what He wants for them.

A. How Jesus felt about His Apostles

> Vs. 6-10 – "I have manifested Your name to the men whom You gave Me out of the world; they were Yours and You gave them to Me, and they have kept Your word. Now they have come to know that everything You

> have given Me is from You; for the words which You
> gave Me I have given to them; and they received them

> and truly understood that I came forth from You, and
> they believed that You sent Me. I ask on their behalf; I
> do not ask on behalf of the world, but of those whom
> You have given Me; for they are Yours; and all things
> that are Mine are Yours, and Yours are Mine; and I
> have been glorified in them.

Jesus reviews what He knows to be true concerning His Apostles. They were chosen by the Father (they could refuse His choice of them, like Judas did, but they accepted the choice). They were given the words of the Father through Christ. They have received and believed the Father's words concerning Jesus. In doing so they have glorified, exalted, honored Jesus in themselves through their faith.

Because of this, Jesus specifically prays and asks special things for them. He does not ask for the world, but because they believe in Him and have His word, He asks for them. This prayer and its request are born of deep love and affection for His Apostles.

B. What Jesus wants for His Apostles

> Vs. 11 – I am no longer in the world; and yet they
> themselves are in the world, and I come to You. Holy
> Father, keep them in Your name, the name which You
> have given Me, that they may be one even as We are.

As in other places, Jesus summarizes in this verse what He desires for His Apostles and then explains it in the following ones. Jesus is leaving them to return to the Father so He asks the Father to protect them in and by the Word. The term "name" comes from a word that means authority. God's authority and character are synonymous with His Word and these ideas are all rolled into a single word, "name." "Name" and "word" are interchangeable. The knowing, understanding and keeping of God's Word is the basis of unity between the Father and Son.

Jesus prays that the Apostles will be kept from spiritual harm and enjoy the same unity as He does with the Father as they know, understand and obey the Word. We see from this part of the prayer how important the work of the Holy Spirit will be: He leads them to knowing and understanding the Word (John 14:26; 16:13). He enables one to overcome sin, which is disobedience to the Word (Romans 8:13).

> Vs. 12 – While I was with them, I was keeping them in Your name which You have given Me; and I guarded them and not one of them perished but the son of perdition, so that the Scripture would be fulfilled.

While Jesus was physically present He spoke and taught them to obey the Word and as a result the only one lost was one whom the Scriptures foretold would do so. It is not that God forced Judas out, it is that God knew in advance how Judas would react and wrote about it long before as a way of confirming the Scriptures' divine source.

> Vs. 13-16 – "But now I come to You; and these things I speak in the world so that they may have My joy made full in themselves. I have given them Your word; and the world has hated them, because they are not of the world, even as I am not of the world. I do not ask You to take them out of the world, but to keep them from the evil one. They are not of the world, even as I am not of the world."

Whatever interactions concerning their salvation and their safety that the Father and Son may have had to which the Apostles would not know (it was only between the Father and Son), this information is now public (to the world). They can hear for themselves what God the Father and the Son want for them and this knowledge and experience should provide not only comfort but great joy. Jesus bears witness before the Father in heaven that these men are believers: they are not of the world; they are worthy of His care and protection; they share His own rejection and persecution from an unbelieving world.

He does not ask that they go with Him now in a glorious resurrection and ascension a few days hence, they must stay, they have a great work to do. Rather, He asks that they be protected against the wicked schemes of the devil who will certainly try to destroy the young church and its leaders in years to come.

> Vs. 17-19 – Sanctify them in the truth; Your word is truth. As You sent Me into the world, I also have sent them into the world. For their sakes I sanctify Myself, that they themselves also may be sanctified in truth.

To "sanctify" means to set apart for God's exclusive use. Thus the priests in the Old Testament were "sanctified" or set apart for exclusive service to God in the temple.

In verse 17 Jesus summarizes a request He has made and explained before. He asks the Father to "set apart" the Apostles for the exclusive ministry they are to undertake. He asks that this "setting apart" be done through the truth that is God's Word.

We know that Jesus has already promised this and explained how it will happen: through the Holy Spirit.

- John 14:26: He will bring into remembrance.
- John 16:13: He will lead to all truth.
- John 14:16: He will comfort, strengthen and enable.

Jesus separates Himself fully through the cross, resurrection and ascension. In the same way the Holy Spirit will come and set them apart as well through His work in and for them.

Jesus was set apart or commissioned by the Word to bring the Word of God to men; now after He has completed His mission, He sends the Apostles out into the world by the authority of the Word to bring the Word to the World. The same Word that sent and empowered Him will now set apart, send and empower the Apostles through the agency of the Holy Spirit.

3. Jesus' prayer for future disciples – vs. 20-26

Jesus has asked the Father to protect, commission and empower His Apostles to complete their mission as He is about to complete His own. He now looks further into the future and offers a prayer for all those generations of believers who will come after because of the ministry of the Apostles. Here he is praying for us. This is what He asks for.

> Vs. 20-21 – "I do not ask on behalf of these alone, but for those also who believe in Me through their word; that they may all be one; even as You, Father, are in Me and I in You, that they also may be in Us, so that the world may believe that You sent Me.

He prays that the growth and unity of the church will provide an ongoing witness to an unbelieving world. He does not mention it, but the opposite is certainly true: going away from the Word leads us away from God and each other and this makes us ineffective in reaching lost souls.

> Vs. 22-23 – The glory which You have given Me I have given to them, that they may be one, just as We are one; I in them and You in Me, that they may be perfected in unity, so that the world may know that You sent Me, and loved them, even as You have loved Me.

What "glory" did the Father give the Son? It cannot be divine glory because the Son is already God and cannot be added to in any way. The "glory" is the divine presence in a human body, and a divine mission for this body. John says in John 1:14, "And we beheld His glory" in referring to Jesus' bodily presence.

Jesus shared His presence in physical form in order to become one with His Apostles. He became one of them while retaining His divine nature. Through their witness of His physical presence in His ministry of teaching and miracles, His physical death, resurrection and ascension, the Apostles will be able to share this glory with others.

They will be able to share the very real love of God experienced between the Father and Son, with themselves (because God was physically with them) and also with others through their witness. In this way the unity of the Father and Son has been experienced by the Son in human form with the Apostles; and later by the Apostles and other Christians; and finally between Christians themselves.

We all carry a part of Jesus' experience with His Apostles in our relationship with other Christians because we share His Word.

> Vs. 24-26 – Father, I desire that they also, whom You have given Me, be with Me where I am, so that they may see My glory which You have given Me, for You loved Me before the foundation of the world.
>
> "O righteous Father, although the world has not known You, yet I have known You; and these have known that You sent Me; and I have made Your name known to them, and will make it known, so that the love with which You loved Me may be in them, and I in them.

Jesus builds on the idea that disciples share the experience of Him by asking the Father to bring all believers to heaven so they can experience firsthand the divine presence of Jesus. Now we know Him through the writings of the Apostles, then we will know Him from personal experience. We will see what the women and the Apostles and the 500 saw and heard and touched after His resurrection.

Jesus finishes by reiterating that the world knows nothing of the things He has spoken of. He has known, obeyed and shared the Word. He has also shared it with His Apostles. He will share it in the future with them through the power of the Holy Spirit who will shed the knowledge and love of Him within themselves until He comes.

Jesus completes His prayer with the implicit promise that they may not be able to behold His glory soon, but through faith He will be within them to love and comfort them, and not only them but all believers. It will ultimately be this love by and of Christ that will be the strongest bond producing unity.

Summary

Jesus finishes up this teaching and encouragement section by praying:

- That the Father honor and glorify Himself and the Son by going through with His plan to save mankind at the cost of His own life.
- He reaffirms His love for and confirmation of the Apostles' faith and asks God to protect that faith as they go out on their gospel mission.
- The Lord ends with a request that the church grow and maintain its unity until such time that the vision of Christ seen through faith in the Word becomes a reality when Christ exalts the church to be with Him at the right hand of God in heaven forever.

27.
THE PASSION
PART 1

JOHN 18:1-38a

In the previous chapter, we finished studying Jesus' final words of teaching and exhortation before His suffering and death (The Passion). In His teaching and prayer:

1. He promised to send the Holy Spirit to comfort and empower the Apostles in His absence.

2. He prays that God will go through with the plan to save mankind through His death and that this action glorify them both.

3. He expresses love for His Apostles because of their faith and prays that God protect and enable them to do the mission they have been entrusted with.

4. He prays that the love and unity between Themselves based on the Word will extend to the Apostles and all future disciples because of that same Word.

Once completed, Jesus will go across the valley to pray alone in the Garden of Gethsemane and this is where we begin.

Judas' betrayal – 18:1-11

Vs. 1-2 – When Jesus had spoken these words, He went forth with His disciples over the ravine of the Kidron, where there was a garden, in which He entered with His disciples. Now Judas also, who was betraying Him, knew the place, for Jesus had often met there with His disciples.

Having ended the supper the group leaves the safety of the upper room. It would be normal for Jesus to leave the city and cross the valley of Kidron (not very deep or long, about 1 mile and a half) to take the road that led to Bethany on the other side. Bethany is where Mary, Martha and Lazarus lived and where Jesus normally stayed when He was in Jerusalem.

The Garden of Gethsemane was a place where travelers stopped to rest before pushing on the final mile to Jerusalem. You could see the holy city from the garden.

So far it would be normal for the Lord and the Apostles to stop and rest at this halfway point between Jerusalem and Bethany. Perhaps this is why Judas knew where to find Jesus.

Vs. 3-9 – Judas then, having received the Roman cohort and officers from the chief priests and the Pharisees, came there with lanterns and torches and weapons. So Jesus, knowing all the things that were coming upon Him, went forth and said to them, "Whom do you seek?" They answered Him, "Jesus the Nazarene." He said to them, "I am He." And Judas also, who was betraying Him, was standing with them. So when He said to them, "I am He," they drew back and fell to the ground. Therefore He again asked them, "Whom do you seek?" And they said, "Jesus the Nazarene." Jesus answered, "I told you that I am He; so if you seek Me, let these go their way," to fulfill the word which He spoke, "Of those whom You have given Me I lost not one."

Note that John does not give any details concerning Jesus' prayers and dialogue with the Apostles in the garden. These are well covered in Matthew, Mark and Luke. John describes in the simplest of terms Jesus' betrayal and arrest. Judas was accompanied by a mix of Roman soldiers and temple security guards and went to the garden knowing he would find Jesus there. They had lanterns to search the area since it was dark in the garden.

Note that Jesus is the one who steps forward and takes them by surprise by asking them to name who they seek. They are so startled that in backing away they trip and fall. Note also that even in this episode Jesus is asking them to confess who they believe Him to be and they answer, "Jesus the Nazarene," which is this purely human name. They show Him no respect as a teacher or a prophet, certainly not the Lord and Messiah, just Jesus, the man from Nazareth.

Jesus repeats that He is the man they seek and demands that they let the Apostles go, not just for safety's sake but also to fulfill what He Himself had promised them in the past. During His ministry Jesus promised that none except Judas would be lost among His Apostles (John 6:39; 17:12). That they escape now is fulfillment of that promise.

Vs. 10-11 – Simon Peter then, having a sword, drew it and struck the high priest's slave, and cut off his right ear; and the slave's name was Malchus. So Jesus said to Peter, "Put the sword into the sheath; the cup which the Father has given Me, shall I not drink it?"

Peter, showing his misunderstanding of the moment, is ready to fight, ready to start the revolution to usher in the new kingdom, the new order of things. Jesus commands him to stop and in a reference to His prayer in the garden about the cup of suffering

He has agreed to take, Jesus reaffirms His willingness to go to the cross because this is the Father's will. Oh yes, there will be a revolution and a great change, but it will be accomplished by His death and resurrection, not through civil war.

John does not mention it, but in Luke 22:51, Luke says that Jesus touched the man's ear and healed him.

Jesus before the Priests – vs. 12-27

There were three sessions before the High Priests but John reports only one.

1. There is the session before Annas who was the former High Priest and father-in-law to the present High Priest, Caiaphas. John describes this one. Annas had retired but as in many situations with leaders, he kept the title of High Priest and its influence long after he was not officially in power. (I.e. Ex-Presidents still called Mr. President)
2. Annas sent Jesus to his son-in-law Caiaphas, the official High Priest that year, and along with the other leaders of the Sanhedrin, they question Jesus in the late night.
3. Caiaphas convened another early morning meeting at which Jesus was condemned.
4. Jesus was taken to Pilate who at first sent Him to Herod and then later questioned and sent Him to His death on the cross.

In his gospel John only describes the session with Annas and Pilate with a brief mention of Caiaphas.

> Vs. 12-14 – So the Roman cohort and the commander and the officers of the Jews, arrested Jesus and bound Him, and led Him to Annas first; for he was father-in-law of Caiaphas, who was high priest that year. Now Caiaphas was the one who had advised the Jews that it

was expedient for one man to die on behalf of the people.

Between the lines we are made to understand that Annas has been charged with making a preliminary examination, probably to establish charges against Jesus. John mentions Caiaphas' statement to show that the end of this trial was a foregone conclusion.

Vs. 15-18 – Simon Peter was following Jesus, and so was another disciple. Now that disciple was known to the high priest, and entered with Jesus into the court of the high priest, but Peter was standing at the door outside. So the other disciple, who was known to the high priest, went out and spoke to the doorkeeper, and brought Peter in. Then the slave-girl who kept the door said to Peter, "You are not also one of this man's disciples, are you?" He said, "I am not." Now the slaves and the officers were standing there, having made a charcoal fire, for it was cold and they were warming themselves; and Peter was also with them, standing and warming himself.

John shifts the scene to the courtyard where he reveals that Peter and another disciple had followed from a distance. John is probably referring to himself here in the third person, as he has done before.

These events are taking place in spring and it would have been cold in the middle of the night. John records one of the three denials he will make concerning Jesus (again the cycle).

Vs. 19-24 – The high priest then questioned Jesus about His disciples, and about His teaching. Jesus answered him, "I have spoken openly to the world; I always taught in synagogues and in the temple, where all the Jews come together; and I spoke nothing in secret. Why do you question Me? Question those who have heard what I spoke to them; they know what I said." When He had said this, one of the officers standing nearby struck Jesus, saying, "Is that the way You answer the high priest?" Jesus answered him, "If I have spoken wrongly, testify of the wrong; but if rightly, why do you strike Me?" So Annas sent Him bound to Caiaphas the high priest.

Annas, with the title High Priest, is searching for a charge so that Caiaphas can have something to work with when the Sanhedrin is convened (70 elders who ruled with the permission of Rome). This questioning and a meeting of the leaders at night was against the law, but they went ahead with it anyways.

Jesus responds truthfully that what He has taught has been done so openly and anyone who has heard it can give Annas the information he wants. In other words, they had no right, and no need to bring Him bound to an illegal questioning because anything they needed to know was already public record.

This accusation made Annas look foolish and to protect him one of the guards strikes Jesus with his hand (the worst insult for a Jew) in order to silence Him. Note that he does not challenge what Jesus said, he only defends the position and honor of Annas. Also, it was highly irregular for a guard to strike a bound prisoner while he is making a defense. Jesus does not retaliate, He merely forces His attacker to consider his motive for striking Him. Seeing that their questioning was getting them nowhere, Annas and those with him decide to send Jesus on to Caiaphas for a more "official" hearing.

Vs. 25-27 – Now Simon Peter was standing and warming himself. So they said to him, "You are not also one of His disciples, are you?" He denied it, and said, "I am not." One of the slaves of the high priest, being a relative of the one whose ear Peter cut off, said, "Did I not see you in the garden with Him?" Peter then denied it again, and immediately a rooster crowed.

John switches back to pick up the scene in the courtyard with Peter. John records two more denials where Peter's accusers are circling closer to his true identity. With the cock crowing we have another fulfillment of Jesus' word about Peter, as well as an indication of what time it is. Peter had been the first to openly claim his faith in Jesus as the Christ and now he is one of the first to deny Christ openly when the threat of persecution is at hand.

Jesus before Pilate – vs. 28-38a

John does not describe any of the details of the trials before Caiaphas and the leaders, this having been done by the other evangelists (Matthew 26:59-68; Mark 14:55-65; Luke 22:66-71).

As I said, trials at night were illegal and the death sentence could not be pronounced on the same day as the trial; there had to be at least one day intervening. The leaders got around this by having an early morning session in addition to the late night one in order to officially pronounce the death penalty.

Since the Jews were not allowed to carry these out under Roman law, they brought Jesus to the Roman governor in order to convince him to execute Jesus. Roman courts were open from dawn to sunset and so in the early morning (7 – 8 AM) Jesus was brought to Pilate.

> Vs. 28-32 – Then they led Jesus from Caiaphas into the Praetorium, and it was early; and they themselves did not enter into the Praetorium so that they would not be defiled, but might eat the Passover. Therefore Pilate went out to them and said, "What accusation do you bring against this Man?" They answered and said to him, "If this Man were not an evildoer, we would not have delivered Him to you." So Pilate said to them, "Take Him yourselves, and judge Him according to your law." The Jews said to him, "We are not permitted to put anyone to death," to fulfill the word of Jesus which

He spoke, signifying by what kind of death He was about to die.

The Jewish leaders, the guards, other followers and Jesus stand outside the governor's quarters not entering a "Gentile" abode for fear of defilement. They would be ceremoniously unclean and thus unable to participate in some of the remaining Passover activities. *The leaders broke laws to condemn unjustly the Messiah but were not willing to break a ceremonial rule to eat food at the Passover.*

Roman law and trials required accuser and accused to face each other before a Roman judge to argue over the validity of a charge. Pilate as governor serves also as judge and begins the proceedings with a request to know the "charge."

The Jews know that there is no way a Roman judge would consider a case based on Jewish religion so they make a generic charge against Jesus as an "evildoer."

Pilate, refusing to be manipulated, tells them to therefore judge Him according to their law… they do not need him!

Then the Jews come out with their true intention: they are looking for the "death penalty," something only a Roman judge can grant. John inserts an editorial comment here reinforcing the fact that even if Jesus is bound and silent at this point, He has already spoken about this event and foretold of its coming. In other words, Jesus controls even this situation because He called it in advance.

Vs. 33-38a – Therefore Pilate entered again into the Praetorium, and summoned Jesus and said to Him, "Are You the King of the Jews?" Jesus answered, "Are you saying this on your own initiative, or did others tell you about Me?" Pilate answered, "I am not a Jew, am I? Your own nation and the chief priests delivered You to me; what have You done?" Jesus answered, "My kingdom is not of this world. If My kingdom were of this world, then My servants would be fighting so that I would not be handed over to the Jews; but as it is, My kingdom is not of this realm." Therefore Pilate said to Him, "So You are a king?" Jesus answered, "You say correctly that I am a king. For this I have been born, and for this I have come into the world, to testify to the truth. Everyone who is of the truth hears My voice." Pilate said to Him, "What is truth?"

Once Pilate hears of their request for the death penalty, he takes custody of Jesus and brings Him into the Praetorium (courtyard) inside the government complex of buildings. He officially begins the trial with the questioning of Jesus.

Pilate begins with the accusation that could potentially carry the death sentence. To declare oneself a leader or king without Roman approval could lead to execution. Jesus tests Pilate to see if he himself really believes this accusation or if Jesus looks like one who would do this. Pilate is insulted replying that he is the governor and judge, he is not a Jew personally involved in the matter. However he sees that the Jews are out to kill Jesus and he wants to know what they are so worked up about.

The cycle continues as Jesus, this time before this pagan Roman official, proclaims His true nature and position as not being part of this physical world. He is very logical. If He were a king of this world there would be fighting and civil war (which the Jews accuse Him of stirring up to gain favor with the Roman governor). But Jesus knows that Pilate has not had any such reports about Him. The Lord acknowledges the part of the accusation that is true, He is a king, and corrects the part which is not true, He is not a secular or worldly king.

Pilate understands this, but now curious, he asks the Lord to explain more about the type of king He is. He probably expected Jesus to deny the charge, but when He does not, Pilate now wants some clarification.

Jesus proclaims His kingship more fully and in a way that would engage and challenge this pagan before Him. He makes a confession of His true person, a divine king that has come to the world to bring the truth. The invitation to Pilate is to pursue this truth: a truth that every person who seeks the truth will pursue. The question left open to Pilate is, "Are you a truth seeker?"

Pilate's response is so sad because it is missing one little word that would have made all the difference. If he would have said, "What is the truth?" this would have opened the door of his heart to let Jesus plant the seed of the kingdom. But he answered, "What is truth?" which recognized what Jesus was saying, but refused to engage in a discussion about it.

His point was like most educated Romans at the time: skeptical, suspicious and self-serving. The best truth was that which provided opportunity for self. Everybody has a "truth," but can there really be one certain truth?

In our next chapter, we will continue Jesus' public Roman trial before Pilate.

28.
THE PASSION
PART 2

JOHN 18:38b-19:30

In the previous chapter, we studied John's description of Jesus' final days. John focused on the Lord's betrayal by Judas and His trials before the Jewish leaders.

I explained to you that Jesus:

1. First appeared before Annas, the former High Priest and current High Priest's father-in-law, in a preliminary hearing.

2. He was then sent to appear before the official High Priest, Caiaphas, and the Sanhedrin in order to be formally charged and sentenced.

3. Jesus went to Caiaphas twice, once late at night and once early in the morning.

4. Next, the Jews brought Jesus to Pontius Pilate, the Roman governor, in order to persuade him to carry out the death sentence, something the Jews were forbidden by law to do.

5. John does not mention this, but Luke (Luke 23:8-12) notes that Pilate, learning that Jesus is from Galilee, sends Him to stand before Herod (who ruled the northern

section and was in Jerusalem at that moment) and let Herod deal with Him.

6. Herod gets nowhere since Jesus remains silent.

7. Pilate takes custody of Jesus and begins to question Him about His claims, and Jesus in turn begins to question Pilate concerning his faith. It is at this point that Pilate breaks off the conversation and returns to the Jews in order to inform them of his views concerning Jesus and their request to have Him executed.

Pilate has not been moved to believe in Jesus as the king of another world, but he also has not been persuaded to believe the charges brought against Him by the Jews either.

The trial before Pilate – 18:38-19:16

Vs. 38b-40 – And when he had said this, he went out again to the Jews and said to them, "I find no guilt in Him. But you have a custom that I release someone for you at the Passover; do you wish then that I release for you the King of the Jews?" So they cried out again, saying, "Not this Man, but Barabbas." Now Barabbas was a robber.

Pilate really believes that Jesus is innocent of the charges and not subject to death but he does not release Him either, a concession to the Jewish leaders who are pressing him for some type of action.

The other gospel writers provide us with information that at this point Pilate, learning of Jesus' origins in Galilee, decides to send Jesus to be questioned by Herod the Tetrarch of Galilee. Herod was one of the sons of Herod the Great (who was king when Jesus was born). When he died, Herod's kingdom was split up among his sons and Herod Jr. received the portion of land in the north around Galilee to rule over. The term "Tetrarch" is a Greek term that was used by the Romans to refer to one who ruled over a part of a province, as Herod did.

Jesus meets briefly with Herod but nothing is found to Pilate's advantage so Jesus is returned to the Roman governor for further action. It is at this point that Pilate attempts to set Jesus free within a Jewish law or tradition to minimize the negative impact that this might have. He should have simply let him go because he found Him innocent, but Pilate was afraid to do so.

The custom during the Passover season was to present two prisoners and let the people choose one to be freed. The insult to Jesus is that He is innocent and put against a man who is a convicted thief and murderer (Matthew 27:16; Mark 15:7).

Pilate is confident at first that the people will choose Jesus, the popular teacher and healer over this convicted killer. But Pilate cannot help provoking the Jewish leaders by offering Jesus up as "their king." You can imagine the laughter of the Roman soldiers, the anger of the Jewish leaders and the resentment of the people when called on to choose between their "king" and a common criminal.

To his surprise the crowd, well salted with the Jewish leaders' followers, rejecting any defense of Jesus, cry out to save Barabbas. Frustrated in his attempt to free Jesus in this way Pilate will try another course of action.

> Chapter 19, vs. 1-5 – Pilate then took Jesus and scourged Him. And the soldiers twisted together a crown of thorns and put it on His head, and put a purple robe on Him; and they began to come up to Him and say, "Hail, King of the Jews!" and to give Him slaps in the face. Pilate came out again and said to them, "Behold, I am bringing Him out to you so that you may know that I find no guilt in Him." Jesus then came out, wearing the crown of thorns and the purple robe. Pilate said to them, "Behold, the Man!"

Seeing that the Jews are wanting blood, Pilate goes ahead and tortures the Lord. The mocking, the crown of thorns and the robe are an attempt to humiliate and discredit Jesus before the Jews.

After the ordeal with the soldiers, Jesus is led back out, naked (this is how prisoners were scourged) except for the crown of thorns and an old robe (probably one worn by one of the soldiers). Pilate once again pronounces Him innocent and introduces Him in a mocking manner as "...the man." The idea is that they should have no fear of this person who may claim to be a king. The Romans have cut Him down to size and demonstrated that He is only a man.

Pilate has three goals:

1. He does not want to execute a man who is clearly innocent and thus cause a possible uproar with the people.
2. He wants to placate the Jewish leaders who want him to "do something" about this troublemaker.
3. Pilate cannot help insulting and belittling these people that he despises and, who he knows, despise him.

In his mind, torturing and humiliating Jesus and then releasing Him to the Jews will accomplish these three goals.

> Vs. 6-11 – So when the chief priests and the officers saw Him, they cried out saying, "Crucify, crucify!" Pilate said to them, "Take Him yourselves and crucify Him, for I find no guilt in Him." The Jews answered him, "We have a law, and by that law He ought to die because He made Himself out to be the Son of God."
>
> Therefore when Pilate heard this statement, he was even more afraid; and he entered into the Praetorium again and said to Jesus, "Where are You from?" But Jesus gave him no answer. So Pilate said to Him, "You do not speak to me? Do You not know that I have

authority to release You, and I have authority to crucify You?" Jesus answered, "You would have no authority over Me, unless it had been given you from above; for this reason he who delivered Me to you has the greater sin."

His attempt to get the crowd to agree with him in releasing Jesus has failed as they respond to the torture with cries of crucifixion. Pilate again repeats that he finds no basis to execute this person and tells them to do it if they want Him dead so badly. This, of course, is a provocation to the Jews because he and they know that they have no such authority.

But the Jews perceive a weakness in Pilate's reply. He says, "I find no guilt in Him," and the Jews reply that they have a law and by that law He should die. In other words, if you have no law or reason to convict Him, we do, use our law to do the deed.

At this point they reveal the true reason for their desire to have Him executed: His claim to divinity. This startles Pilate because as a pagan he had no belief or understanding of the Jewish Messiah and His claims, but his own background was filled with Roman gods, mythologies, etc. Could this man be one of these? He was skeptic, but Jesus' demeanor and reputation were unusual and this latest revelation by the Jews frightened him. Could he have inadvertently tortured one of the Roman gods that were said to mingle at times with men? If so, what would the gods do to him because of this?

Pilate returns to question Jesus and this time the questioning is more urgent and personal because Pilate himself may be involved. Pilate asks where Jesus is from, he wants more details about His identity but Jesus gives no reply. He has already told him who He is and Pilate has not believed, so further questions are not answered.

Frustrated, Pilate alludes to his power to free or execute Him, hoping that this threat or offer will move Jesus to explain further His identity. Jesus does not expand a person's knowledge of Himself without faith. First, you believe, then you know. Jesus

298 | MIKE MAZZALONGO

responds by commenting on Pilate's perception of his own power. He tells him two things:

1. Pilate does not have the authority over His life, someone else has given him this authority and power. We know that God is the one who permits and appoints secular leaders, good or bad (Romans 13).

2. Even the wrongs he is doing now are secondary to the wrongs committed by the Jews who originally arrested and falsely tried and accused Him.

Jesus answers like a true king and passes judgment on the way these lesser officials have conducted themselves.

> Vs. 12-16 – As a result of this Pilate made efforts to release Him, but the Jews cried out saying, "If you release this Man, you are no friend of Caesar; everyone who makes himself out to be a king opposes Caesar."
>
> Therefore when Pilate heard these words, he brought Jesus out, and sat down on the judgment seat at a place called The Pavement, but in Hebrew, Gabbatha. Now it was the day of preparation for the Passover; it was about the sixth hour. And he said to the Jews, "Behold, your King!" So they cried out, "Away with Him, away with Him, crucify Him!" Pilate said to them, "Shall I crucify your King?" The chief priests answered, "We have no king but Caesar."
>
> So he then handed Him over to them to be crucified.

The end game in Pilate's effort to release Jesus comes into view as the Jews zero in on his own vulnerability. Until this time, their focus has been on Jesus and their desire to have Him executed.

The Jewish leaders have outwitted him in providing all he needs to carry out the execution:

1. They have provided a charge of sedition (claiming that He was a king).

2. They have given him a legal framework to condemn Him since Pilate cannot do it based on Roman law. He can condemn Jesus using their interpretation of Jewish law.

3. They also provide motivation by suggesting that releasing Jesus would be contrary to Caesar's (Pilate's ruler) wish.

4. The Jews finish their assault on Pilate by declaring that in doing this thing he will win their greater loyalty to Rome.

And so against his conscience (3 times found no guilt), the law (innocent are released) and better judgment (fear), Pilate sends Jesus to His death thinking that in doing so he will appease the Jewish leaders, avoid civil turmoil and secure his own position in government. He was Caesar's governor but a riot and sustained complaints about his loyalty to Rome and competence could be a threat to his position.

Another cycle is complete as Jesus with His silence, His words and His demeanor proclaims His identity. This Roman official disbelieves and acts on this disbelief by sending Jesus to an execution that was illegal (not allowed to execute a person found innocent at trial).

The crucifixion – vs. 17-30

Vs. 17-22 – They took Jesus, therefore, and He went out, bearing His own cross, to the place called the Place of a Skull, which is called in Hebrew, Golgotha. There they crucified Him, and with Him two other men, one on either side, and Jesus in between. Pilate also wrote an inscription and put it on the cross. It was written, "JESUS THE NAZARENE, THE KING OF THE JEWS." Therefore many of the Jews read this inscription, for the place where Jesus was crucified was near the city; and it was written in Hebrew, Latin and in

Greek. So the chief priests of the Jews were saying to Pilate, "Do not write, 'The King of the Jews'; but that He said, 'I am King of the Jews.'" Pilate answered, "What I have written I have written."

John does not give a lot of detail concerning the further torture and process of crucifixion, this having been done by the other gospel writers. He actually follows more on his theme of Jesus' identity in describing the on-going debate between the Jewish leaders and Pilate.

Pilate gets the last word by combining what the Jews claimed Jesus to be and what Jesus Himself said about His identity. His intent was to further insult the Jews, their intent was to both kill and discredit Jesus, but in the end what was written in languages for all the world to read was the truth. Here on this cross is: Jesus, the man from Nazareth; Jesus, the Son of God; Jesus the God/Man. Despite the protest of the Jewish leaders, Pilate manages to get the final say and in doing so proclaims the truth that both he and the Jews missed.

Vs. 23-27 – Then the soldiers, when they had crucified Jesus, took His outer garments and made four parts, a part to every soldier and also the tunic; now the tunic was seamless, woven in one piece. So they said to one another, "Let us not tear it, but cast lots for it, to decide whose it shall be"; this was to fulfill the Scripture: "They divided My outer garments among them, and for My clothing they cast lots." Therefore the soldiers did these things.

But standing by the cross of Jesus were His mother, and His mother's sister, Mary the wife of Clopas, and Mary Magdalene. When Jesus then saw His mother, and the disciple whom He loved standing nearby, He said to His mother, "Woman, behold, your son!" Then He said to the disciple, "Behold, your mother!" From that hour the disciple took her into his own household.

There were five pieces of clothing worn by Jewish men: a head covering (turban) to protect from the sun; a tunic which was worn close to the body; a pair of sandals for the feet; a girdle or sash which was worn around the waist to secure a fifth piece which was an outer robe; the loincloth was not valuable and of such nature as to be discarded. It was the custom that the soldiers who carried out executions divide the victim's personal effects between them.

John, along with the women, was an eye witness and says that four soldiers each took one piece of clothing for themselves and rather than tear up and ruin a good quality (seamless) robe, they threw lots for it. The significance of this seemingly unimportant detail is that it fulfilled a prophecy concerning the details of the Messiah's death made by David some 800 years before (Ps. 22:18). Again without a word or gesture, Jesus is proclaiming His identity to those before Him (soldiers and especially Jewish leaders and teachers) and they respond once again with disbelief.

Note that there were 3 Mary's at the scene:

1. Mary, Jesus' mother.

2. Mary, the sister of the Lord's mother and wife of an early disciple Clopas, who many believe to be the brother of Joseph, Jesus' earthly father (two sisters marrying two brothers).

3. Mary from Magdala, a town in Galilee. Jesus cast spirits out of her and she was a faithful disciple.

Jesus arranges for the care of His widowed mother, as is His duty as the eldest son. He leaves her in the care of one who had a special love for Him, now this love will be there to care for His mother. At that moment only one Apostle and friend was near, even His earthly brothers and sisters, who would later believe, were gone. So to John went this special responsibility.

This is not hard for me to understand. When our children were young, even though we had family, our will dictated that in the

302 | MIKE MAZZALONGO

event of our deaths, our children would be cared for by brothers and sisters in the church and not our unbelieving families.

Jesus does the same here in leaving the care of His mother in the hands of the one faithful person who was there at that moment.

> Vs. 28-30 – After this, Jesus, knowing that all things had already been accomplished, to fulfill the Scripture, said, "I am thirsty." A jar full of sour wine was standing there; so they put a sponge full of the sour wine upon a branch of hyssop and brought it up to His mouth. Therefore when Jesus had received the sour wine, He said, "It is finished!" And He bowed His head and gave up His spirit.

All things accomplished, meaning all the things that the Father through the Scriptures foretold that He would do, including this suffering and death on the cross.

The request for wine (even sour wine) enables His parched lips to utter His final words recorded here and in Luke before His death.

Note also that He controls even this portion of the proceedings in that He gave up His spirit, it did not simply leave Him. He had control over His moment of death because of 2 reasons:

1. He had no sin and so death could not overpower Him, He decided when His spirit would leave.

2. He completed all of the things set before Him by the Father and recorded in Scripture, and would not give up the spirit before all of these were accomplished.

With the sacrifice of His perfect life, Jesus fulfilled the requirements of the Law, paid the moral debt for our sins and opened the door to forgiveness for all men based on His sacrifice.

29.
DEATH / BURIAL / RESURRECTION

JOHN 19:31-20:18

In our last chapter, we carefully looked at the final close encounter that Jesus had with an individual before His death. The four authors each reconstruct the time Jesus spends with Pilate and give an account of the Lord's appearances before the Roman governor.

This was the only other Roman (centurion was the first) person Jesus comes in contact with and the clash of the two cultures (Jewish and Roman) is seen in their exchanges. In the end we see Pilate, a victim of his own pride, disbelief, and thirst for power as he is outmaneuvered by the Jewish leaders in sending Jesus, a person he knew to be innocent, to His death.

But the illegal hearings by the Jews and trials with Pilate do allow Jesus one more chance to witness His divinity before both the Jewish and Roman leadership and supply the reason for their own condemnation in the end. You see, it was they who were on trial, they who were being judged by God as the choice to believe or not to believe was presented before them, and they convicted themselves by not believing and as a result sent the Savior to His death.

It is ironic and sad that their disbelief and consequential actions produced the event (Christ's death) that would forever more save those who would believe. This is an example of God's divine economy at work producing a profit from a loss.

Death and burial – Chapter 19:30-42

John's account focuses primarily on the interaction between Jesus, the Jewish leaders and the Roman governor, Pilate. John's purpose is to profile the belief and disbelief expressed before Jesus' witness. He does not, therefore, spend much time describing the torture and death of the Lord. His description of the death of Jesus in verse 30 is given as yet another way to support Jesus' claim of divinity.

A. Jesus' death – vs. 30-37

> Vs. 30 – Therefore when Jesus had received the sour wine, He said, "It is finished!" And He bowed His head and gave up His spirit.

In this verse John claims three things with the death of Christ:

1. That it was the culmination of many things ("It is finished"). The prophecies about His life and work and the purpose for all He did was deliberate and planned out. This was not a fluke or a bad turn of events. It was the goal and all that was supposed to precede it had been completed.

2. That it was a success. All things were completed in the way God had wanted them to be done. Jesus had told His disciples beforehand that this was the reason He had come to die and not to die would have been a failure. His death, although ugly, humiliating, and painful, was the successful end to the life He was sent to live.

3. That He was still in control (He gave up His spirit). I said last week that since He had no sin, no matter how bloodied and bruised He was, no one could take His soul from His body. Jesus, Himself, released His soul from His body to show that He submitted to death for our sakes, but He was not a slave of death like we are. (Even with His death He builds our faith.)

And so, after his brief description of Jesus' moment of death on the cross, John goes on to a more detailed description of His burial.

> Vs. 31-34 – Then the Jews, because it was the day of preparation, so that the bodies would not remain on the cross on the Sabbath (for that Sabbath was a high day), asked Pilate that their legs might be broken, and that they might be taken away. So the soldiers came, and broke the legs of the first man and of the other who was crucified with Him; but coming to Jesus, when they saw that He was already dead, they did not break His legs. But one of the soldiers pierced His side with a spear, and immediately blood and water came out.

The Jewish law required that those who had been executed needed to be removed before sundown so as to not pollute the land. The Romans normally left their victims to rot on their execution crosses as a visual reminder of their brutality and as a warning to others. The Jewish leaders ask Pilate to accommodate them in speeding up the death process by breaking the legs of the victims so that they can be removed. They were on the eve of the Passover and could not begin their preparations before the bodies were out of the sight of the general population.

Pilate quickly agrees, wanting the matter to be over. The orders are passed on and the two other criminals have their legs broken but, as we already know, Jesus is dead and so the soldiers do not bother breaking His legs. Instead, to assure themselves of His death they pierce Him with a spear and John notes that blood and water come out of His side. Much has been written about the medical or symbolic nature of this blood and water. This may be interesting, but John notes in his book that the significance of these events lay in the fact that these things happened as a fulfillment of Scripture.

> Vs. 35-37 – And he who has seen has testified, and his testimony is true; and he knows that he is telling the truth, so that you also may believe. For these things came to pass to fulfill the Scripture, "Not a bone of Him shall be broken." And again another Scripture says, "They shall look on Him whom they pierced."

John repeats the theme of his book, that the events that have taken place, even those events taking place concerning the mutilation of His lifeless body, are a source of witness for our faith. In this case, the sparing of His bones and piercing of His side, a fulfillment of prophecy concerning the Messiah and His treatment at the hands of others (Exodus 12:46; Zechariah 12:10). All of this is made even more unusual because the soldiers disobeyed a direct order from the governor in not breaking His legs and spearing Him instead. Their action fulfilled God's plan. John points to this as yet another witness of God's divine act in sending Jesus.

B. Jesus' burial – vs. 38-42

After the gruesome events at the cross, John switches scenes and introduces the characters that buried the Lord.

> Vs. 38 – After these things Joseph of Arimathea, being a disciple of Jesus, but a secret one for fear of the Jews, asked Pilate that he might take away the body of Jesus; and Pilate granted permission. So he came and took away His body.

Joseph of Arimathea was part of the Jewish council, Sanhedrin (Luke 23:51), but who was opposed to their actions and who secretly believed. Prisoners who were executed were taken down and thrown into a common felon's grave. The Romans would allow the families of prisoners to bury them upon request, however no such request was made by Jesus' family.

Joseph sets aside his fear and goes to Pilate to request the body. This could not be kept secret for very long and Joseph would be revealed as a disciple for this act.

This action on Joseph's part also fulfills another prophecy about Jesus, that He would be buried with the rich (Isaiah 53:9). Joseph, as a leader in Israel, was wealthy and by placing Him in his own tomb Jesus was buried in a rich man's grave and not the poor criminal's common grave.

We also see the cycle of faith turning again as Joseph, one of the Jewish leaders, breaking with his fellow Jews to express his faith in Christ, even at His death! This was great faith indeed because the Lord is now dead. It would have been easier to disbelieve at this point than to believe.

> Vs. 39 – Nicodemus, who had first come to Him by night, also came, bringing a mixture of myrrh and aloes, about a hundred pounds weight.

Nicodemus, also of the Sanhedrin, also a secret disciple, screws up his courage and steps forward along with Joseph to provide the spices for burial. Joseph brought the linen wraps and Nicodemus the spices. This suggests they knew and agreed on each other's participation. The weight of the spices, the position of the buriers and the quality of the grave show that Jesus had a king's burial.

> Vs. 40-42 – So they took the body of Jesus and bound it in linen wrappings with the spices, as is the burial custom of the Jews. Now in the place where He was crucified there was a garden, and in the garden a new tomb in which no one had yet been laid. Therefore because of the Jewish day of preparation, since the tomb was nearby, they laid Jesus there.

Joseph and Nicodemus receive the body from the Romans and bring it to Joseph's family burial place located in a garden nearby. Burial places were carved out of hillsides or caves, unlike today where we bury in the ground. It was a new tomb where the rock was carved out to produce a chamber in the side of a hill. Usually, for a rich man's tomb, they would also carve a mantle and door facades on the top and sides of the entrance. A "round" stone like a wheel was carved and placed before the entrance to the tomb. It was rounded so it could be rolled away to place more bodies in the tomb later on when necessary.

It was too late in the day to complete the burial process (perfume the body, etc.) so they laid the body in the tomb and intended to come back and finish after the Sabbath. And so Jesus, even with His lifeless body, evokes a response from those who come near Him to believe or disbelieve, even in the way they react to His dead body.

The resurrection – 20:1-18

None of the gospel writers describe the actual resurrection because there are no witnesses. Jesus was quickened from the dead and silently left the tomb through its walls in His resurrected state.

Matthew talks about an earthquake and an angel rolling away the stone, but this was after the fact and done to witness the completed deed.

John spends little time describing the scene and focuses on the reaction of the women and their witness to the Apostles and the Apostles' reaction to the empty tomb.

> Vs. 1-2 – Now on the first day of the week Mary Magdalene came early to the tomb, while it was still dark, and saw the stone already taken away from the tomb. So she ran and came to Simon Peter and to the other disciple whom Jesus loved, and said to them,

"They have taken away the Lord out of the tomb, and we do not know where they have laid Him."

Joseph and Nicodemus were probably coming later in the day to prepare the body but the women, including Mary Magdalene, came at dawn. There were several women but John focuses on the experience of only one. By this time Jesus has risen, the earthquake has rumbled, an angel has rolled the stone away and the soldiers guarding the place have run away in fear.

The women note the empty tomb and Mary Magdalene goes to tell the Apostles that someone has taken away the Lord's body.

Vs. 3-10 – So Peter and the other disciple went forth, and they were going to the tomb. The two were running together; and the other disciple ran ahead faster than Peter and came to the tomb first; and stooping and looking in, he saw the linen wrappings lying there; but he did not go in. And so Simon Peter also came, following him, and entered the tomb; and he saw the linen wrappings lying there, and the face-cloth which had been on His head, not lying with the linen wrappings, but rolled up in a place by itself. So the other disciple who had first come to the tomb then also entered, and he saw and believed. For as yet they did not understand the Scripture, that He must rise again from the dead. So the disciples went away again to their own homes.

Peter and John rush to the tomb to verify what she has said. Peter gets there last but enters first and what he sees are two signs of resurrection:

1. The wrappings are there exactly as they had been placed around the body. If the body had been stolen, the wrappings would have been kept not stripped off. In John's description the wrappings form an empty shell as if someone had passed through them.

2. The handkerchief placed over the face was not taken or thrown down but carefully folded and placed in a corner, all done purposefully.

Note that what John is describing here is his and Peter's coming to faith in an "after the fact" way. They both knew but did not grasp (understand) the Scriptures that said that the Messiah would rise from the dead (Ps. 16:10). They had both acknowledged their faith in Him as Messiah, but with the crucifixion their faith had waned (even though the Scriptures and the Lord said He had to die, they did not believe it would happen). Now with the evidence of the resurrection before them they realize that all of it was true and that their faith had been so small.

John explicitly says that, "…he saw and he believed", placing himself in the company of Thomas. That he and Peter part company without joy or enthusiasm and return to their own homes shows that they are stunned into silence by the event and their own personal failure to remain believing throughout the entire ordeal.

It is not that they were completely disbelieving like the Jews, it is that their faith, which they thought to be so strong, was tested and found to be lacking. (i.e. Peter ready to die for the Lord (John 13:37), John ready to be at the right or left of the Lord in His kingdom (Matthew 20:21).

The proof of the resurrection at the tomb brought this home to them and humbled them to silence as the truth of the moment sank in. The feeling in today's culture would be expressed by saying "It is really true!"

> Vs. 11-13 – But Mary was standing outside the tomb weeping; and so, as she wept, she stooped and looked into the tomb; and she saw two angels in white sitting, one at the head and one at the feet, where the body of Jesus had been lying. And they said to her, "Woman, why are you weeping?" She said to them, "Because they have taken away my Lord, and I do not know where they have laid Him."

Meanwhile, Mary is still under the impression that someone has actually stolen the body. Peter and John have silently slipped away and she remains. She now looks into the tomb and sees the angels who she questions after they address her. She thinks they will help her find the corpse.

> Vs. 14-15 – When she had said this, she turned around and saw Jesus standing there, and did not know that it was Jesus. Jesus said to her, "Woman, why are you weeping? Whom are you seeking?" Supposing Him to be the gardener, she said to Him, "Sir, if you have carried Him away, tell me where you have laid Him, and I will take Him away."

At this point Jesus Himself appears to her asking the same question as the angels and she answers in the same way. In her sorrow she recognizes neither the nature of the angels nor the person of Jesus whom she thinks to be the gardener and asks if perhaps he might know where the body is so she can properly prepare and bury it.

> Vs. 16-18 – Jesus said to her, "Mary!" She turned and said to Him in Hebrew, "Rabboni!" (which means, Teacher). Jesus said to her, "Stop clinging to Me, for I have not yet ascended to the Father; but go to My brethren and say to them, 'I ascend to My Father and your Father, and My God and your God.'" Mary Magdalene came, announcing to the disciples, "I have seen the Lord," and that He had said these things to her.

We see Jesus break through her grief by simply calling her name, and this personal address opens her eyes to see who is truly addressing her. Her response, Rabboni, which was a Galilean form of the word Rabbi (Mary was from the north) shows that she recognizes Him. Rabboni means "my master" or "Lord" and was used as a title of respect for Jewish teachers.

This response is accompanied by Mary's joyful and relieved clinging to the Lord. This would probably be her clinging to His lower legs or feet as an act of enthusiastic and heartfelt worship. She thought He was gone but He is there alive and she clings to him in relief, not wanting to lose Him again.

Many see Jesus' response as harsh or impatient when it is actually one of encouragement and revelation. Jesus is reassuring her that she will not lose Him, there is no need to cling to Him. As a matter of fact He will be closer to her in the future than He ever was (Holy Spirit). He tells her that He has not yet ascended to the Father (He will not leave her right away, she will see Him again, she can let go). She needs to compose herself and go tell His "brethren." This term was meant as a word of encouragement to the Apostles who must be feeling badly about their small and failing faith. She is to tell them that they may have missed the resurrection, but if they come to Him they will witness the last step of His earthly ministry, and that is His visible bodily ascension to heaven.

John recounts that Mary followed the Lord's instructions and sought out the Apostles to announce to them the good news of the resurrection. In this we see, among others, two interesting points:

1. God gives the privilege of seeing and announcing the resurrection to a woman which is a high honor and indication of His love for women.

2. Another example of the cycle of miracle and belief. Mary looked at the angels and did not recognize them; looked at Jesus and did not recognize or believe her eyes at first. When He called her name, she finally believed what was before her.

Today, through the Word, many see the miracle of the resurrection and are called through the gospel, but not all respond with faith to the risen Jesus like Mary did.

30.
APPEARANCES TO THE APOSTLES

JOHN 20:19-21:25

In our last chapter we looked at John's description of the Lord's death, burial and resurrection. We noticed that he spent little time describing the details of these things focusing rather on the reaction of various individuals to these events.

- Pilate who condemned Him.

- The soldiers who tortured and mutilated His body and in so doing fulfilled prophecy.

- Joseph and Nicodemus who buried Him.

- Mary Magdalene who was the first disciple to discover the empty tomb after His resurrection.

- Peter and John who were the first Apostles to see the evidence of His resurrection at the empty tomb.

- And once again, Mary Magdalene who returned to the tomb and was the first to actually see and speak to Jesus after His resurrection.

John examines all of these as he describes their varying degrees of faith as they witness and are affected by every stage of the Lord's death, burial and resurrection.

As we pick up John's gospel in chapter 20:19, we will see how John describes Jesus' actual appearance and interaction with His Apostles after His resurrection.

Three appearances

The Bible records at least eleven appearances by Jesus after His resurrection:

1. Appearance to Mary Magdalene
(Mark 16:9-11; John 20:11-18)

2. Appearance to the other women with her
(Matthew 28:8-10; Mark 16:8)

3. Appearance to Peter
(Luke 24:34; I Cor. 15:5)

4. Appearance to two disciples on the road to Emmaus (Luke 24:34)

5. Appearance to the Apostles without Thomas
(Mark 16:14; Luke 24:36; John 20:19-23)

6. Appearance to the Apostles with Thomas
(John 20:24-29)

7. Appeared to the Apostles by the Sea of Galilee
(John 21:1-24)

8. Appearance to the Apostles on the mountain to give the great commission
(Matt. 28:16-20; Mark 16:15-18; I Cor. 15:7)

9. Appearance to 500 and James
(I Cor. 15:6-7)

10. Appearance to the Apostles at the moment of His ascension
(Mark 16:19; Luke 24:50-53; Acts 1:9-12)

11. Appearance to Paul the Apostle after His ascension
(I Cor. 15:8)

These may not be the only appearances, but they are the only ones that the Bible records. John in his final chapters only chooses to describe 4 of the 11 appearances, and then makes a few summary statements to end his gospel.

Jesus appears to the Apostles 20:19-23

John has already described Jesus' first appearance to Mary Magdalene and now switches the scene to the Apostles. In the meantime, the Lord has appeared to the other women, and privately to Peter.

> Vs. 19-20 – So when it was evening on that day, the first day of the week, and when the doors were shut where the disciples were, for fear of the Jews, Jesus came and stood in their midst and said to them, "Peace be with you." And when He had said this, He showed them both His hands and His side. The disciples then rejoiced when they saw the Lord.

Note that even if the Apostles knew about the resurrection from the reports of the women, Peter, and the disciples from Emmaus, they were still frightened and confused, holding up in locked quarters. They feared being killed by the Jews in the same way their leader was. If He could be killed, how could they survive? Note also that Peter is not able to calm their fears, even with the news and proof of Christ's resurrection.

Jesus simply appears among them. He is no longer limited by human weakness and now demonstrates the power of His glorified state.

He greets them with a common greeting, but coming from Him a greeting that means so much more. His appearance will truly bring peace to their troubled hearts. They are convinced it is He and not a ghost or some hallucination or dream when He shows them the scars on His hands and side. This is the first time they rejoice, they did not at the news given to them by the others concerning the resurrection.

> Vs. 21-23 – So Jesus said to them again, "Peace be with you; as the Father has sent Me, I also send you." And when He had said this, He breathed on them and said to them, "Receive the Holy Spirit. If you forgive the sins of any, their sins have been forgiven them; if you retain the sins of any, they have been retained."

In these verses, Jesus does three important things:

1. He commissions them on behalf of the Father to continue His work of calling all men to God.

2. He gives them the Holy Spirit to dwell within them thus fulfilling His promise to them in chapter 16. They had already been baptized to fulfill God's command through John the Baptist, now that Jesus is risen they receive the gift of the Holy Spirit. After they begin to preach the gospel, those who respond will receive the same gift of the Holy Spirit from Jesus in the waters of baptism (Acts 2:38).

3. He grants them the authority to carry out the great commission. Through their preaching and teaching, sin will be forgiven or retained depending on the response of the hearers.

The appearance to Thomas – vs. 24-29

The next appearance occurs a week later, to the Apostles again but this time with Thomas present.

> Vs. 24-25 – But Thomas, one of the twelve, called Didymus, was not with them when Jesus came. So the other disciples were saying to him, "We have seen the Lord!" But he said to them, "Unless I see in His hands the imprint of the nails, and put my finger into the place of the nails, and put my hand into His side, I will not believe."

John explains Thomas' reluctance to believe. His disbelief does not drive him to sin or to abandon his fellow Apostles. He merely sets conditions on God before he will completely accept the news of Christ's resurrection. "I will believe it when I see it."

> Vs. 26-29 – After eight days His disciples were again inside, and Thomas with them. Jesus came, the doors having been shut, and stood in their midst and said, "Peace be with you." Then He said to Thomas, "Reach here with your finger, and see My hands; and reach here your hand and put it into My side; and do not be unbelieving, but believing." Thomas answered and said to Him, "My Lord and my God!" Jesus said to him, "Because you have seen Me, have you believed? Blessed are they who did not see, and yet believed."

Jesus appears again and provides the proof Thomas requires. He admonishes Thomas and encourages him to believe. Thomas shows his belief by declaring his faith and worshipping Jesus. This is another way of demonstrating our faith, by worshipping the Lord.

In His response the Lord admonishes Thomas because he refused to believe based on the sight and witness of others (the women, Peter, the disciples from Emmaus, the other Apostles), he wanted to see for himself.

While Jesus was with them this was possible and the Lord graciously granted Thomas' demand, such is the Lord's love and mercy. However, in the future, faith would be based on the sight and witness of others (the Apostles and their writings) and Jesus pronounces a blessing on those who would believe in this way. Thomas was there, he saw, but the blessing Jesus pronounces does not include him, only those, like us, who believe without seeing.

Conclusion and Summary #1 – 20:30-31

> Vs. 30-31 – Therefore many other signs Jesus also performed in the presence of the disciples, which are not written in this book; but these have been written so that you may believe that Jesus is the Christ, the Son of God; and that believing you may have life in His name.

John ends his gospel, for all intents and purposes, in verse 29. He ends it with a proclamation of faith from one who has seen the evidence before him. One last example of the cycle of faith we have seen repeated over and over again in his gospel.

His first closing, therefore, is a summary statement that describes what the purpose of his book was. The things written in this book are only a portion of the miracles, teachings, events in the life of Jesus, but they have been recorded as a witness to bring the reader into the cycle of faith. All the stories of faith or disbelief lead up to asking the reader himself to decide if he or she will be counted among the believers or the disbelievers.

Appearance to the Apostles by the sea – 21:1-24

In chronological order this would be the seventh time Jesus appeared but John selects this as his third example. It is unusual that after his concluding and summary statement John would add another description of Jesus' interaction with the Apostles after his resurrection. Some scholars say that this chapter was added by someone else at another time. Biblical research shows, however, that no copies of John's gospel have ever been found without the 21st chapter. This means that it has always been in this format. John, then, is the author of chapter 21 but the manner in which it was written may have varied from the first 20 chapters. We will discuss this later. Chapter 21 could be considered an "epilogue," the part that comes after the main story.

Vs. 1 – After these things Jesus manifested Himself again to the disciples at the Sea of Tiberias, and He manifested Himself in this way.

John sets the scene and the event that will take place. Note that Jesus appears in Jerusalem, in Galilee and in between; to women, to men, to individuals, groups, indoors, outdoors, night and day over a period of 40 days. Unlike other religious leaders or prophets where there is just one appearance and it is usually to only one person in a secluded spot. Jesus appears everywhere to many.

Vs. 2-3 – Simon Peter, and Thomas called Didymus, and Nathanael of Cana in Galilee, and the sons of Zebedee, and two others of His disciples were together. Simon Peter said to them, "I am going fishing." They said to him, "We will also come with you." They went out and got into the boat; and that night they caught nothing.

The Apostles are still together but are waiting for the next step in their ministry: they have seen the Lord and they have received the indwelling of the Holy Spirit. Peter is agitated, impatient with all of this waiting so he decides to go back to the familiar task of fishing. They may have needed money or food because their supporters may have gone into hiding after the crucifixion. A familiar scene begins to develop as they fish all night and catch nothing.

Vs. 4-6 – But when the day was now breaking, Jesus stood on the beach; yet the disciples did not know that it was Jesus. So Jesus said to them, "Children, you do not have any fish, do you?" They answered Him, "No." And He said to them, "Cast the net on the right-hand side of the boat and you will find a catch." So they cast, and then they were not able to haul it in because of the great number of fish.

Jesus again appears and calls out to them regarding their catch and they respond to Him by trying the other side of the boat. The miracle is instantaneous as a full catch is made on the other side of the boat.

> Vs. 7-8 – Therefore that disciple whom Jesus loved said to Peter, "It is the Lord." So when Simon Peter heard that it was the Lord, he put his outer garment on (for he was stripped for work), and threw himself into the sea. But the other disciples came in the little boat, for they were not far from the land, but about one hundred yards away, dragging the net full of fish.

Much like Mary Magdalene whose grief and anxiety kept her from recognizing the Lord, Peter's focus on the task at hand prevents him from recognizing the Lord until John points Him out. Peter's enthusiasm cannot wait for the boat as he plunges into the sea to make his way to the shore. The others follow in not wanting to lose the catch.

> Vs. 9-11 – So when they got out on the land, they saw a charcoal fire already laid and fish placed on it, and bread. Jesus said to them, "Bring some of the fish which you have now caught." Simon Peter went up and drew the net to land, full of large fish, a hundred and fifty-three; and although there were so many, the net was not torn.

They had caught fish but Jesus already had a fire going with fish and bread prepared for them! The better translation of what Jesus says to them is, "…before you eat with Me, go take care of the fish you have caught."

They have caught a lot of fish that are not yet sorted. Their breakfast is cooking so Jesus tells them to take care of the catch. They do so and after the smaller or inedible fish are thrown back in, 153 fish are kept. There is no symbolism in the number of fish. John provides these small details to complete the vividness of the scene, the very real and natural activity that was taking place in an extraordinary moment. A regular fishing trip and a regular breakfast with a regular group except that Jesus, the resurrected Lord, is present. In other words, the event is extraordinary but not bizarre or dreamlike.

> Vs. 12-14 – Jesus said to them, "Come and have breakfast." None of the disciples ventured to question Him, "Who are You?" knowing that it was the Lord. Jesus came and took the bread and gave it to them, and the fish likewise. This is now the third time that Jesus was manifested to the disciples, after He was raised from the dead.

John continues his very matter-of-fact like description of a very special moment as the Apostles sit quietly eating the food Jesus has prepared for them. They know who He is and how exceptional this all is and John adds that this is Jesus' third appearance to them as a group. John is the only gospel writer to describe all three appearances of Jesus to the Apostles as a group without other people present: without Thomas, with Thomas, and near the Sea of Galilee.

> Vs. 15-17 – So when they had finished breakfast, Jesus said to Simon Peter, "Simon, son of John, do you love Me more than these?" He said to Him, "Yes, Lord; You know that I love You." He said to him, "Tend My lambs." He said to him again a second time, "Simon, son of John, do you love Me?" He said to Him, "Yes, Lord; You know that I love You." He said to him, "Shepherd My sheep." He said to him the third time, "Simon, son of John, do you love Me?" Peter was grieved because He said to him the third time, "Do you love Me?" And he said to Him, "Lord, You know all things; You know that I love You." Jesus said to him, "Tend My sheep.

We know that Jesus has already appeared to Peter alone (Luke 24:34; I Cor. 15:5) but have no information on that meeting. Since Jesus has already included him among the faithful Apostles when He told the women to "…tell His disciples and Peter" (Mark 16:7), we can surmise that Peter received forgiveness for his sin of denial at that time. He was also with the Apostles when Jesus appeared and gave them the Holy Spirit and authorized them to go into the world as Jesus was sent into the world (John 20:19-23).

This dialogue between them, therefore, was recorded to publicly restore him, confirm his apostleship and ministry, and acknowledge his repentance and approval by the Lord. He does this by asking three questions:

Question #1: Do you love Me more than these?

This is a reference to his former boasting self ("I am ready to die for you"), a claim that his love was superior to the other Apostles. Jesus asks, "Is your love still greater than these?"

Answer #1: Peter, humbled by his past failures, answers more in line with the truth. The Lord knows the extent of his love. He no longer claims any more than what the Lord knows to be true. To this more honest and realistic response Jesus gives him the commission of pastoral leadership. This does not make Peter the leader of the Apostles; he is not to feed the other Apostles, he is to lead and feed the flock (believers) like the other Apostles. They had not betrayed Jesus as he had done, they did not need to be restored to their apostolic role as he did.

Question #2: Do you love Me?

This time there is no comparison to others. After all that has happened (the denials) do you really love Me? Peter's actions were not born of love, but out of fear and self-preservation.

Answer #2: Peter answers in the same way, putting his confidence in Jesus and the Lord's ability to see Peter's heart, knowing that the love he does have is true. Jesus builds on this to point Peter again to the flock directing him to invest his love of

Jesus into the care of the flock. In other words, this is how you will prove your love for Me: take care of My sheep. The first command redirects Peter to his task, the second gives him the motivation for it.

Question #3: Jesus asks a third time about his love.

Answer #3: Peter's anguish is based on the fact that this third question makes clear the purpose for all the questions, and that is to purge the three previous denials in a public way. Peter left the circle of the apostleship with three categorical denials of the Lord. Jesus reinstates him publicly with three affirmations of love, and confidence that Jesus knows his heart. The Lord finishes again with an admonition to care even for the smallest and weakest of His flock. Now that Peter knew about failure, weakness and total dependence, he was ready to care for these same souls within the family of God.

> Vs. 18-24 – Truly, truly, I say to you, when you were younger, you used to gird yourself and walk wherever you wished; but when you grow old, you will stretch out your hands and someone else will gird you, and bring you where you do not wish to go." Now this He said, signifying by what kind of death he would glorify God. And when He had spoken this, He said to him, "Follow Me!" Peter, turning around, saw the disciple whom Jesus loved following them; the one who also had leaned back on His bosom at the supper and said, "Lord, who is the one who betrays You?" So Peter seeing him said to Jesus, "Lord, and what about this man?" Jesus said to him, "If I want him to remain until I come, what is that to you? You follow Me!" Therefore this saying went out among the brethren that that disciple would not die; yet Jesus did not say to him that he would not die, but only, "If I want him to remain until I come, what is that to you?" This is the disciple who is testifying to these things and wrote these things, and we know that his testimony is true.

These verses are self-explanatory, even meant to clear up confusion that existed before the book of John was written (80-85 AD). Jesus prophesizes the kind of death Peter would experience, a martyr's death. He had boasted that he was willing to die this way before his denials, now Jesus tells him that he will. (Peter was martyred in Rome in 64 AD by Nero, crucified upside down.) Now that he was reinstated, his future death for Christ would glorify God.

Jesus bids Peter to follow Him away from the others and John is seen behind. Peter questions Jesus about John and his future. Jesus answers that John's future is in His hands just like Peter's, and if the Lord wants him to remain alive until the second coming, this is out of Peter's hands.

John explains that the early disciples understood this to mean that John would definitely be alive until Jesus returned. He corrects this error by saying that if Jesus wanted this, it would be so, but this was not a promise. He identifies himself as the witness of the events and writer of the book in order to erase any doubts the reader might have.

Conclusion and Summary #2 – 21:25

> Vs. 25 – And there are also many other things which Jesus did, which if they were written in detail, I suppose that even the world itself would not contain the books that would be written.

John's second summary closes the book but leaves open the question of Jesus' life and work. There is enough here to base a decision of belief, but this is definitely not all there is. There is more that you do not know about than what has been recorded, but these other things, like what has been written here, you will have to accept by faith.

31.
REVIEW & QUIZ

This is the "bonus" chapter in this book on the gospel of John. We have taken our time with this study, going over every verse and following some key concepts throughout the gospel.

In this bonus chapter I would like to do 2 things:

1. I want to give you a short quiz in order to drive home the essential points of this book. This is just a personal exercise and no one will see it but you. Answers can be seen at:
    http://bibletalk.tv/gospel-of-john-review

2. I would also like to provide one more summary of John's gospel and a few more practical lessons we can take away from it.

QUIZ

1. Pilate
2. Tetrarch
3. Samaritans
4. Personal Evangelism
5. Annas
6. Passover
7. High Priestly Prayer
8. Jesus' death
9. Mary Magdalene
10. Joseph
11. Peter
12. Governor
13. Caiaphas

1. Match the correct word above with the statement below.

A. People who were considered as "half breeds" by the Jews. _____

B. The process of bringing people to Christ. _____

C. One of the men who buried Jesus. _____

D. The person Jesus appeared to first after His resurrection. _____

E. A Greek term referring to a ruler who was responsible for one quarter of a Roman Province. _____

F. The man who found Jesus innocent three times. _____

G. The father-in-law of the ruling high priest when Jesus was tried. _____

H. The term used to describe Jesus' lengthy prayer on the night of His betrayal. _____

I. The condition required for the Holy Spirit's coming. _____

J. What Jesus & the Apostles were doing the night of His betrayal. _____

2. Fill in the blanks with the correct word in the following sentences.

A. The sub-title of this book on the gospel of John has been, Jesus the _____ / _____.

B. The reoccurring themes in John's book were referred to as _____ of belief or disbelief.

C. Jesus provided proof of His divinity through His _____.

D. The Lord's first miracle occurred at _____.

E. John was from the northern part of Israel near the sea of _____.

F. Jesus often stayed with His friends, Mary, Martha and Lazarus who lived in _____.

G. _____ was the ruling high priest at Jesus' trial.

H. The Bible records a total of _____ appearances by Jesus after His resurrection.

I. Jesus promised the Apostles that He would send them the _____ who would lead them to all _____.

3. TRUE or FALSE.

☐   John was the son of a wealthy fisherman.

☐   Jesus' miracles were done to create respect for God in the people.

☐   John is the only gospel writer to record all three of Jesus' appearances to the Apostles after His resurrection.

☐   The "Follow-Through" of faith is obedience.

☐   John has carefully recorded all that Jesus said and did.

☐   Jesus did not have to be baptized because He was the Son of God.

☐   Jesus' last public miracle was the feeding of the 5,000.

☐   The beginning of John's gospel is usually referred to as the "Introduction."

☐   The purpose of John's gospel is that his readers will respect Jesus.

☐   This is the best textual Bible class you have ever had.

Total Points = 30

Your Score _____

Summary of John's Gospel

The gospel of John, as I have tried to show you, has one main theme repeatedly presented in every single scene depicted by John. From the opening verses in the prologue where he describes Jesus' position with God before the creation of man to the post resurrection appearances, John is continually presenting Jesus as the divine Son of God.

This is the entire point of his gospel, that Jesus Christ, by His miracles, His ministry and His resurrection has proven that He is indeed divine.

Someone might say, "Well isn't this the intention of the other gospel writers as well? How is John special?" Each gospel writer had a point of view and audience target with his book and John was not different.

- Matthew demonstrated that Jesus was the Messiah according to the prophets. This is why he refers so much to the Old Testament in his gospel. He wanted to show the Jews that Jesus' miracles, ministry and resurrection were all done in accordance to what the prophets said would happen when the Messiah came.

- Mark's gospel is the eyewitness account of Peter the Apostle. We read Peter's words in Mark, who served him as secretary. Mark's work focuses on Jesus' power, recording more of Jesus' miracles than the other writers. The point to anyone who read was that the kingdom of God had come with awesome power in Jesus.

- Luke wrote his work from a historical perspective. He tells the same story but is careful to include details that will fix the incidents of Jesus' ministry in a proper historical framework. In the 1st century, Luke's gospel and the book of Acts were circulated as one book and seen as a definitive history of early Christianity and the church.

- In comparison to these, John is the only writer who directly engages his reader. His gospel is up close and

330 | MIKE MAZZALONGO

personal. From beginning to end he focuses not only on Jesus' miracles, teachings and ministry, he also focuses on how people react to these things.

John describes how men, women, rich, poor, Jewish, Roman, High Priest or common fisherman react to the Lord. And John leaves no room for compromise, people are seen as believing Jesus or rejecting Him. In the end, after countless examples of faith or disbelief, he leaves the reader asking himself, "Do I believe or disbelieve?"

And so after reading John's gospel there is little doubt as to his point (that Jesus is divine) or to his purpose (making everyone choose to believe or reject Christ).

Lessons

I hope that you have gained greater understanding of this gospel. I hope also that your faith has been strengthened as we have studied the lives and responses of others who have seen and believed in Jesus. I hope also that you will remember these last few lessons from John as we close out our study:

1. This gospel is for us today

It is easier to detach ourselves from the other gospel writers, saying that one wrote for the Jews (I am not a Jew), one wrote as an eyewitness (I was not there), one wrote for history's sake (I am not into history). But John had his eye clearly on every person who would read his book then as well as now. There is no escaping the fact that if you read this book, you are compelled to render a decision, whether you like it or not.

I used to say that if I was working with a non-Christian I would read Mark to him first because it is easy, short and to the point. But after studying John I understand why so many choose this gospel to begin teaching others, it is the one that asks the reader to decide whether they will be included with the believers or the unbelievers.

2. Christianity is about Jesus

We get wrapped up in issues, programs, systems, projects, budgets and debates. John's gospel, however, brings us back to the basics of our religion: the person of Jesus. John develops only one idea, one point of view in the 21 chapters of his book. That main idea is that Jesus is God!

Everything else about our faith and our practice of it begins and ends with this one basic truth.

When we begin having personal or corporate problems as individual Christians or congregations, we need to go back to this fundamental truth that John puts forth: Jesus is God!

- We need to think about it.
- We need to reaffirm our faith in it.
- We need to focus our attention on it in worship.
- We need to reteach it before looking elsewhere for solutions.

3. The best is yet to come

Note that for all those who said "yes" to Jesus, there was a reward given beyond their expectations. From the woman at the well who found a new purpose, to the blind man who found a new voice, from Mary Magdalene who found her beloved teacher risen from the dead, to Peter who found forgiveness and renewal.

All those who John describes as accepting Jesus were blessed for their faith. But Jesus speaks to all of us today when He says, "Blessed are they who have not seen but have believed." (John 20:29). Like Thomas, we have not seen, but are addressed directly by Jesus Himself (the rare instance where God, in context, speaks directly to the present generation).

Jesus bypasses John's commentary and promises us that we too will receive a blessing if we believe. Let us weigh the evidence and not be doubting, brethren, let us believe and continue to do so in order to receive the best gift yet to be given: fellowship with the Lord Jesus without end. Now **this** is a blessing worth waiting for.

BibleTalk.tv is an Internet Mission Work.

We provide textual Bible teaching material on our website and mobile apps for free. We enable churches and individuals all over the world to have access to high quality Bible materials for personal growth, group study or for teaching in their classes.

The goal of this mission work is to spread the gospel to the greatest number of people using the latest technology available. For the first time in history it is becoming possible to preach the gospel to the entire world at once. BibleTalk.tv is an effort to preach the gospel to all nations every day until Jesus returns.

The Choctaw Church of Christ in Oklahoma City is the sponsoring congregation for this work and provides the recording facilities and oversight. If you wish to support this work please contact us at the address below.

bibletalk.tv/support